LABOUR, LIFE AND LITERATURE

Photo by John A. Stelling, Peckham Road, London

Frederick Rogers.

From the painting by Ernest Stafford Carlos

LABOUR, LIFE AND LITERATURE

SOME MEMORIES OF SIXTY YEARS

BY
FREDERICK ROGERS
AUTHOR OF "THE SEVEN DEADLY SINS," "OLD AGE PENSIONS,"
"THE ART OF BOOKBINDING," "COWPER IN
THE TEMPLE," ETC.

WITH A PORTRAIT

LONDON
SMITH, ELDER & CO., 15, WATERLOO PLACE
1913

[All rights reserved]

I DEDICATE THIS BOOK

TO

MY SISTER

SUSAN ESTHER ROGERS

TO WHOSE LOVING LOYALTY I HAVE

OWED ALL THE HAPPINESS

OF MY LATER LIFE

PREFACE

It is among the advantages of growing old that we grow indifferent to praise or blame. We have lived our life, and whether our neighbours are offended or pleased at our way of living gives us little concern. In our active years this is not so. A thousand things born of custom and opinion influence us, and we have to determine whether we will dodge them, submit to them, or clear them away. To submit is easy for lazy souls, and none of us escape entirely the sin of sloth. To dodge them is inglorious, but it is often done, and to clear them away is to appeal to our heroism at once. But the latter process is very often the reverse of heroic when it is translated into action, and becomes quite uninspiring at times. It is usually done in the fashion whereby a bull endeavours to clear away a stone wall. There is much roaring, a fine display of courage, and possibly a touch of heroism in the heart of the bull, but in the result the stone wall remains, and the bull does not.

Life produces an eternal crop of new problems for us to face as we solve the old, but it is no impossible riddle notwithstanding its background of mystery, and it can be understood if it is lived sanely. Its harvest is of our own sowing, and for our failures, mistakes and shortcomings no one is to blame but ourselves. We never admit this, but it is true all the same. We cast the blame of our faults on circumstance or environment, as Adam cast the blame of his fault on to Eve and she hers on the serpent, and pick a quarrel with life to hide our own blundering.

In these pages there is no quarrel with life, there is an appraisement of it as it presents itself to me after nearly threescore and ten years of its experiences. In the words of an ancient writer, "I come now to the spacious fields and palaces of memory, wherein are treasured unnumbered images of things of sense, and all our thoughts about them. . . . There too I meet myself, and whatever I have felt and done, my experiences, my beliefs, my hopes and my plans."

In writing these reminiscences I have tried to show the workman's life as I have lived it and seen it lived. I have taken my share to the full in labour activities; but when I began my work there was no money in the Labour Movement, and I worked for it after hours, earning my living by working at my trade at the same time. In the most complete sense of the words my life has been that of a man of action, but I have found my chief joy in the world of thought and imagination. With all its ups and downs, life has been to me a wonderful panorama, a rich banquet, a many-coloured and marvellous thing. One of its many paradoxes is that happiness is not found by those who set out to search for it, but is often found by those who do the work nearest to hand, because they feel it wants doing, and try to do it as well as they know how.

Changes are nearing our social fabric—and our own nation and the world are moving out to new ideals. The greatest enemy to every kind of social reform is individual sin, and no social reform worth having will be reached while men ignore that. But the world is sane, in spite of symptoms to the contrary, and it will not cast away the lessons of old experience and ignore truths that all the generations of mankind have proved, in its restless moving forth. Its wealth and its pleasures are not destined always to remain in the hands of the few, and the claim of the many to a larger share of them is sound in logic and equity alike. But when it is made and substantiated it may well prove a doubtful boon, and may not bring the happiness which it is expected to bring. The sages of the ancient world and the mystics of the Middle Ages had reached a fundamental principle when they proclaimed that "being" not "having" was the truth that humanity needed most, and that few wants, discipline, and a plain and simple life were the open secrets of human happiness. But being has few chances in a world that must needs live by doing, and plain living and high thinking are a yearning rather than an achievement. And still the old conflict with the World, the Flesh, and the Devil rages as fiercely as ever it did, except for those who give up the fight and let the unholy trinity win.

I have worked for literature because I have loved it, understood it, and made it my constant companion. The wonder and the glory that can be revealed in the art of expression, the exhaustless charm that may come with rhythmically ordered words, and the fairy world of imagination and thought which I have entered through these doors have created within me a passion and a thirst that will be slaked only when the springs of life itself run dry.

Of the world of thought that I have passed through, or lived in, I have written of necessity—the desire that impelled me was not of my own creating. Those who read it will regard it with favour or disfavour, as it may chance. I am not concerned to repel the charge of being dogmatic, should anyone care to bring it against me. In the last resort there can be no clear expression of objective truth without dogma, and—regarded from another standpoint—dogma is a vice of youth and a privilege of age. Nor shall I be concerned to repel any charges of egotism, should they be brought against me, though I am quite ready to admit that what I have said about my own personality may quite easily be the least important parts of these reminiscences. But I at least hope that the incidents I have remembered and described may prove worth reading as a first-hand record of adventures—intellectual and social—in a workman's life.

Many of the chapters in this book have appeared in serial form in the pages of the *Treasury*, and I desire to record my thanks to the editor and publishers of that magazine for permission to reprint them. There are, however, new chapters and large additions which have not been published before.

FREDERICK ROGERS.

LONDON,
Oct., 1913.

CONTENTS

		PAGE
I.	Early Memories	1
II.	Dr. John Watkins, 1867–71	16
III.	The Tragedy of Edward Baker, 1867–79	22
IV.	A Recollection of Father Ignatius	32
V.	James Allanson Picton, 1868–78	35
VI.	The First Education Act	49
VII.	Labour Movements	63
VIII.	University Extension	76
IX.	A City Tradesman	86
X.	Journalism	91
XI.	"Time and Change are Busy Ever"	107
XII.	Mind and Character in the Workshop	125
XIII.	Henry Irving and the Drama	128
XIV.	Social Ideals	137
XV.	Toynbee Hall	142
XVI.	Irish Experiences	147
XVII.	The Co-operative Movement	154
XVIII.	The Elizabethan Society	157
XIX.	The Bookbinders' Strike, 1891–92	178
XX.	Blacklegs and a Parson	191
XXI.	Christ and Modern Commercialism	196

		PAGE
XXII.	Browning Hall and Old Age Pensions	203
XXIII.	Men and Logic	229
XXIV.	Side Issues and Manœuvres	238
XXV.	Pensions Achieved	257
XXVI.	Of Books and other Matters	271
XXVII.	American Literature	280
XXVIII.	For Better or for Worse?	294
XXIX.	"In the Midst o' the Bigness o' Things"	309
XXX.	Evening	320
	Index	329

LABOUR, LIFE AND LITERATURE

I

EARLY MEMORIES

THERE is no valid reason why a man should write about his own life, but there are a good many excuses, and one is that from time immemorial other people have done so before him. Life is always the most interesting thing in life, and one's own experience of the joy and sorrow of living is interesting to one's self, and may therefore be interesting to other people. The life here described has been busy, varied, and has had, in its more mature years, a fixed and definite purpose. Activity has often proved the secret of happiness, and there was wisdom in the reply of a simple soul to the query in the title of a once popular book, " Is life worth living ? " " Yes, life is always worth living if you have something to do." And I have always had something to do. Never in the worst times of my workman's days had I very much share of the horror of an artisan's life, being " out of work." And if failures and mistakes have brought clouds and shadows, effort and struggle have brought more than their full measure of satisfaction and joy.

I was born in Gower's Walk, Whitechapel, on the 27th day of April, 1846. Gower's Walk is a little narrow turning with four-roomed houses in it, which is now called a slum. It is in Goodman's Fields, Whitechapel, and was then simply a poor but entirely respectable street. My father was a linendraper's assistant at the time of my birth, and had been a sailor; but my earliest memories of him are as a labourer in the docks, and the first locality I remember is that of Mile End. Mile End to-day is a crowded, congested district, whose inhabitants are largely Jews. My memory recalls, if somewhat dimly, pleasant houses in Mile End Road, with front gardens and flowers. There was little traffic, omnibuses were few and expensive, and two of the old-world coaches still ran—a blue coach to Dunmow, and a red one to Woodford. A good-sized park, with large, overshadowing trees, which reached to Green Street, where we lived, was where runs what is now St. Peter's Road. The leaves of the trees in Charrington's Park, as it was called, fell into our garden, and there were legends among old ladies of rabbits in the park, but I never saw any.

A famous day in East London in my childhood was Fairlop Friday. An old rhyme of the nursery order fixes the date indelibly in my mind:

> "And the boats go round, and you tumble on the ground,
> On the first Friday in July."

Boats on lorries, decorated with flags and streamers, and carrying members of various seafaring societies, drove from Wapping and Whitechapel to Hainault Forest, and spent the day there, returning at night to an accompaniment of music and coloured fires. In the forest was a large oak called Fairlop Oak, and under this tree and round about it was held Fairlop Fair. All sorts of stories were rife as to the origin of the custom, and people of large imagination found its source in pagan ritual, and talked learnedly of Druid traditions. Its real founder, however, appears to have been one Daniel Day, who lived in the eighteenth century, and was a block and mast maker of Wapping. He used to take his employees there once a year, and regale them on beans and bacon under a spacious oak, finishing the day in dancing and merrymaking. Day's hospitality attracted such a crowd that a kind of fair was instituted, and out of this grew the custom of Fairlop Friday. The tumbling on the ground was supposed to refer to the traditional drunkenness with which the festival was credited. Fairlop Friday was dying out when I remember it, and beginning in my memory with four boats, it dwindled down to two, and gradually passed.

Another strange spectacle which I saw two or three times in Mile End Road was a prostitute's funeral. The women of the streets in East London used to stick close together, and had a custom or club, or perhaps both, which showed itself in their funerals. Bow Cemetery was the great burying-place for East London, and a " grand funeral," as it was called in local speech, always fetched the inhabitants out in crowds. There was nothing grand in such a funeral, but there were occasional elements that were strangely picturesque, and children in East London learned quite early what the evil thing meant. When one of the sisterhood of Rahab died it was not unusual for her comrades to give her a funeral similar to that given to one whom death prevented from becoming a bride. There was a suggestion in this, unconscious perhaps, but none the less real on that account, of the homage Rahab pays to Lucretia. A hearse surmounted with white feathers bore the coffin, and as many of her sisters as cared followed it in couples to the grave. They were clad in the old hideous black hoods and scarves, but white ribands ornamented them, as would have been the case if the person buried was engaged to be married. Usually, also, a guard of men of the kind who were called "bullies" walked on either side of the women, to prevent—so it was said—any hooting or stone-throwing on the part of the virtuous matrons of the neighbourhood through which the procession passed.

One of the most remarkable spectacles of the kind was that of a woman who had been stabbed to death by a sailor in Ratcliff Highway. The man was duly hanged for his crime, and the woman's funeral was a remarkable episode of the tragedy. It passed down to Bow Cemetery one afternoon just as we were coming out of school. Rumour had been busy as to the form it would take, and stories were current that so many women would follow dressed in red, so many in white, and other details of a more or less romantic kind. The body was borne in a funeral car, with the usual white ribands and feathers; the custom of flowers had not, so far as I remember, come in then, and the car was followed by a band playing the "Dead March" in Saul, and some two hundred of the sad sisterhood, with their guard of men. They were however, all dressed in deep black, and the procession made a deep impression on the neighbourhood.

There was a good deal of open ground in Mile End and Bow, and children had no scarcity of playgrounds. Charrington's Park covered an expanse of ground now occupied by roads and streets, and the entrance to it was nearly opposite Stepney Green. Many other open spaces were in the immediate locality, and there was no lack of fields to play in, or of grazing cattle in them to drive about when the spirit of mischief possessed the playing boys. For a long time my father's wages were 15s. a week, and seven of us were kept out of it, and my mother added to it by ironing. Poor we certainly were, but I have no memory of want, and my home in childhood was a happy one.

The first public function in which I remember taking part was my baptism, which took place in St. Peter's Church, Stepney, when I was ten years old. I had no conception of the meaning of the rite: nothing, so far as I remember, was ever taught me about it. An energetic curate of the name of Stevens, who worked with the Rev. T. J. Rowsell, afterwards Canon Rowsell, of Westminster, had succeeded in getting a large number of children of all ages to be baptized, and I have a vivid recollection of standing erect on the little platform which held the font, and of the water falling into my eyes. My schooling was partly that of a dame school in the street in which I lived, and partly of a British school near by, but I went to work in the year of my baptism, my first place being that of errand boy to an ironmonger, and my wages two shillings a week. For this sum I had to work from eight to eight each day, except Saturday, when I worked from eight to ten, having out of this, however, an hour allowed for dinner and half an hour for tea. I do not remember a time in my life when books were not a passion with me. I learned to read as soon as I learned anything, and the books that attracted me chiefly were works of imagination, though I read a good deal of English history when I got the chance, chiefly of the school-book kind. The "Pilgrim's Progress" was the first book to make any real impression on my mind. I used to read it to my grandmother when quite a child, and there is a dark street yet in East London along which I have run with beating heart lest I should meet any of the evil things Bunyan so vividly described.

It was not so easy for a London errand boy to get reading then as it is now, but I got a good deal. As a small boy I had many shifts and changes in my endeavour to get my living, and one of the most interesting was that of a sandwich boy. My work then was to promenade the City with some half-dozen other lads, with a board back and front of us, on which were set forth the merits of some one's fireproof safes. This work was regarded by me as a step in advance, as my working day ended at six o'clock instead of eight, and I had three shillings a week instead of two. And it introduced me to the City, which till then I did not know. It was against by-laws to carry boards in the City unless the carrier of them walked in the road, and to walk in the road was to incur risk from vehicles, and I did eventually get run over. But the thing we had to do was either to risk being run over or else come to quarrels with the police. And finally, although the oldest of our little band was but thirteen, we developed considerable skill in dodging the officers of the law, though now and again a policeman's hand or foot would come heavily against some part of our persons. City churches were not open for private prayer or any other purpose on week-days in the 'fifties, and in the empty but sheltering porches of one or two of them we lads dined.

Seated on our boards, out of the wind's way, we ate our scanty meal, and spent the time allotted to us for the dinner hour. It was all dreary and wretched enough, no doubt; but children feel the monotony of things but little, and the factories, and the shops, and the busy City life, brought a touch of idealism into our boyish lives, and showed us the possibility of escape in the future from the work we were doing then.

One of the most powerful forces in the shaping of my mind at this period, was the cheap theatre. There were five cheap theatres in East London—the Standard in Shoreditch, the Britannia in Hoxton, the City of London in Norton Folgate, and the Pavilion Theatre and the Effingham Saloon in Whitechapel. The Effingham was, I believe, the last of the saloons, which were cheap and popular places of amusement where you might drink and smoke during the performance. I was brought up in the belief that playhouses were bad places, and therefore very early desired to see what they were like. My chances of theatre-going were few, and when I did go I do not remember that I ever saw anything particularly bad. The most popular form of entertainment was the domestic drama, at all the theatres above mentioned except the Standard. At this theatre excellent performances of the "legitimate" drama were frequently given. Charles Kean, Samuel Phelps, James Anderson, Henry Marston, William Creswick, Mrs. Herman Vezin, Miss Heath, Miss Atkinson, and Miss Marriott were all well known to East London playgoers from appearing on its boards; and as a boy I have passed happy Saturday nights, watching Miss Marriott as Hamlet or James Anderson's Ingomar, for the small sum of fourpence—threepence for admission, and a penny for apples by way of refreshments, play-bills being a needless luxury to a youngster who could study them outside and remember as many of the chief actors' names as he wanted without much trouble. The playbill of the domestic drama often possessed quaint and amusing literary characteristics which were probably necessary in appealing to the less educated, but assuredly not less appreciative audiences of those days. The chief characters, occasionally all the characters, were described in rhymed couplets on the bills, as follows :

> "Mary, a workgirl, poor but honest : Miss Jones.
> Her hands were rough, her eyes were blue,
> Her work was hard, her heart was true ;"

or somewhat more humorously in, I think, a play called the "Watercress Girl" in which various types of street characters were described :

> "Cast Iron Poll, nutty Liz, and thirsty Nan,
> They go their rounds with taters, and a can."

The old cheap theatre was cheap in all things—sentiment included. The Effingham saloon was famous for domestic drama, honest, wholesome stuff, if its sentiment was cheap, and the popular edible there was the baked potato. If you had sixpence on Saturday night you could get four hours' good amusement for threepence and for another threepence get a perfect debauch of baked potatoes ; and in this connection an amusing story recurs to me. In a front seat in the Effingham sat a young woman of the fishwife and coster type, and two or three seats behind her—he had come in late—sat her sweetheart. Between them was a shy, reedy-looking youth of about eighteen; and to him the young coster made the request, " Young feller, yer might jest touch that young 'oman on the arm." It was done, and the young lady demanded to know, with expletives, what he meant by "shovin' 'er elbow; like his cheek it was." But the deep voice of her lover boomed forth above the clamour of the orchestra, "Sal, 'ave a tater?" The youth became the means of passing the edible; the three became friends for that evening, and all was peace.

The leading actor and actress at a cheap theatre were popular personages amongst youngsters as well as grown-ups; and to have seen in Whitechapel, and off the stage of the Effingham, Mr. Sam Sawford, or Mr. C. J. Bird, was something for us to talk about as we tramped through the City gutters, with a "board at our back and a board at our belly" as we used to describe ourselves. The titles of those old domestic plays were less sensational and, as it seems to me, more natural and therefore more attractive than plays of a similar character in our own day. "A Poor Girl's Temptations, or a Voice from the Streets," "Fifteen Years of a British Seaman's Life," "Waiting for the Verdict," and the "Guilty Mother," were immensely popular, and on the whole deservedly so. If there was fustian in them, there was good stuff mixed with it. It was a time when tags and catch phrases were in vogue, and a phrase that always "brought down the house" in the nautical play above mentioned was "A man who has shown his face to the enemies of his country should never show his back to the boatswain's cat." The plays at the Effingham Saloon were occasionally of an inferior character to those of the other houses, but the acting was good of its kind. "Lady Hatton, or the Suicide's Tree," "The Man with the Iron Heart," "Sweeney Todd, the Barber Fiend of Fleet Street," and, of course, "Jack

Sheppard" were among the plays that delighted my childhood at the Effingham. The house generally was voted "low"; and as, at one time in its career, it had a threepenny pit, its audiences were probably rougher than at some theatres. But—except for the fact that I lied occasionally in order to conceal the fact of my having been there from my natural guardians—the only memories I have of the old Effingham are pleasant ones, for it was a place where I got cheaply healthy, if occasionally commonplace, amusement.

With the exception of the "Pilgrim's Progress" I did not come into contact with much good literature till I was nearing sixteen. I read without guidance, and simply chose what interested me most. But there was a closer connexion between popular literature and the cheap theatre than there is to-day; and to know the one meant, sooner or later, knowing the other. Where stories like the "Will and the Way" and "Woman and Her Master" achieved a phenomenal success in the *London Journal,* and the "Woman of the World" sent up by leaps and bounds the circulation of *Reynolds's Miscellany,* they were quickly dramatized for the City of London or Pavilion Theatre, and sometimes proved as popular on the boards as in the weekly journal.

It is the custom to condemn unsparingly the stories of highwaymen which formed so much of the mental food of errand boys and other lads who could read in those days, and, to some extent, does so still. As literature it is rubbish; but I doubt if it ever did the harm it has been credited with. Occasional acts of dishonesty among young boys do not prove much, and the same lad would probably do the same thing whether he read robber romances or newspapers. We are bound by ethics and common sense to supersede bad literature by good, simply because bad *is* bad, but we must go deeper than mere romance-reading to touch the sources of juvenile crime.

The half-dozen boys with whom I tramped the streets and gutters of the City read, as I did, much literature of the Dick Turpin and Jack Sheppard class, but none of us became burglars or criminals. I certainly do remember, when I was reading that entirely respectable novel by Mayne Reid, "The Scalp Hunters," being seized with an overwhelming desire to scalp my little sister; which desire, however, I was much too fond of her to gratify. Two pieces of great literature came to me in my boyhood's days—"Don Quixote" and Lewis Filmore's translation of Goethe's "Faust." I have both those books still. I read the "Faust" through from beginning to end, not because I was able at sixteen to appreciate Goethe, but because I was interested in the Devil. "Don Quixote" took me a year or two, and I did not realize its greatness till long after; but its stories of adventure and its romance and humour appealed to me strongly enough.

It was not till 1860, when I entered my fourteenth year, that I came into touch with the trade with which I was to be identified for the rest of my life, and in that year I obtained employment at Messrs. Rock Brothers and Payne, an old City firm of stationers, and remained in their employ three years. I was now no longer errand boy; I had indoor employment, a different set of companions, a considerable advance in my salary—it was four and sixpence a week—but I had also very much more physical work. Boys in those days, when lifts were not, or only occasionally were, spent much of their time in carrying loads from the lower to the upper part of the factory, and this formed a considerable portion of my work, and no work could have been worse for a growing boy. But life was tolerable there. I had intellectual lads among my companions, and in the life outside the factory I got a close and intimate knowledge of a once popular London spectacle, now happily removed from public sight for ever—the gallows. The factory where I was employed was at Ludgate Hill; I had to pass the Old Bailey every morning on my way to work, all the details of a public execution became rapidly familiar to me, and I have never beheld a more degrading spectacle. But, hideous as the whole scene was, it had for a long time a strange fascination for me. The first execution I saw take place was that of James Mullins for the murder of Mrs. Emsley, on the morning of November 19, 1860. The murder was a peculiarly brutal one. It was an East London murder, having taken place at Bow, a neighbourhood every corner of which was familiar to me, and it had been a long time before the public. It therefore had for me an interest of its own, apart from an ordinary crime. The shouting, half-drunken crowd, the great black structure in its midst, the solemn notes of the death-bell, the roar of execration that greeted the wretched creature who came out to die, the quivering, struggling thing that a moment later was swinging in the air, and, but for the twitching limbs and the working in and out of the hands, bearing little semblance to anything human, all combined to form a picture horrible and degrading to all who witnessed it. And when the drop had fallen, the " last dying speech " was brought out from under countless cloaks and shawls and was there and then on sale for a penny. The Evangelical preacher was there to improve the occasion and to distribute tracts, and at one hanging—not that of Mullins—I saw General Booth (then the Rev. William Booth, and not then the head of the Salvation Army) holding a prayer meeting under the scaffold. Barrett, the Fenian, was the last man hanged at the Old Bailey in public, and I was under the gallows then, though no longer working in Ludgate Hill. But there was no great crowd at that hanging, and I think that the Bill for executions in private came at the psychological moment, and exactly expressed public feeling.

When I went into a stationer's warehouse, I realized how much brutality a young boy had to accustom himself to and put up with if he wished to get on and learn a trade; and I resolved to learn book-binding. In his daily work a lift with the foot or clout of the head was a common and ordinary experience, and if he went wrong in learning his business, you did not teach him principles, you pulled his ears. And if, as often happened, in protest against this unscientific treatment, he indulged in profanity, it was usual to read him a solemn lecture on the wickedness of swearing. But boys got their revenges now and then. At one workshop where I was employed there was a peculiarly vicious brute of a workman who took a special dislike to me. He was a huge, middle-aged man, slow of movement, I was a small boy of a little over fifteen, and he had a diabolical method of twisting my ear in a way that caused me most acute pain. I was afraid to go straight for him, and for a long while could not find out a way to retaliate; and then I learned from another boy that my enemy suffered terribly with corns, and I knew that the Lord had delivered him into my hands;

and I waited. In the 'fifties an endeavour was made to introduce Lancashire clogs into the London market. They never took on, but they were cheaper than leather boots, and I wore them for a year or two, and I was wearing a pair in the year that this brute and I worked together. Something I said or did gave him offence, and once again my wretched ear was being nearly twisted out by the roots. But this time my revenge was at hand. Crash went my wooden-shod feet, as heavily as I could bring them, on to his corns, and with a yell of agony he let my ear free, and I fled. I have never doubted the substantial truth of the statements made by Protestant novelists as to grand inquisitors gloating over the cries of their victims. I can remember still the holy joy that filled my young soul as I stood at a safe distance and listened to the gorgeous and flamboyant language that flowed from his lips concerning myself.

From sixteen to nineteen my health began to fail, but I stuck to my work because to do so meant learning a trade which I liked. But I ceased to take any share in the sport or play of other lads, and I had no youth in the sense in which they had it. When my work was done I was too worn-out to play and was glad to get home. The perfect devotion of a loving and noble-hearted mother lightened my pain, but doctors and hospitals grew familiar objects to me, but never seemed to help me in any way, and life was an ache and a burden. In the workshop I was called lazy, the fact being that I became weaker and more of an invalid with every year that passed. Healthy lads are callous, and very often cruel to those who are not healthy, and rarely make companions of them, and I had few friends of my own age. But books were an unfailing solace, and by the kindness of older men and women good books found their way to me. Ainsworth and Dumas filled me with delight; the lurid and picturesque romances of G. W. M. Reynolds had their charm; once or twice I came across an odd play of Shakespeare; and one or two of Marryat's novels carried me far away from the workshop and its world. The historic parts of the Old and New Testament attracted me, and the men and women of the sacred books were as familiar to me as the men and women of Alexander Dumas. These things did not bring back health, but I could forget my pain if I could creep into a quiet corner with a book and rest my tired body when my day's work was done. A dull, slow, sickly boy, with no hope or prospect in life, and careless alike whether it continued or ended; these are my recollections of my twentieth year.

II

DR. JOHN WATKINS, 1867–1871

LIKE all great cities, London has its full share of curious and picturesque personalities, and Dr. John Watkins, F.R.C.S., F.R.G.S., and F.A.S., of 2, Falcon Square, City, was one of the most remarkable among them. Falcon Square in the 'sixties was rapidly ceasing to be a residential square, and its eighteenth-century houses were being converted into offices and warehouses. The residence of Dr. Watkins was one of the last among them which remained as a dwelling, and it had been in the possession of himself and his family for over a century. He had a wide reputation which was based on a wonderful remedy he had for curing diseases of the bones and nerves, and also ophthalmia. What this remedy was he kept to himself, and, so far as I know, it died with him. What he did with it was to restore sight and strength to thousands who had lost both. And many among them were the poorest of the poor, for the doctor was a philanthropist as well as a scientific man, and during certain hours of the day gave help and healing without fee or reward. When I knew him he must have been between seventy and eighty years of age, but he possessed a striking and splendid personality. A tall, squarely built, upright frame, surmounted by a magnificent head with flowing white hair and beard; bright, sparkling eyes, from which the glint of humour was never absent; a resonant and sympathetic voice that somehow made your heart go out to the man as its notes fell upon your ear; a quick, springy step, and a hearty, merry laugh: this was Dr. John Watkins. A staunch Conservative, as I learned later, conventionality and he were, nevertheless, sworn foes. His "philosophy of clothes" led him to dress in an ill-fitting black suit, made purposely so, in accordance with his views as to clothing, which set fashion and art alike at defiance. But dress how he might, he was ever a gentleman, and gentleness and sympathy were in every line of his kindly old face.

He did not take long to decide about my case when I went to him. It was a very bad case. He had never seen a case of spinal disease quite like it before, and he did not know that he could do much for me. But, if I was willing to persevere and visit him regularly, he was willing to do his best. I was a free patient; I had no means of paying him any fees; but the old man's words had brought a great flood of hope back to my heart, for hope does not need much wooing at twenty, and I was ready to place myself in his hands and do his bidding blindly as a slave. And so morning by morning I came to Falcon Square by five o'clock, gave myself up to his treatment, and went on to my work close by at 7.30, and slowly strength and health came back to me through his kindly care.

To go backwards and forwards to the doctor's house for—with intervals—a period of four years, to listen to his wonderful conversation, and to know something of the struggle, the pain, and the loving self-sacrifice that manifested itself among the sick poor there, was to get an education which, if not exactly liberal, was to me, who had had none, immensely valuable. The back parlour of the doctor's house was the room wherein the patients sat after they had been "dressed" by him, and it was usually thronged, even at the early hour I went. When the first relay of patients, male and female, were dealt with, it was his custom to come into one room one day and another room on another day, and sit among us and talk. It was a strange and curiously stored mind that was opened to us, though many there could only listen in open-mouthed wonder as it was displayed before them. He was Welsh, and had the eloquence and the vivid imagination with which it is usual to credit his race. His scientific knowledge seemed to me wide, but his knowledge of ecclesiastical lore from the Protestant standpoint was tremendous. Rome and its religion were to him accursed things, and the only bitterness I ever saw him display was in dealing with the Catholic faith. He was not bitter to its followers, only to their creed. For him the perfect religion was that of the Church of England; and every dissenter was, in his eyes, a secret emissary of the Jesuits. It was in his waiting-room that I first came across a copy of the English Prayer-book, and it was his eloquent tongue that made the beauty and the reverential order of its services apparent, though in those days I knew nothing of either religion or literature, and against the former had an unreasoning prejudice. Seeing that I was fond of reading, the doctor took to lending me the *Rock*, then a newspaper and much believed in by him, and I read it in order to be able to discuss its contents with him; though there was always a large leaven of cynicism in my comments on the religious strife with which its columns were full. He, however, was far too kindly-natured to notice my assumptions of knowledge and occasional youthful arrogance, and rather enjoyed putting me in a corner in argument, which he did always with the most charming good humour. It must have been an easy task, for with all my reading I knew nothing. Mere chance and desultory reading, however assiduously pursued, never educated any man yet; and I, without training or guidance, and reading because it was the best pleasure I had found, was, after all, not much more than a human box that was full enough of information, but it was there in strange confusion, and I had no knowledge whether it was valuable or no, or how to use it if it was valuable.

We sick folk were a motley group in the old doctor's waiting-room, but there was enough of the milk of human kindness among us to destroy such pessimism as filled my mind then, though I did not realize it at the time. Like many young fellows, I was critical about things, and not a little morbid, and, if I had a profound belief in myself and my own virtues, was fully prepared to pronounce sentence on the world in general, and to say that it was very bad. And yet in the crowd of sick folk by whom I was surrounded, many beautiful expressions of the sympathy and the goodness that may always be found in the human heart were constantly before my eyes. A feeble, tottering old grandmother came morning by morning and month by month, as guardian to a half-blind orphan grandchild, and the delight of the poor old dame as the young girl's sight was restored was a beautiful thing to see. A lame sailor—an alien and foreigner—was brought each day by a bright-faced, ragged lad, who must have done the work for sheer love, since the poor foreigner, who could not even speak the language coherently, was a crippled derelict stranded down Poplar way, and was penniless and out of work. But the most touching episode of all was the loyal friendship of two young lads, one a sturdy fellow of sixteen, vigorous and full of abounding life, the other a helpless cripple of some fourteen years, without the use of his lower limbs. The healthy lad carried his companion on his shoulders for something over a mile each morning, waited while the doctor " dressed " him, and then carried him back again. Once or twice he had to go away and send some one to fetch his companion, and once, when the person sent did not come, I carried the cripple lad home myself—a poor, feeble little fellow, with a pinched but pleasant face and a merry tongue. I learnt a great deal that Sunday morning as I struggled along with my human load. I discovered that I was not so strong as the lad who sturdily bore the burden day by day, though I was some years older; but the chatter and the thanks of the crippled child made my journey a very pleasant one. The poor lad was not cured, and I never knew whether he lived or died. The loyal friend who brought him was poor like himself, and presently had to go to work, and the cripple found no other helper, and his visits to the doctor ceased.

As the years passed they brought strength to me, but they brought feebleness to Dr. Watkins. It was a beautiful evening of life that I was privileged to see, and perhaps in some small measure to lighten. He was still faithful to his poor; but he had no assistant nor helper, and grew slower in his work, and many left who could not spare the time he required now. I went regularly on Sundays and as often in the week as I could; for I loved the kindly souled old man who had restored to me the life I thought

I had lost. And when he, who had brought sight to so many, found that even his skill availed nothing against the infirmities of age, and reading became impossible to his failing eyesight, he was glad for me to read to him, and to me it was a joy unspeakable to serve my venerable friend. I, as usual, read the *Rock* to him, but its controversial side ceased to interest him, and he cared more for its paragraphs relating to archæology, its religious verse, and its snatches of sermon lore. Life was fading, but not intellectual vigour, and not hope. The venerable face would light up with what seemed to me an almost unearthly radiance as I read some old religious poem or fragment of verse. Now and again his wonderful conversational powers would come back—not to argue on points of Protestant theology, but to burst out into eloquent rhapsodies on the old legends, or the poetry of the Cymric race, or to muse with the musings of a wise and clear-sighted age on problems of life, death, and eternity. They were wonderful mornings, though I only realized the charm of them after they had gone for ever. And they were soon to go, for the old man grew rapidly more and more feeble, and by and by he kept his room and his patients saw him no more. I knew none of his family—to them I was only a free patient with whom they had no further concern when the doctor ceased his work. But week by week I called to know of my aged friend, and at last came the message that filled me with a sorrow that none of my friends could understand, because none knew of the depth of the friendship between him and myself. One of the noblest hearts that ever throbbed in human bosom had ceased to beat: John Watkins had passed to his everlasting rest.

III

THE TRAGEDY OF EDWARD BAKER, 1867–1879

In these early years of my life I sought no friendships, because I was fit for none. Companionship with vigorous, hearty lads of my own age, though I often secretly desired it, and envied those who could share in their sports and their mirth, was impossible for me. But some friendships came unsought, and among them was the friendship of Edward Baker. It was the accident of working at the same bench, when I was learning my trade, that brought us together. He was a man some dozen years my senior, intellectual from a workman's standpoint, well read, and of a sympathetic nature. He belonged, however, to a somewhat lower grade than the rest of the workmen so far as his handicraft was concerned; and I, partly from the reserve natural to me, and partly from the priggishness common to youth, was disposed to be as stand-offish to him as I was to most other people. But an act of great— and by me much-needed—kindness thawed the ice about me, and we soon became fast friends. We had many interests in common. Far ahead of the rest of the workmen in our shop in intellectual capacity, he occasionally found himself isolated and misunderstood in his little world, and was the more ready in consequence to welcome the conversation of one who could sympathize with and understand him a little, even though that person was but a youth, as I was when we first met. It was from Edward Baker that I first really learned to think about religion. The conversations with Dr. Watkins about the English Church and its Prayer-book were valued by me for the speaker's sake, but I do not know that they made any great impression on me beyond that. Memories of them at a later time helped when I took systematically to the study of history and literature, but I am not conscious of any impression made then of a religious kind.

My attitude toward religion at this period was one of dislike. It stood in the way, so I believed, of a pleasant life; and, with increasing vigour, the pleasures of life appealed to me, and in my pursuit of them I was no less selfish than other young fellows of my age. But while I half wanted religion not to be true, I was never able to stifle the belief that it was, and I saw that, if it was, it was the chief thing in life.

Edward Baker was a Freethinker—the first of his kind that I had ever met, but, curiously enough, with a great fondness for going to church. He hated Nonconformity with a vigorous hatred, but was always following after the great preachers of the English Church. It was in his company that I first listened to Henry Melville, at St. Paul's Cathedral, preach a sermon on the Doctrine of the Trinity, in the presence of Her Majesty's Judges and before a Unitarian Lord Mayor. With him I went to hear C. J. Vaughan at the Temple Church and Charles Bradlaugh at the Hall of Science. He never joined a Freethinking Society until the National Sunday League was formed; of that, however, he became an active member, and introduced me to the leaders of an organization which met in St. George's Hall, Langham Place, and was called the "Church of Progress." I went often to the Sunday meetings of this body, and they consisted of pleasant musical evenings, the music being chiefly sacred with a popular talk of some thirty minutes long, thrown in like the powder in the jam.

I heard many men of note and ability on its platform, though of doctrine or systematic teaching there was not the slightest shred, nor was there meant to be. It was no uncommon thing for the speaker of one night to contradict absolutely the speaker of the previous week, but the aim of all the speakers seemed to be to speak the truth they knew, though some of them said they knew very little. Spiritualists and agnostics, now and then a Broad Church clergyman, Unitarians and secularists, and once or twice a university professor—all were welcome on the platform of the "Church of Progress." It had but a short life, even though, as Edward Baker often told me, its aim was to "catch the upper ten." Most Radicals that I knew then had, notwithstanding much platform-shouting to the contrary, a slavish desire for the patronage of the "upper ten." But the upper ten thousand never came near the "Church of Progress," though now and then a man of as high and intellectual a *calibre* as Huxley was to be heard within its walls. How it came to its end I never quite knew, but it is not even a memory now except possibly with myself.

It was Edward Baker who first turned my attention to politics, and it was in his company, in October, 1871, that I first heard William Ewart Gladstone on Blackheath. It was on a Saturday afternoon, and my friend and I left our work at two o'clock and went off to the heath, and the sight was one I never forgot. Down in the hollow of the heath a platform was erected, and on the heath itself, far as eye could reach, there stretched a mighty crowd; and on the platform stood Gladstone. Without an effort—so it seemed to me—the great orator held his audience for nearly two hours. I stood so far off that the features were indistinct, but was spellbound by the music and the magnetism of the wonderful voice. I had listened to great preachers and to atheistic lecturers, and my imagination had been stimulated by the one and my prejudices by the other, but I had never heard a speaker like this man. I knew little and cared less of the merits of the case he discussed. I was only conscious of the presence of a great human personality under whose spell I was, and from whom I could in no way escape. The magic of sound was in the wonderful voice, and if the things he said were unintelligible to me, the voice brought with it something of inspiration and of uplifting power. The only detail that remains in my memory of the speech was some rhyming reference to the Straits of Malacca, which caused much comment in the Press. All else was glamour, magnetism, charm, call the influence what we will, but it made a mark on my memory which was never quite effaced. Probably about six years after the time to which I refer, Mr. George R. Sims wrote in an early number of the *Referee* his impressions of a meeting at Greenwich and a speech by Gladstone. He is an honoured member of the Conservative party now, but in 1877 his writings added to the gaieties of Radicalism. He felt the charm of the great orator as I did, and I append his description to my own:

As I stood on Saturday afternoon at Greenwich listening to the glowing words of the grandest orator and statesman of modern times, I felt lifted into a holy region of politics, where

Tories cannot corrupt or Jingoes break through and yell. This age is too vile and mean and debased to understand the pure and elevated patriotism of plain William Ewart Gladstone. Had he a Star and a Garter, a title and a coronet, rings outside his gloves, and the blazing orders of Jericho plastered about his coat, the mob and the gutter gang would be better able to understand him. The infamous handbills issued by the agent of the Conservatives, and the invitations to hoot and stone the man who has given his whole life to his country, are the atrocities bred of imperial mouchardism and political organization. What a glorious speech! As I listened to the rolling periods I fancied that I was a little angel sitting at the feet of some celestial being. I quite forgot that I was at Greenwich, and that I was only,

DAGONET.

It was through Edward Baker that I first came into touch with the Working Men's Club movement, and it arose out of a desire to hear Frederick Temple, the then newly appointed Bishop of Exeter. He had written an essay in a then notorious, but now forgotten, book, " Essays and Reviews," and was credited with Rationalist proclivities. A violent storm raged round his appointment, and the opposition to it was of a sensational and sordid kind. The man himself was entirely dignified and self-restrained, and ignored the flattery of Unitarian lecturers and the vilifications of orthodox Churchmen with equal impartiality. Probably not many men in public life were better able to estimate at their true value platform heroics and gallery applause than Frederick Temple.

The occasion when Baker and I heard him was a meeting of the Working Men's Club and Institute Union, or what then stood for it, at Exeter Hall. It was in the small hall, and as I did not know what a workman's club was then, the proceedings did not interest me much. Baker had his own club at Camden Town, to which he afterwards took me. It was a teetotal club, and the evenings I passed there, listening to music and recitals, with occasional speeches interspersed, were pleasant, healthy, and harmless enough. He was eloquent over the beauties of the Bishop's speech, but for once in a way I did not share his admiration, though I have no doubt the speech was as excellent as he said.

It was Edward Baker who introduced me to a phase of London life, which is described with much skill in the "Mark Rutherford" volumes—I refer to the Freethought Societies in the neighbourhood of Tottenham Court Road. In the early years of our friendship Baker certainly had a faculty for making the best of the various organizations created for the "elevation" of the working classes. He was fond of music, and had some knowledge of it, and was a perfect directory of free and cheap concerts and lectures all over London. Occasionally he and I would afford a shilling for the sacred concerts at Exeter Hall, given, I think, under the direction of Joseph Barnby. He was passionately fond of the writings of Dickens and Scott; of Dickens I had read a little, but of Scott I knew nothing till I met him. He was a help and a guide to me in the selection of literature, although he had no literary knowledge, and simply followed his instincts. But they were splendidly true, and he never directed me to anything that was bad, so far as literature was concerned. Looking back through the vista of the years, I can see that the little Freethought Societies to which he took me from time to time had to the full their share of the comedy of life. I used to laugh at them pretty considerably then, occasionally causing sadness in the mind of my good friend; but there can be no doubt that the majority of their teachers were honest up to their lights. But what guttering rushlights some of them were!

A handful of people, meeting in a little tin lecture-hall or back parlour of an old house, with perhaps one educated man among them, were all perfectly certain that the little knowledge they had was sufficient to set aside the experience of the centuries, and start the world straightaway on an entirely new career. Their chief outcry was against dogma, but none were more dogmatic than they. Liberty was their great ideal, but licence—at any rate among their younger frequenters—was its interpretation. One organization called itself the "Advanced Unitarians," though I never was able to see what there was to advance to when Unitarianism was left behind. Its teacher was an undertaker of the name of Antill, whose business was, I think, in Kentish Town. He had the reputation among his followers of being a very worthy man, but he was to me a strange, cold creature, and never achieved any very great platform success.

As I got to know the life of Edward Baker intimately, I realized that he was an exceedingly upright and honourable living man. He was quiet and reserved, and took some time to know closely, and he never got out of the second-rate position he occupied in his trade. But he was thrifty and hardworking, never drank or gambled, made the best use of all his opportunities, and was usually much better off than a good many people in the shop with better wages than himself. And during the first years of our friendship he was happy in his home life and passionately devoted to his wife. It was a considerable time before he introduced me to her, but before I knew her I knew how perfect his devotion to her was. No knight of the days of chivalry ever gave a more loyal or more complete love to the king's daughter he hoped to win than this workman gave to the partner of his heart. To him she was perfection; for her happiness he would have sacrificed life itself. In appearance he was commonplace, and, except on Sundays, was usually shabbily dressed, as were most workmen then. His face was plain and deeply pitted with smallpox, but I have seen it become almost beautiful when talking of his wife. In her he had found the ideal of his life, and with her his happiness was complete. When I got to know her I knew where his Freethought principles came from. She was a woman of singular ability, and with many masculine elements in her character, and after a time it seemed strange that the two should have wed. Her nature was as cold and hard as his was sympathetic and tender, and not many of the younger men whom he asked to his house from time to time shared his belief in the purity and the faithfulness of his wife. Intellectually forceful and brilliant—and in these things the superior of her husband—she was also coarse-minded and sensual to a degree, and had at times the ways of an animal rather than a woman; and his love for her seemed to me hardly a natural thing. But it helped me in later years to understand the lines of Shakespeare:

"Thou blind fool, Love, what dost thou to mine eyes,
That they behold, and see not what they see?
They know what beauty is, see where it lies,
Yet what the best is take the worst to be."

A change in my employment separated my friend and myself, and we only saw each other at holiday times. Then I met him after a long interval, and a strange and a terrible alteration had taken place in him. The woman he believed pure as snow had proved an adulteress and a thief, had stolen the few paltry pounds he had kept in a cracked teapot against a rainy day, and had gone to America with a drunken brute who had been a criminal and deserted his own wife to go.

This tragedy of humble life was only comedy to his fellow-workmen, though they would have helped him generously had he been in pecuniary need. Under the crushing weight of his awful sorrow he did not, as so many of them would have done, drown his misery in drink. He endured the agony and waited for the end. It had crushed him body and soul, but it had not destroyed the inherent goodness of his character. There was, however, one tremendous change. He who had been to all women "a very perfect gentle knight" became a hater of them all, warning all men younger than himself to trust no woman or believe in her. This was comedy, too, to commonplace minds, and we had all common-place minds in the workshop. He was only a workman dying quietly of a broken heart, but around him, and around the crumbling ruins of his life, there was the tragic and awful dignity which enshrouds those who are burning in the fires of destiny. Illness and poverty brought the end at last. I had been working late many nights in succession when the news came that he was dying in Holloway Workhouse, and that if I would see him it must be at once. I set out for the workhouse on a glorious July afternoon, and reached it late as I had far to go. As I approached his bed the setting sun had surrounded it with golden light. But the face on the pillow was calm and still; life's agony was over, and Edward Baker was dead.

IV

A RECOLLECTION OF FATHER IGNATIUS

It was in the 'sixties that I first heard Father Ignatius. He preached every Friday in the dinner hour at the Church of St. Edmund the King and Martyr, in Lombard Street, and I was learning my trade at a firm hard by. I did not go because I had any interest in religion, but because I had been warned against him as a dangerous man. Edward Baker it was who was the indirect cause of my going to hear the monk. I knew from Baker all the arguments in favour of popular rationalism, and the ideas put forth by Mr. Blatchford as new to-day were commonplaces to me in the early 'sixties. I was too young to confute them, and as I had not far to go to the church I resolved to hear what the other side had to say. To go once was to go often. A boy of seventeen who has left an elementary school at ten is not likely to have any opinions on theology of consequence, and I had none. But Ignatius was an orator, alive at every point of his being, and his words awoke within me feelings and emotions I had not been conscious of before. His personal magnetism was wonderful—so wonderful that after awhile I became afraid of it, and thought there might be something in my friend's warnings after all. I went into the church once dirty from my work, and having, as I usually had, to stand, was in full view of the preacher. Almost immediately, he began to talk about work and workshops. A couple of countrymen came in clad in their smockfrocks, and before long the preacher was talking of fields and meadows and country life. He had a genius for fresh and natural speech, and listening to him then life grew larger to me, and fuller of purpose and meaning. I have little memory of his words; it was rather the inspiration that somehow came with them, that got into my nature and bore such fruit in after years as I could not dream of then. I still went occasionally with Baker to the free-thought lecture halls, and he in turn went with me to the church; but I became a somewhat contemptuous (and probably very ill-informed) critic of what I heard at both places.

It was after a lapse of thirty years or more, in 1896 or 1897, that I again found myself visiting City churches with fellow-shopmates, and listening to dinner-hour discourses by Father Ignatius. We had both learned much in the intervening years, but I had travelled many paths, and he had remained faithful to one. Of the things that had filled my life—literary studies, trade-union work, labour developments, social reform—he knew almost nothing; he was still the preacher with his solemn message, but it was with a difference. The faith, the fervour, and the religious passion that had held me in the opening years of my youth were with him still, and it was for these I cared, for I had come to see that, immensely valuable as were all the material reforms that I had been working for, there was yet something lacking to give purpose and meaning to our human lives, and when I sought to discover what it was, the only answer which satisfied my soul was that given by the principles of the ancient faith. It was not Ignatius, but Father Stanton, who made me see that the supreme enemy of social reform is individual sin; but Ignatius made me feel again the power and passion of those ancient principles as I had not felt them for many a year. He had become full of anecdotes, there were moments which suggested mental aberration, but there were moments, too, when the religious genius of the man welled up into speech and shone out of his inspired face, and held his hearers as under a mighty spell. The old bitter Protestant hatred of everything it did not understand, which he fought so well in other years, had died down, or nearly, so far as he was concerned; and I have seen members of the Salvation Army and Nonconformist ministers in Romaine's old church of St. Andrew-by-the-Wardrobe and have seen him in his monk's garb in the centre of a band of Salvationists at the church porch, chatting to them with all his old lovable charm. He was called "a modern mediævalist," but in his veneration for the letter of the Bible, and in his belief in verbal inspiration, there was more of the Puritan than the mediævalist, and the attraction which his preaching had for Nonconformists when they had got over their prejudices against him is not difficult to understand. He stands a lonely and striking figure in English religious life, tender and loving as a gentle-natured woman, brave as any soldier that ever hurled himself against the bayonets of the foe, and with a spiritual strength and passion in him which cannot be kindled by any power which man commands, but when it exists is surely what Robert Louis Stevenson has called "a kind of riches of the soul."

V

JAMES ALLANSON PICTON, 1868–1878

THE warnings of Edward Baker against Father Ignatius and the influence of Dr. Watkins combined to turn my thoughts more and more in the direction of religion, and it was through reading the *Rock* to Dr. Watkins that I first heard of James Allanson Picton. That paper adopted an attitude of violent hostility to what is called the three R's—Ritualism, Romanism, and Rationalism. Mr. Picton was minister of an old-fashioned Independent Chapel in St. Thomas's Square, Hackney. Its congregation had drifted into Rationalism without knowing it, under the ministry of his predecessor, the Rev. W. Kirkus. On April 13 and May 11, 1868, the *Rock* quoted passages from the *Inquirer*, a Unitarian paper, to show that orthodox dissent was moving swiftly towards Rationalism, and Mr. Picton's sermons were adduced as evidence of the fact. This was, to Dr. Watkins, a profound truth, but I had no clear conception of what Rationalism meant. I only knew it as a bogey word among religious folk, and I made up my mind to go and hear Picton and find out.

It was then that I realized there was a conflict in my mind between two ideas. One was the desire to throw over religion utterly, and make my own moral code; and the other was the feeling that, without intellectual dishonesty, this could not be done. The old doctor's influence went deeper than I knew, and perhaps through it I could never quite stifle a conviction. I could, and often did, put it behind my back and ignore it, but it had a way of asserting itself when least expected. My baptism made me a member of the Church of England, and I liked her services; and a favourite way of spending Sunday afternoons was to go to St. Paul's Cathedral, sometimes with Edward Baker, sometimes alone, and there I often listened to Liddon in the days of his youth and vigour.

The fact that the *Rock* laid strong emphasis on the danger of Mr. Picton as a religious influence, but had nothing else to say against him except this, and his political views, made me curious to hear him, and so I went. I found him an exceedingly intellectual and scholarly preacher, and after a visit or two found myself under the spell of his oratory. If I had any ideals or ambitions in my twenty-second year, they were all in the direction of scholarship. To be a learned man seemed to me the noblest thing on earth, and I certainly hoped to be one, though I had no perception how.

But I was a workman, with a workman's view of life—dressing, looking, and behaving like a workman—and the people to whom Mr. Picton preached were painfully respectable, after the manner of lower middle-class Nonconformists, and I went backwards and forwards to the chapel for two years before any soul there spoke to me. This gave me no concern, however; for a shilling a month, which was the price of my sitting, I was getting a moral and intellectual stimulus which I enjoyed. Of

Nonconformity as such I knew little and cared less. Mr. Picton himself was a loyal Nonconformist, but he took it for granted, apparently, that his congregation understood Nonconformist principles, for he never taught them. He used the Church of England Prayer-book at all morning services for some years, until a service book on Unitarian lines was adopted, so that the respect for the Prayer-book learned by me in Dr. Watkin's surgery was not destroyed. His preaching was what was called "advanced" for Dissenters. It was intensely critical, but he held on for a long while to the dogmatic inspirations, and always to the moral ideals of the Christian faith. Its effect upon me was to sow the seeds of personal discontent; to make me realize that my life might be better than it was, and perhaps to cause me to endeavour to make it so. I probably fulfilled the outward conditions which won respect in the class to which I belonged. I certainly was very loyal to the workman's conception of respectability, but when I got to know the people who worshipped at St. Thomas's Square I was sufficiently a prig to conceal so far as I could the fact that I was a workman.

In 1870 Mr. Picton published a volume of sermons entitled "New Theories and the Old Faith," a book which made a considerable sensation in the Nonconformist world. It was a narrow and spiteful world, as I knew it, notwithstanding the many good people who were in it. It had no generosity of spirit, no breadth of intellectual outlook, but was always ready to believe the worst of those from whom it differed, and to grow frightened and hysterical over anything it did not understand. There were a good many things it did not understand, and among them was the book written by Mr.

Picton. I had heard the sermons delivered in the previous year, and was spellbound by Mr. Picton's eloquence of speech. I could not criticize; I could only listen, enjoy, and fancy I understood. He was well versed in all the criticisms made by science on religion, and it was largely believed in those days, especially by the frequenters of atheistic lecture-halls, that through the influence of science religion would be utterly destroyed. No one in the ranks of Nonconformity—I then knew little of the Church—was able to deal with the arguments of the scientist, though a scholarly and eloquent gentleman—the Rev. Dr. Kennedy, of Stepney Meeting House—did, to the satisfaction of himself and his chapel, succeed in demolishing Darwin. Mr. Picton seemed to me to be quite able to deal with them, though really he dealt with them by accepting them. His book was referred to by Darwin in complimentary terms, and was also eulogized by Dr. James Martineau as a remarkable book illustrating the influence of scientific thought on religion. It dealt with the relations of the doctrine of Evolution to the Christian faith. Until I listened to Mr. Picton I had not the slightest idea what the doctrine of Evolution meant; listening to him it became for me a religious idea. He was a man full of religious fervour, and with a passion for truth and right living which could not fail to impress those with whom, in pursuance of his religious duties, he came into contact, and which certainly had a powerful influence on myself. Unlike the majority of Nonconformist ministers I had heard, there was no posing, nothing histrionic about his pulpit oratory; every word he uttered was natural and sincere. In his highest flights of eloquence there was never the slightest suggestion of playing to the gallery or of rant, and herein he stood out in sharp contrast to another leader of Nonconformity with whom his name was associated—Dr. Joseph Parker, who always appeared to me not so much a preacher as a good actor spoilt. About the time when Mr. Picton published "New Theories and the Old Faith" Dr. Parker published a book called "Old Truths in New Forms." The two books were reviewed together, and of their authors a religious paper of the time said: "Dr. Parker flirts with Christianity, but Mr. Picton has forsaken it altogether."

Beautiful as Mr. Picton's book was, its tendency was away from Christianity, and, followed to its logical conclusions, led to the renunciation of the Christian faith. He was illustrating an old truth, though to me then an undiscovered one, that an heresiarch may be, and often is, a very noble man, whatever may be the result to society of his views. But that which the reviewers called irreligious in tendencies seemed to make the religious side of my character strong, and to build up conviction within me. The positive side of his teaching, scholarly, thoughtful, and high-minded as it was, sank deeply into my nature, and the negative side then, and for several years after, fell away and did not influence me at all. Something of this was due, I have always thought, to the influence of the Book of Common Prayer. It is full of noble and inspiring ideas and, as the old surgeon made me see, rightly understood and lived up to, its teachings make for a manly life, and this aspect of it was taken by Mr. Picton whenever he touched it at all.

Each year the keen pleasure that came with the pursuit of knowledge and the mastery of a good book grew stronger and stronger. And, although I had no money to buy any but cheap books, I somehow always succeeded in reading any book I really wanted to. In 1869 I came across a cheap set of Gibbon's "Decline and Fall of the Roman Empire"; it took me two years to read through, for I worked long hours in those days, and was only gradually getting back my lost health, but the long bright summer mornings, when I could read from four to six, and then have plenty of time to reach my work by eight, are pleasant memories yet. It was not till 1872 that I began to make any friends outside the workshop, with the exception of Dr. Watkins and Edward Baker; books were my only companions, and I was entirely happy in their company If a book was mentioned by Mr. Picton of which I had not heard, this was to set me off in pursuit of it. He was a great lover of Tennyson, and was constantly quoting "In Memoriam," and occasionally, though he was never a Browning worshipper, Robert Browning. These two writers were hard to get; it was not till 1879 that Tennyson was to be had in half-crown volumes, and there was no cheap selection of Browning till I caused one to be published in the year of his death.

From 1868 to 1872 I was feeding my inner life with little more than my instincts to guide me in my choice of intellectual and spiritual food. And my trade began to appeal to me on its imaginative side. My actual work was that of an account-book binder, and book binding as distinct from account-book binding was work I seldom did, except when I bound books of my own. But I always loved to see and to handle a well-bound book, was never tired of hearing about the masters in my craft who had bound famous books, knew rapidly all their names, and spent many an hour in the British Museum and places of a similar kind, poring over not the insides, but the outsides of the wonderful books of mediæval days. I began to see that idea of the mediæval church— " the holiest relic must be within the costliest shrine "— had created a magnificent artistic instinct which expressed itself in the glorious bindings of the religious volumes, and I wondered whether our own modern trade would ever create an art so living and true as that I saw in museum cases! So far as my experience had gone then I saw no evidence that this would ever be.

I liked my trade, and enjoyed working at it. There were times, when I was sweated or overdriven, to which this would not apply. But machinery was not then the power it is now, and the speed of the workshop was not set by the motor or the gas-engine; it followed a natural order, and was set by the human energies and the human hand. I often experienced the pleasure and enjoyment which comes to a man when he has done a good piece of work and knows he has done it well. I did not find life in a workshop a very intolerable thing, though I know full well the limited company or the driving employer can often make it so now. The workman who kept his ideals within his income stood a chance of expanding both ideals and income later on, and I often saw it done. Many things might militate against this—ill-health, large families, changes of intellectual outlook— but unless these things happened workshop life could have as many pleasant things as unpleasant in it at the time of which I write. And it had its share of the beauty as well as the comedy and pathos that is ever inseparable from the incidents of human affairs, and never at any time in my experience did I meet with more generous social effort to help comrades in trouble than in my workshop days. Workmen had the advantage—for it *is* an advantage when we really want to do our best to solve a social problem—of being unhampered by theories; and I never knew any harm come from the generous and straightforward efforts to help their fellows in trouble, even though all they did was often in flat violation of everything that was then regarded as the science of political economy.

The various forms of social life which grew out of the life of the workshop had always their interest and charm. The beanfeast was an established institution, which, in well-ordered shops of men, had many advantages. It occurred on a Saturday, and as no workman expected to get more than a day's holiday at a time, unless he were out of employment, the beanfeast and the day following could be, and was, utilized so as to make a two-days' holiday, and perhaps I never enjoyed more, though I have enjoyed as much, any spell of rest by the sea, or among the green fields, as in those early days when my two-days' holiday in June was a thing to be looked forward to in the first half of the year, and a pleasant memory in the second. Balls, concerts, and entertainments of various kinds, often displaying considerable talents among the men of the workshop, helped to give variety to a life that might have been monotonous, and often was so when the artisan lacked pleasure in his work. And as the speed of life increased, pleasure in work departed, though perhaps it never quite departed for me, as I always held the belief that it was possible to get more out of even workshop life than a good many of my fellows managed to get, and I set myself assiduously to work to put my belief into practice.

To some extent, no doubt, circumstances favoured me, for during the whole of my life as an artisan I worked in the city of London, and London of itself is even now one of the most interesting cities in the world, and at the period of which I write it was an education to those who could read the lessons which it taught. The glamour of London—the mysterious influence which is created by ancient houses, by old-world nooks and corners, the sense of hallowed presence which clings to ancient temples of religion, the thing we call (for want of a better word) atmosphere—was upon me from the first. The churches which gave me shelter under their friendly porches when, as a child, I carried advertising boards about the streets, became centres of historical knowledge to me as I grew older, though the only guides I had in finding that knowledge were my instincts and an appetite for knowledge which nothing could slake. It was in or about the year 1870 that the Guildhall Library was thrown open as a free library, and that to me was an introduction to what seemed an illimitable world. As a matter of fact, the library, though it had a wealth of good books, was limited and old-fashioned—a fact which, if I had been a student of any special subject, I should have soon found out. But I was only a desultory reader, though desultory reading is always the most delightful kind of reading. And as I worked within five minutes' walk of Guildhall for five years, and within fifteen minutes' walk for two, I had plenty of opportunity of browsing among its books. And in whatever way the library was limited it had a wonderful collection of material about London.

It was in the Guildhall Library, about a fortnight after it was open free, that I first made the acquaintance of Browning's poetry. I had read a great deal of English poetry without system or guidance, and for a time was entirely under the spell of Byron. My favourite poem was "Mazeppa"—not his best work by any means. But I never tired of that wonderful ride, the wolves and the torrents. Manfred, largely because of its supernatural element, I think, gripped me too, and I saw several times Adah Menkeu as Mazeppa, and Phelps as Manfred. But Browning was expensive and never on the cheap bookstalls, and people said no one could understand him, so I resolved to spend a Saturday afternoon in trying to do so.

The book I chose was "Paracelsus," and it was accident—if there is such a thing as accident in human affairs, and I have always doubted it—determined my choice. I began at the beginning and resolved to read it steadily through, and soon I was lost to the outside world. People might call Browning obscure if they liked; I saw no obscurity in "Paracelsus." Its wealth of poetic imagery fascinated my imagination, and its wonderful thoughts captured my mind, and for two and a half hours I gave myself up to the book, reading and re-reading till I mastered the meaning of the words. The library closed at five then, and I got there about half-past two, and sat, all unintentionally, under the bell which then rang out at closing time. I was no longer a workman, but was in the Middle Ages with the travelling scholars, when clang, clang, went the bell and brought me back to the world again, and the conclusion of "Paracelsus" had to wait till the following Saturday. But it was not until I met Canon and Mrs. Barnett that I really mastered Browning.

London and its opportunities were educating me as universities do other men, and gradually I found my everyday environment was capable of being moulded to meet the needs of my intellect and my imagination, and I set myself to work to organize my spare time. My working day as a vellum binder was from eight till seven; and I had the incalculable blessing of the Saturday half-holiday. It was then I did the greatest amount of my reading—in the summer under the trees in Victoria or Hyde Park, in the winter in the Guildhall Library. There was a great plane tree which for many years was a sacred object in Victoria Park, for it was beneath its shade I first made the acquaintance of Emerson and read Huxley's Essays, and when in later years I visited the park and found the old tree gone to widen the pathway, a lump rose in my throat, and I felt almost as one feels who has lost a friend. It was in the Guildhall Library that I had the greatest run of books, and there I revelled in the lore of London, and from it naturally to that of England with a kind of intellectual debauchery.

Legends of London streets, old ballads, trials and criminal records, bits of ecclesiastical history, old customs and folklore, biographies of ancient citizens, and the wealth of history which had grown up round the chief city churches were all devoured by me with greedy avidity, and the monotony of life disappeared as I realized I could live in so many worlds at once. The dinner-hour soon became a means of ministering to my intellectual hunger, and of stimulating my imagination. It was a custom among the workmen in my trade to have their dinner in the workshop, and usually to read or doze after the eating was done. It was a custom I never followed. It broke the monotony of the day to get out into the streets, if only for an hour; it changed the air of the workshop for a fresher current, and—for me as I read about them—London's streets and buildings became full of a new life and meaning. Twenty minutes for my simple and frugal meal—for I was always simple in daily habits, and ate, as I spent, frugally—left me forty minutes each day to do what I chose. And those midday spells were rich in pleasure and enlightenment. The city companies' halls, with their fine old fronts, stately doorways, and picturesque appearance generally, were an education to any who closely studied them. And the ancient dwelling-houses—many of them the one-time home of famous men; the link extinguishers and circles for holding the oil-lamps; the carvings over the doorways and in the nooks and corners, were familiar to me as the faces of my friends. And the city was full of strange human personalities in those days, many of whom I knew. Men still lived in it, and loved and wedded, and brought children into the world in it, though it was fast becoming a mere place for buying and selling and getting gain.

One of the most curious characters was a poor weird, half-crazed creature who got her living by selling street wares, and was called "Pennywinkle Joe." She was an ugly and scarcely human creature, and the wares she sold were chiefly periwinkles—hence her name. But this poor, uncouth piece of womanhood had been debauched by a scoundrel, and the birth and death of a child brought a curious change into her half-developed life. The mystery of birth and being had touched her soul with a sense of joy and anguish, and the eyes that looked out from under the sloping forehead had a haunting wistfulness in them after her trouble, a kind of half-expressed and dumb appeal for pity and sympathy which could never be forgotten by any who had looked into their depths. I never knew what became of "Pennywinkle Joe." The sloping forehead and the wistful yearning eyes, disappeared from the streets : perhaps at the bidding of kindly death. Another sad-faced, lonely being, whose name I never knew, was a woman who got her living by making those curious cloth designs called penwipers, which were sold in stationers' shops. A mere cloth doll, all shreds and tatters, which served to wipe the pens of their surplus ink when laid aside by the writer, the living got by making them must have been wretched enough. And she herself was a walking penwiper—her dress and whole get-up was like the things she sold. She was never known to talk and gossip with any one. She simply did her business and went on her way ; but her face had been beautiful once, and there was some mystery hidden at the back of that silent life and those weeping, wandering eyes.

Hardly a man—scarcely human was he—who was known as "Joe Ray's Beast," and yet he could command women and their love. Joe Ray kept a low public house of a popular kind on the borders of the city, and the beast was waiter, potman, and general bully thereat. The creature had acquired a reputation among the people of the district of a decidedly uncanny kind. Part of his career had been spent in one of her Majesty's gaols ; for what crime was never clearly set forth, though garotting was the offence most often alleged. When I saw him in

1868 he was a man of massive build and hideous, ape-like countenance, and the story told as to the origin of his name was that for a wager he had bitten nine puppy-dogs' heads off. It was told in circumstantial fashion, and, looking at the face of the "Beast," it was not difficult to believe the story true. Another poor helpless creature whom I knew in the neighbourhood of Tottenham Court Road was Annie. A little woman, ragged and dirty, and with a face from which every trace of beauty had vanished; she got her living chiefly by begging, though it appeared after her death that she was well connected and was supplied with a small income by relatives; poor Annie was a pitiful object to see. Always more or less drunk, she falsified all the medical teetotal theories, lived a long life in London streets, and died on a dust-heap, grey and aged, at last. "Poor Tom all alone" I never saw, though I knew many who had seen him. He was a match-seller, half demented, who stood holding out his matches and was never heard to say anything but "Poor Tom all alone."

I could not and cannot explain my interest in phases of life like these. I always realized that a very thin dividing line separated the derelicts from the respectables—one strange hag-like creature was said by the police to have been the daughter of a bishop—and I could imagine circumstances under which I might have become a derelict myself. I never believed in the aphorism of my Socialist friends—"Man is the creature of his environment." Man is only the creature of his environment while he doesn't know the ropes; when he does know them the environment becomes his creature. But some never know them, and others knowing them ignore them and pay the penalty—as did poor Annie among the derelicts,

VI

THE FIRST EDUCATION ACT

My first great enthusiasm came with the Elementary Education Act of 1870, and it led me into public life. The fires of that enthusiasm were lit by Mr. Picton. The Act was entitled "A Bill to provide for Public Education in England and Wales." It was introduced to Parliament by the Right Hon. W. E. Forster on February 17, 1870; read a second time on Friday, April 1; sent up to the Lords on July 25; passed by them on August 2; and received royal assent on August 9. Mr. Picton was one of its most ardent supporters, and preached many sermons in its favour. He was one of the few Nonconformists in London who was strictly consistent and logical in his view of it. His policy was that of the National Education League—viz. "Free, compulsory, and secular"—but that league belonged to Birmingham, and carried little influence in London. His fellow-Nonconformists were not so consistent. They wanted—and got—what they called "undenominationalism." Mr. Gladstone, the Premier, called this a "moral monster." It was an emasculated religion containing only those doctrines about which all the sects agreed. Picton attacked vigorously and all through his life, both by speech and pen, the inconsistency of his Nonconformist brethren, and said that "what most evangelical Nonconformists objected to was not so much

State support of religious teaching, but only the patronage of religious teaching other than their own. To an Independent or a Baptist it was intolerable that he should pay rates for teaching Church doctrine. But when they found they could have their own creed taught under the name of unsectarian religion, they had no difficulty whatever in making Unitarians, Rationalists, and Catholics pay for it." They hated him because his words were true, and with an easy conscience accepted the doctrine of a State-supported Nonconformity in the schools, while rejecting that of a State-supported Church.

I was always an ardent supporter of popular education, and the Act appealed to me at once. I had not thought the question out then, and having no ideas of my own, was very receptive of those that came from Mr. Picton. In my brief school days the method of teaching was simply to memorize passages from the grammar or geography, and repeat them at the proper time. If the monitor could explain anything in them he did. It was a crude method enough, but it was that which laid the foundation of the excellent memory I have had all through my life. And I had a kindly, sympathetic master, and the personal character of the teacher counts for more than machinery in the purposes of education.

The new Act accepted the principle of popular election as the final court of appeal in educational matters, and no method less likely to promote educational efficiency could possibly be devised than that. It was, however, the best method that could be arrived at then; the school boards were a new experiment, and most people wished them well, and some of the ablest men in public life gave themselves whole-heartedly to the work. Professor Huxley was a member of the first board, but not of the others. Able, active, and conscientious, his influence was entirely on the right side during his membership; but ill health and the pressure of his scientific work caused him to resign. Leading Nonconformists like Mr. Samuel Morley, M.P., and Mr. (afterwards Sir) Charles Reed; Churchmen like Mr. W. H. Smith, Rev. W. Rogers, Rev. John Rodgers, Rev. Evan Daniel, and the Rev. Robert Gregory, who was afterwards Dean of St. Paul's, and later on the Rev. C. E. Brooke, of Kennington, did splendid work. Canon Gregory was chiefly known as a vigorous fighter for the Church schools. The school boards were famous also in giving an opportunity for the first time for women to take part in public work, and, contrary to popular expectation, they were not failures at it, though some of them did develop into frightful cranks. Mrs. Garrett Anderson, Miss Helen Taylor (step-daughter of John Stuart Mill), and a lady who before her marriage was known as "Miss" and after it as Mrs. Fenwick Miller, were among the leading women who were in the public eye, and the last lady was the most interesting—from a stage point of view—of them all. Young, good-looking, brilliant, and daring enough to talk frankly on public platforms on matters relating to physiology—it required courage for a woman to do this in the 'seventies—and very much of a demagogue, Mrs. Miller in those days enjoyed a popularity which, while it lasted, was one of the most remarkable incidents of the time. The Commonwealth Club in the Bethnal Green Road was packed to suffocation when she lectured on physiology. Then she was a doctor of medicine, but in later years became a successful journalist.

The schools boards lasted up to the year 1902–3, when the Education Act of that year abolished them and placed popular education in the hands of the county councils. Their abolition had become inevitable, but I supported them both by tongue and pen while they lasted, and my enthusiasm for the education of my own class was just what I wanted at that time, and changed me from a self-centred young fellow to a public-spirited one, and also taught me the price a workman had to pay if he took part in public work. If I gave time to school-board duties it was stopped out of my wages, and in the eyes of my comrades I was rather a fool. I worked chiefly with Nonconformists, and individual Nonconformists often did splendid work for the schools, but Nonconformity as a whole was more influenced by hatred of the Church schools than by desire for education. Mr. Picton and a few like him upheld a noble educational standard, and I supported it till I became conscious of its limitations, but they were in a minority among their brethren.

There was very little real enthusiasm for education among the working classes themselves, though popular shibboleths and party catchwords were shouted loudly from their platforms. In the workshop my enthusiasm was chaffed good humouredly, or laughed at outright, and an utterance of a man who was a leader of Labour in his own little circle—" Look here, youngster, we don't warnt eddication, we warnts work "—expressed with tolerable accuracy the opinion of the working classes as I knew them in London in the early 'seventies. There was a good story current in 1873 of a workman who, on being told by a school-board visitor that he must send his child to school, replied, " What, educate that kid ? Not if

I know it. Why, there's one forger in the family now." I do not, however, give this as representing working-class opinion. But the Act became law, notwithstanding democratic apathy, and that it did so was due to the determination among the best men of all parties—Liberals, Conservatives, Churchmen, and Nonconformists—that the ignorance among our population should not continue if law could remedy it. But I never saw evidence of any great outburst of democratic feeling on behalf of education, though later writers on the Liberal side have proclaimed that there was. Archbishop Tait, preaching in St. Helen's Church, Bishopsgate, pleaded for its support by Churchmen in words that yet remain in my memory—" You talk of Christianizing the children of our great cities : you must humanize them before you can Christianize them ;"— and James Allanson Picton said that " conventicles in every street, and prayer-meetings in every court, would yet, without the spread of better education, and without some great changes in the relations of Capital and Labour, leave the next generation as squalid and hopeless as this." Tait was Archbishop of Canterbury, and Picton a loyal educational reformer, and each was entirely consistent and logical from his own point of view; but consistency and logic were not much in evidence in the policy of the early debates of the school boards, and the average educational reformer in London hated Picton only a little less than he did the Archbishop.

The passing of the Elementary Education Act of 1870 was one of the greatest pieces of social legislation that my life has seen. It was the public—and unconscious— recognition of a principle, alien to the popular politics of the time, but which had to be absorbed by the politicians, that voluntary effort on the part of well-disposed groups of people, however strenuous and sincere it might be, is not sufficient to solve any social problem of magnitude, and that it is the duty of the State to step in where individual effort fails. Individual effort had been at work on the education problem since the middle of the eighteenth century, and in the result the nobleness and the pettiness of the individual alike stood revealed. And collective effort—*i.e.* the effort of religious and charitable organizations—had been at work since the end of that century, and the net result of it all was that in London alone in 1870 school places were required for, in round numbers, two hundred thousand children. There was a strange irony, which I at first did not perceive, in the spectacle, often to be seen, of an eloquent and sincere Nonconformist denouncing the State as an unholy thing from the religious platform, so unclean that the Christian conscience was held to be polluted by its touch, and lauding it on the education platform as the only saviour of the nation from ignorance and crime.

In 1873 I was taking active part in educational work, being on the committee of management of a group of large schools in East London, and in November of that year, at the London School Board election, made my first plunge into public life. In the election of 1870 I took no part except that of a looker-on, although Mr. Picton was candidate for Hackney, and was elected on the school board of 1870, and the two succeeding boards of '73 and '79, by a large majority. But I resolved soon after 1870 had passed I would be in the forefront of the next election, and perhaps my final determination was fixed by my first visit to the city of Oxford.

It was in the summer of 1873, and, apart from Bank Holidays, was my first long holiday. The workman of to-day gets his week or fortnight at the seaside in the summer as a matter of course if things go well with him. The theory of the workshop then was, if the employer could spare you for a week, he could spare you altogether. I broke through theory, asked for a holiday of three days, and got it. Added on to Saturday afternoon and Sunday, this gave me four days and a half, and I resolved to see Oxford and walk there. I could find no companion for such a mad expedition (so my friends called it), and therefore went alone. Starting off when I left my work on Saturday afternoon, with a stout oak stick in my hand, and riding some dozen miles out of London by train, I was in Windsor time enough to spend a long evening in the park before I went to bed.

It was perfect summer weather; I was on classic and historic ground which I had never visited before, and I gave my imagination full freedom to travel as it would. I believed in ghosts, but never feared them, and I should have gloried to have seen Herne the Hunter with his rattling chain, or the mumming fairies that pinched fat Falstaff black and blue. But I was alone in the moonlight, with fancy and imagination for companions, and yet not half so lonely as I have sometimes been in crowds. The great trees waving gently in the night wind murmured friendship and welcome. I was hearing for the first time Nature's mysterious voices; I seemed to have a fellowship with the shy and shadowy deer, the flitting bats, and gliding night-moths; and the noiseless noises that came with night and moonlight filled my soul with strange dreamings and longings. I was free from the workshop and alone with Nature, and I was happy with a happiness which made me envy no man, and which no man but myself understood.

On Sunday I started on my walk again, not following the beaten track, but following, where I could, the line of the river, which I had not seen beyond Richmond before, and revelling in the glory of the meadows and the dancing beauty of the stream. It seemed to know me and I it, and when I found myself away from all things human but myself, I shouted to the great river as if it could hear my words, and sang snatches of song to its waters, and then finally plunged my body in their cool translucent waves, and lay naked among the grass and buttercups to dry. I had reached the pinnacle of human joy as I knew it then—as a young man knows it when Nature has a voice of friendship and a hand-grip for him; it is a joy that passes as the years pass, but while it was with me my cup of happiness was full, pressed down, and running over. I could not then, and cannot now, explain the magnetism that Oxford had for me. The time was to come when I should know it as well as those who had lived in its colleges and taken its honours, but this was unrevealed in 1873. I had no knowledge of what a university might be. It had for me all the charms of mystery and distance and ancient national life. It was an undiscovered country which I alone, with no guide or helper, meant to explore for myself.

It was early on Monday when I entered the city, and I found it was in the long vacation, and empty of its youthful life. With the help of a popular guide-book, I was soon busy exploring its colleges and their gardens—gardens which in their full beauty the young men rarely see, as they leave before it really comes and only return when it is passing away. The spell of the city soon began to work, and it was a widely different spell to that of London and its busy streets. Nathaniel Hawthorne had taught me what to expect in the college gardens, and I went in and out wherever I found open doors. I must have been a trespasser often, but no one bade me go, and I quickly felt I had made no mistake in spending my holiday there. The High Street, with its ancient towers and churches, broke like a vision from an older world upon my delighted eyes. I had read of such streets, but had never beheld them before. No ambitious boy, coming to his university for the first time, felt keener delight than I at all he saw, and yet everything was dim and vague and uncertain to my mind. But it was a symbol of the intellectual growth of England for me ; history and romance filled my mind, the phantoms of the great dead were with me, and a yearning to be, or to do, something worthy of those out of whose life the ancient city grew possessed me, and so, dreaming, aspiring, and enjoying, my holiday passed.

I was back at my bench on Thursday morning, and the inspiration I had received had lifted my life. My school-management work was filled with a new significance, and my activities therein received a new spur. The members of my committee, of whom I was the youngest, were local tradesfolk of the small shopkeeper class, and its chairman the Rev. T. J. R. Temple. He was a worthy, kindly soul, who had no ideas about education and pretended to none, but, with his colleagues, aimed simply to carry out departmental orders and keep down the rates. I was gaining experience, and did not trouble so much about the rates as my fellows, but the general management of the school, the appointment of teachers, and the periodical examinations were all of engrossing interest to me, and I soon got to know what a miserably defective thing our educational system had been. The work meant often much pecuniary sacrifice to me, which, however, I did not begrudge. Days or half-days away from my work—albeit on public service—were stopped out of my wages, and sometimes perhaps my enthusiasm grew cool, but never for long.

One consequence of passing the Education Act of 1870 was the closing of a number of the inferior schools, chiefly private ones, though occasionally denominational. This was a good thing in itself, but it naturally caused hardship to some estimable people. The schools supported by the various religious bodies were, on the whole, fairly efficient up to the educational standard which then obtained. The best among them were the Church of England schools, and after them came the Wesleyan and the Roman Catholic schools. The Congregational and Baptist schools, where they existed, were inferior; in fact the aim of the various religions was less to educate than to proselytize. It was an aim that each religion could logically justify from its own standpoint, but each religion had no scruple in blaming the others for doing what it was doing itself. It was the great crowd of private schools and colleges (so called) which left the mark of incompetency so deeply stamped upon elementary education. Any one who pleased could set up for him—or her—self a private school if it could be made to pay. It mattered nothing that the teacher had no training whatever for the task undertaken, so long as the house possessed a respectable exterior, and was called by its proprietor a " middle-class school." I have seen schools of the kind described, with the legend "middle-class school" cut out of white paper and pasted on the window-glass. The hopeless snobbery of it all was so appalling. Parents pinched and starved to pay high fees to schools like this, in order that their children should not associate with those who went to the denominational schools, and the poor little ones had, in return for the sacrifice, an education that was often far inferior to the worst among the other schools, whether denominational or board.

Naturally enough the majority of these private-venture schools could not stand the competition which came with the schools under the various boards. Equipment, teaching, buildings—all were infinitely better than anything the private schools could show. "Far too good" was the verdict passed by the average man, who cared nothing at all for education or the board schools, and who protested vigorously at one election because the ratepayers' money had been "wasted" in the purchase of a Turkey carpet for a board-room. When the private-venture schools closed it often happened that applications were made by their former teachers for appointment under the board. The teachers were rarely efficient, or came up to the standard required by the new laws, but wherever it was possible to appoint them the thing was done. It was not often possible, and my committee had many struggles between duty and sympathy with the teachers of the older schools. To the average elector this was a very solid grievance, and the new work was done under a strong fire of criticism, which, truth to tell, it needed much. Wherever Nonconformists were in a majority every effort was made to crush out Church schools. I took part in the efforts till I got to know those schools and the splendid work they were doing, as I did in later years. There is no doubt Nonconformists believed—the wish being father to the thought—that it would be the best thing possible for the nation if the system of school boards became universal. But the nation never thought so, and from 1870 to 1903 the members of the Church of England built some six thousand schools of their own, the cost of the buildings being saved to the nation, besides paying rates and taxes for those under the board. The Nonconformists, on the other hand, with the exception of some of the Wesleyans, closed their schools or made them over to the boards. Everything was done by dissent to magnify what it called "the religious difficulty," but I never met with it except on political platforms. During the ten years of my school management it never once arose in the schools.

In 1873 I joined the committee to elect Mr. Picton on the London School Board; canvassing, attending meetings, working on committees, all came alike to me. I was determined to help on the work of elementary education, and careless of myself in doing so. But Dr. Watkins had taught me the way to build up a good constitution, and, even though it was built on the ruins of a bad one, it served me well. Every chapel in Hackney was a committee-room on behalf of those who supported the Education Act, and although it was loudly proclaimed everywhere that there were no party politics in education, I soon discovered when I got into the work that there was nothing else. Nonconformist sermons were simply political speeches, with a dash of religion thrown in, all through the election period, and I remember a sermon on "Godless Politics" which I heard at this time, the politics which were defined as "Godless" being those of the Conservative party. There was no hypocrisy in all this. It came of the strenuous way in which the Nonconformists of that day took life. Their world was narrow and their faith mutilated, but within their limitations they were real with a reality which their opponents in those days could not reach, and a phrase of George Eliot's about life running more strongly in narrow channels often came to me in connection with them.

In 1873 was founded a book society at St. Thomas's Square Chapel, which was to influence strongly my intellectual life. My love for literature did not slacken, but increased with years, and by dint of watching carefully the book reviews and criticisms in the newspapers which I read at the eating-houses where I got my food, I always managed to keep in close touch with the world of books—a closer touch than any workman I knew, except Edward Baker. But there were no free libraries then, where I could see the half-crown reviews, and Mr. Picton often preached *Fortnightly Review* articles as sermons, and told us where he got his inspiration from. The society purchased the chief reviews and other books, and lent them to its members. The "other books" languished, and then, in October 1874, I was made librarian, and in October 1875, subject to the committee and the state of the funds, I was free to select books for the society. This meant in practice that I might purchase any book I wanted to read, if it were not too costly, and until the Society died in 1878 I revelled in the literature I cared about. About a third of the books were chosen by the members, the rest by myself. Among the publications circulated was Ruskin's "Fors Clavigera." Only one man, so far as I could see, cared for Ruskin's "Fors," and I was not that man. Well read as I certainly was, I was frankly a philistine in regard to Ruskin, and saw nothing then in what he said, and in this I undoubtedly expressed the feelings of the few—the very few—workmen who had read his books.

After 1873 I had a crowd of friends outside as well as inside the workshop. I gradually discovered I could do anything I wanted if it interested me sufficiently. That very important condition had to be fulfilled, but given that, the rest was easy. I developed rapidly into a successful public speaker, and the only theory of speech I had was to say in the best way I could what was in my mind, and make the man in the back row hear me; and whatever reputation I may have obtained for oratory has been obtained through these methods. I was not naturally rough tongued, but platform interruptions and repartee soon made me so, and I won the reputation of being dangerous to tackle if I was criticized too freely. It was probably undeserved, as all through my life I have been careless of what people said of me, and have adopted as a safeguard a motto from Thomas Carlyle, "Men may say what they like, and I shall do what I like." Gradually my interest in books became partially superseded by an interest in the ideals of my own class. Working men's clubs, co-operative societies, trade unions, friendly societies, all preferred their claims, and a larger development of my life came through the multifarious activities of the Labour movement.

VII

LABOUR MOVEMENTS

On June 10, 1873, I first became a member of the Vellum-Binders' Trade Society, of which I am still a member. Edward Baker was not a trade unionist, and his influence was to make me hostile to trade unionism. When, however, I began to understand the meaning of the Labour activities around me, I was not long in deciding to which side I belonged in them. A passage from the rules of the "Amalgamated Society of House Decorators" made a strong appeal to me. It said: "What does it profit us that half a dozen of our fellows in a generation should succeed in joining the war against the men who were formerly their comrades, and end perhaps in failing for half a million?" and I resolved to join the Vellum-Binders' Society. It was a small, old-fashioned union, and, like all old-fashioned unions, of decidedly conservative tendencies. It was a London union only, with no branches, and had been in existence since 1823.

I have a clear memory of the night I joined, and the scene. It was at a quarterly meeting that I was made a member, and the Society met in a hall attached to a public-house in Bartholomew Close called the "Rose and Crown" —a smoke-begrimed room, close and ill-ventilated, and reeking with the fumes of bad tobacco. I was never much of a smoker, and as I was interested in the scene before me, refused either to drink or smoke, and contented myself with observation. Much cheap beer was being disposed of, and nearly everybody was smoking; but no one was drunk. On a raised platform at the end of the hall sat the president and officials, and the business of the evening consisted largely of taking subscriptions, calling the names of members and putting down those absent to be fined, and discussing matters relating to the trade. For a time the atmosphere of the hot and noisy room was repellent to me, but not for long. I soon discovered the elements of life and sincerity in the speeches of the eager, excited workmen. Their aim was to protect themselves from oppression by their employers, and although I had found no oppression from any employer then, I realized the possibilities of finding it some time, and my sympathies went swiftly over to those from whom at first I shrank.

It was crude idealism, wild and ill-regulated warfare, that was expressing itself in their speeches that night, but their grievances were real and their fighting straight and fair. " The working classes are the children of society," some one had written; " presently they will grow and will by-and-by reach to manhood and become a power in the State." One of the first things I did was by moving a resolution, which was carried *nem. con.*, to take the meetings of the Society from the tavern to Bishopsgate School, where the Vicar, who was known as " Hang-theology Rogers," gave us welcome, and we met there many years, till the room became too small for us. I took office rapidly, but the " boss " of the Society, for all its democratic principles, was a strong-willed, dogmatic Irishman, by name Daniel Keeley. For a long time he was practically its personal governor, nobody being strong enough and wise enough to supersede him. As a young man I had not the knowledge of the working of a union to oppose him successfully, and had many falls in trying to do so; and then suddenly he changed his attitude towards me—first to patronage and then to friendship—and the work of my union became easy and interesting for some years to come.

It was in the year after I joined my trade union that I came into touch with another phase of Labour activity—the movement for creating workmen's clubs. The difficulty of workmen meeting together for any purpose except in a public-house, which often meant the cultivation of habits of drinking among them, had long been recognized by social reformers of every grade and character. Employers of labour often adopted the vicious method of paying the weekly wage at a tavern, and kept the workmen waiting about in tap-rooms and bars for two or three hours on the pay-night before they brought their wages along. From the beginning of the growth of our factory system the drink-shop has been an agent of the employer in degrading those whom he employed. In the small village in the mining districts, in the factory town or industrial district the mine owner or factory proprietor built and owned the drinking shebeen often enough, and made his profits out of the weakness and folly of the men and women who sought excitement in alcoholic stimulants. Small wonder that they did so when the monotony and the squalor of their lives are realized. The temperance movement, at first alone, then allied with the conventicle and afterwards the Church, strove nobly to grapple with the evil, but often vainly enough. But the men and women created by the temperance movement were often very unlovely specimens of humanity, and few among the ardent souls of the younger generation felt any considerable desire to be like unto them. All the same, the work of the temperance movement was needed, and its influence on the public opinion of the nation was almost entirely to the good.

The workmen's club movement was not a temperance movement—in fact, its enemies declared that it became a decided foe to temperance, and sometimes a creator of drunkards. In this there was exaggeration, and it certainly attracted in its early years a body of earnest and self-denying workers, and won support from well-to-do people of all shades of religious opinion. The history of the movement has been written by the Rev. Henry Solly, partly in a book called " Working Men's Clubs," and partly in a volume of reminiscences entitled " These Eighty Years," and also in a volume entitled " These Fifty Years," by Mr. B. T. Hall. Solly was secretary to it from 1862 to about 1880, and among the supporters of the movement during those years, and for long after, was an Indian civil servant, Mr. Hodgson Pratt. I was brought into touch with it through a man who became famous in it for a time—though as a movement it has produced few famous men—Mr. James Lowe, President of the Haggerstone Club, or, as it afterwards became, the Borough of Hackney Workmen's Club. Mr. Lowe, when first I knew him, occupied, like myself, a sitting in St. Thomas's Square Chapel, and listened to Mr. Picton. He was a visitor of the new School Board, whose business it was to look after absentee children and, if necessary, to summons the parents of those who were persistently away.

He did his work thoroughly, and became very unpopular in consequence. I never quite understood his reasons for coming to chapel; he slept peacefully during sermon-time often enough, and used to tell me Picton was far "over his head." But he was a pleasant, cheery man, and we struck up an acquaintance. The Borough of Hackney Club grew out of a handful of men coming together under the inspiration of the club idea, and trying to put the idea into concrete form. They took a roomy old eighteenth-century house that had been at one time a vicarage, and by the aid of a friendly brewer, who supplied them with liquor, enlarged and altered it and invited membership. The neighbourhood was a working-class one, and members rapidly poured in, and soon numbered over a thousand, besides crowds of visitors on entertainment nights. A good income came to the club; and after a time, Mr. Lowe gave up School Board work and became its president. He was elected president in March, 1874, and held that office till his death in 1884. He also sat on the Committee of the Working Men's Club and Institute Union for many years. His aim was, as indeed was the aim of all the early club-workers, to unite intellectual training with amusement, and combine in one a club and a college, and men of eminence in the literary, scientific, and religious spheres were invited to speak from its platform. But in a good many clubs the bar proved a formidable rival to the lecture-room. When I knew the club, good work was being done by Mr. Lowe, and on one occasion Cardinal Manning gave a lofty and eloquent discourse there on "Some Ideals of Labour," and a little incident remains pleasantly in my mind concerning it. James Lowe, strong leader of men though he was, was simple as a child in all that concerned great persons, and when it was announced that the Cardinal had arrived, whispered to a friend in an awe-struck tone, "How do you speak to the old chap—isn't he his holiness?"

The hold Lowe had over the club he kept to the day of his death, and I have always regarded it as one of the most remarkable things in my experience. He was a man with a good fund of general information, but was not in any large sense an educated man. He was not a great orator; he was a moderately good speaker, and that was all. But the men loved him, and it was because of his eminently lovable disposition. He had the frank geniality which the workman loves, knew his own limitations and never presumed on his position, devoted himself absolutely to the well-being of the club and its ideals, and in his interpretation of them was only just a little ahead of his followers; and this put his popularity on a solid and lasting basis, for the clubmen then had no very large amount of idealism in their composition. They wanted amusement, naturally enough, and wanted it cheaply, and it did not take long to find out that lectures were more often dry than they were amusing, and a concert, a brass band, or a dramatic reading were liked far better than lectures. Still, they were willing to doze through a scientific lecture now and then in the belief that they were doing something intellectual, and to applaud vigorously at the end.

The first lecture I listened to at a club was at the Borough of Hackney, and the lecturer was an eminent physician whose name I have forgotten, but it was on a much-worked subject in those days—"Physiology in

Every-day Life." It was my first experience of popular scientific lecturing, and the lecturer had to the full the popular gift of putting his statements in clear and simple language. In those days science and religion—the clergy and the scientific teachers—were deadly foes, and it was full of sly drives at the clergy, chiefly those of the Church of England, which were highly appreciated by the audience. Speaking of the effect of overcrowded rooms and bad atmosphere, he referred to the habit of sleeping in church. "If you want to alter that," said the lecturer, "my advice is, shorten the sermon and ventilate the church." Not many, probably, of those listening to him ever ran any risk of the ills that might come from badly ventilated churches, but the atmosphere of that lecture-hall, with every second man smoking cheap tobacco, was simply murderous.

James Lowe held the presidency of the club for ten years, and his popularity increased with time. His funeral was one of the sights of East London. The club buried him, and gave him what was called "an excellent funeral," as well as making provision for his widow; but it was not the funeral pageant that was striking, but the endless crowds of people who turned out and lined the streets to see the body pass to its last resting-place. A great statesman, with years of national service behind him, never received truer devotion or more sincere sorrow than did this simple workman, whose only claim to it was honest service, done straightforwardly and loyally, and who never looked for any recognition and was happy in the pleasure he found in his work. For many years the memory of James Lowe was kept green in the Borough of Hackney Club by the custom of wearing violets by the members on the anniversary of his death, and by calling that day "violet day." Mr. Tongue, a successor of Mr. Lowe in the presidential chair, used to say the idea was borrowed from Primrose Day and the custom of wearing primroses in memory of Lord Beaconsfield. "He was our Beaconsfield—as great to us as the Tory peer," he said once in a burst of admiring enthusiasm.

Two other workmen of striking personality were Charles Baines and T. W. Dennard. Baines was secretary of a club in Kingsland Road, not far from the canal bridge, called the Progressive Club. The term "Progressive" has since become a party badge in municipal politics, and is the title of those on our London County Council who have done good work for the social well-being of London. I do not suggest any connection between the Progressive Club and the Progressive Party, but I never met the phrase as anything but an abstract term till, in about the year 1878, I came into touch with Charles Baines and the Progressive Club. He and Dennard were both, in the natural and not in the formal sense of the word, gentlemen, and Baines was a man of considerable culture as well. He had the instincts of a scholar, spoke with a careful and polished style of speech, and was intellectually far above those with whom he worked; but he never lost their confidence, as such men as he often did then. The Progressive Club, however, did not progress. It had none of the spontaneous life and go that marked its neighbour, the Borough of Hackney. It cultivated dancing among its members, and its balls were well attended. Sometimes a political meeting was followed by a ball, and, as a club was a private house in the eye of the law, they could keep their dancing up to as late an hour as they liked. I often went to the Progressive balls and enjoyed their hearty, honest amusement, though the dancing was often of a rough-and-tumble kind.

T. W. Dennard was president of the East London Club, and I was vice-president. It met in an old skating-rink which had failed in its original purpose, and was let cheaply to those who wanted it for a club. Dennard was a type of man I often met with in the ranks of Labour, resembling Baines in courteous and gentlemanly manners, but with less intellectual force and vigour. He made beautiful speeches, with very little in them, but they held the rough and simple workmen by their charm and sincerity. Both he and Baines finished their lives while in their prime. Baines was cut down at a level-crossing by an express train, and Dennard fell a victim to consumption in his early thirties.

It was at the Borough of Hackney Club that I took the chair one Sunday morning for Canon Scott Holland, when he gave a lecture on the opium traffic. In those days he was enthusiastic about the trams at Oxford, then, I think, a comparatively new departure. Time cools many enthusiasms, but I do not know his views on the trams at Oxford now. Bishop Walsham How, the suffragan Bishop of Bedford, was an active worker in the clubs, and I presided at the much-talked-of meeting held at the East London Club on April 30, 1881, where he referred to Sydney Smith's phrase "a gig bishop," and said for his part he could not drive even a gig in the streets of London—he was "a 'bus bishop." The phrase made good material for newspaper scribes for a long time to come.

I have always thought that the woman orator found her own level quicker in the clubs than anywhere; and I recollect Annie Besant, in the days when she was popular among the working classes, going away from the Tower Hamlets Radical Club one morning because there were only a dozen people who had come to listen to her. Much was written in those days about the triumph of feminine charm on the platform, and the "glamour of sex." But an audience of more or less tired workmen was not particularly susceptible to the glamour of sex, and if the female orator had many excellent qualities, "charm" was usually conspicuous by its absence. And whatever there may have been of "charm" in connection with platform women has been destroyed for a generation at least, by the modern suffragette. One of the best women I met in the clubs was Miss Jessie Craigen. She was a violent temperance advocate, a supporter of woman suffrage, a martyr to neuralgia, and a thoroughly good-hearted soul. Among young men with ribald tongues she was known as "Mother Gamp." She dressed in dowdy fashion, and her umbrella formed an aggressive detail of her costume. I remember taking the chair for her at the Tower Hamlets Radical Club at a lecture on "Woman Suffrage," when she was crazy with pain, tried all sorts of drugs to relieve it, but stuck to her lecture all the same.

Conspicuous among club orators was a handsome young civil servant familiarly known as "Old Pick." E. H. Pickersgill was a man of intellectual tastes, a keen student of Shakespeare, and a member of the New Shakespeare Society, and he was also an eloquent exponent of popular politics. In 1885 he won a seat in Parliament for a division of Bethnal Green, and this caused him to resign his situation in the Civil Service, and he became a barrister. During the formation of the first London County Council in 1889 he and I took an active part, speaking together at many East London meetings. His political career lasted, with an interval between 1900 and 1906, when he was out of Parliament, till 1911. He was a loyal worker for his party, but his services were neither of the sensational nor the servile kind, and office never came his way. In the closing years of his life "Old Pick" was very poor, and a little before his death he vacated his seat in Parliament and accepted the position of a London magistrate, but died before he entered on his duties. He was a hard-working public servant, but all he won for his service to the commonweal was a life of struggle, and a little fame; sweetened for a while by human friendship and love.

The club movement showed me very clearly that there was an earnest desire on the part of the educated classes to get into touch with the artisan class if they only knew how. The clubs were at that time the only medium by which they could do so, but they were not the best medium, and they did not attract in very large numbers the more intellectual of the working classes; these were in the trade-union movement or the co-operative world. Dean Stanley was president for many years of the Working Men's Club and Institute Union, took the chair at its annual meetings, and delivered exquisitely beautiful annual addresses, usually far above the heads of his audience, and, perhaps with some consciousness of this, sought afterwards to know them by inviting selected members of the various clubs to the Deanery, Westminster. My first talk with the Dean at one of these visits was on the beauties of Shakespeare's pastoral plays. He had a wonderful power of making himself immediately at home with any one, and the talk is a delightful memory yet. Robert Browning was at one of these meetings—a spruce, smart old gentleman with an inexhaustible knowledge of everything he talked about, and it was a keen joy to ramble in the sunlight of a July evening through the aisles of the ancient Abbey and listen to his talk thereon. The desire on the part of the cultured classes to break down the partition walls which divided them from those whom it was the foolish custom to regard as beneath them began to manifest itself at the Deanery, Westminster, and it was to extend and broaden itself like a great flood in later years, and I was destined to take a part in its development.

Many and amusing were the stories that gathered round the unconventional Dean. His humour was of the quiet subtle order, but it could be crushing on occasions. It was on a Saturday afternoon during the progress of the Turco-Russian War, that I listened to a discussion at the Deanery on the likelihood of England going to war with Russia on behalf of Turkey. The Dean argued that the temper of the nation was against such a possibility. There was a good deal of jingoism among the working classes then, and a young fellow present hotly declared that Dean Stanley was wrong, referred to the various meetings that had been held in favour of the Turks, and finished up by saying, "After all, you know, Mr. Dean, there's no smoke without fire." "No," said the Dean with a quiet smile, "but I have often seen a great deal of smoke from a very little fire."

It was his custom on occasions to have meetings of

ministers of all denominations at the Deanery, who discussed with perfect freedom their points of doctrinal differences. At one of these gatherings where the Unitarian element preponderated, a clergyman who was a new-comer, exclaimed, "Mr. Dean, Mr. Dean, I cannot endure this, I really must say a word in defence of the Holy Ghost." It is quite certain that he gathered men and women of all shades of opinion to listen to his preaching, and it was a Jew who told me the story of a young Jewess who in bewailing Stanley's death said, "I never missed the Abbey when I knew the Dean was to preach, and I never heard a single thing in his sermons that I did not agree with."

Meanwhile my life was being lived actively enough. I was manager of a group of Board schools, active in my trade union and friendly society, the latter being the Stationers' Mutual Benefit Society, and was getting in a goodly amount of reading at the same time. My hours were from eight till seven, and one o'clock on Saturdays, and my wages were, in turn, 32s., 34s., and 36s. per week. Beyond the fact that I kept a home over my parents' heads till their death, I had no calls on my pocket when my own wants were supplied, and they were usually simple and easily satisfied. Cheap books got a great deal of my spare cash, and I soon became a sort of directory of second-hand booksellers. I had overcome the illness of my early years, and I was enjoying life and helping my fellows, and was content.

VIII

UNIVERSITY EXTENSION

The University Extension movement in East London was a further development of a social enthusiasm which began with the work of Edward Denison. He was a son of a Bishop of Salisbury, and was born in 1840 in that city. Going to East London in 1867 as almoner for the Society for the Relief of Distress in Stepney he found himself face to face with certain social facts, and resolved to settle in Stepney in order to study them. 1866–67 were years of excessive distress in East-London, but our humble household was not affected by it. This was largely due to the genius of my mother, as, although my father, my brother, and myself were at work, the total income of the family could not have been large. '67 was the year I first went up to Dr. Watkins, and my time was absorbed in my daily work and my endeavour to bring back health, and I never came into personal contact with Edward Denison, though I did hear in fragmentary fashion of things that were being done " at St. Philip's Church," and had I been in health should probably have found myself in touch with them.

Denison settled at 49, Philpot Street, Stepney, in 1867, and John Richard Green, the historian, was then Vicar of St. Philip's, Stepney, having been appointed there by

Archbishop Tait in 1866. He and Denison suited each other and worked together in perfect harmony. Denison built and partly endowed at his own expense a school, where he taught and gave lectures to the working classes at night. It was uphill work, and he was working practically alone—when will the democracy learn to do justice to the splendid work done for education by English Churchmen?—and in less than three years he was dead. Of frail physique and full of a passionate devotion to the cause of social betterment, he went under as Arnold Toynbee did twenty years later, and only his own immediate friends knew or cared.

But the beautiful life of Edward Denison was not lived in vain. He saw certain social evils which now are universally recognized, but then were disregarded. The custom of giving regular doles to the poor had no principle at the back of it, and led to much demoralization. They grew by degrees to rely rather upon the dole than their own effort, and as a corrective to this he preached the gospel of thrift. It is a true gospel as far as it goes, but he never saw its limitations. All the thrift in the world will never enable a man to get more than twenty shillings out of a pound, and thrift can never make up for bad wages, however far it may make the bad wages go. Edward Baker was as thrifty a workman as ever I knew, but he lies in a pauper's grave.

All the same, nothing will ever take away the glory from the splendid idealism of Edward Denison. Such men as he earn the crown of martydom in our modern world. He does not rank with the ignoble army of newspaper martyrs with their broken windows, sales by advertisement, and other accessories of second-rate melodrama.

His is a loftier throne, and his place is with those who, in the immortal words of George Eliot, " have lived faithfully a hidden life, and rest in unvisited graves."

In the *Progressive Review* of June, 1897, I wrote the following :—

" It was in the autumn of 1877, in a stuffy little back room of a house in the Commercial Road, that there met together for the first time a committee whose aim it was to promote in East London the establishment of classes in connection with the London Society for the Extension of University Teaching. It was a large committee, and sufficiently broad in the character of its representation. University graduates, local clergymen, officials of workmen's clubs, one or two tradesmen, and a group of young workmen whose qualifications were a little enthusiasm and an interest in the subject that brought them together, formed its members. None there, save perhaps the university men, knew exactly what university extension meant. To the group of workmen it seemed a further development of the work of Frederick Denison Maurice, who, saint and sage by turns, standing between the old and the new, and stretching forth the hand of fellowship to each, had filled the hearts of workmen who came within his influence with strange vague longings for a different and a better life for those who lived by the labour of their hands. Others thought of Edward Denison, whose sweet and strenuous life had ended, then a few brief years ago, and speculated if anything would come out of the movement to carry on the work which he began."

These words, which formed the opening paragraph of an article entitled " Twenty Years of a Social Movement," expressed with considerable accuracy what university extension meant to me at the beginning of my connection with it. The London Society for the Extension of University Teaching had come into existence some two years before the date when the Whitechapel committee was formed, and meetings, thinly attended, had been held at Shoreditch Town Hall—in those days a temple of every new movement of a political or educational kind. The chief personality at those early meetings was a Mr. J. E. H. Gordon, a young scientific teacher who lectured on electricity. He was a graduate at Caius College, Cambridge, and a man of rare personal courage, for he was afflicted with what seemed to be a hopeless stammer. But in spite of the stutter he manfully faced his audiences week by week, and they were so unsympathetic as to meet with peals of laughter any more than usually disastrous effort on his part to overcome it.

The Whitechapel committee was formed to further the work of University Extension in Whitechapel. At its head was the Rev. S. A. Barnett, who afterwards became a Canon of Westminster, but was then Vicar of St. Jude's, Whitechapel. Of that committee I was from the first a member, and after a little while became secretary. Its first secretary was Ernest Myers, poet, and brother to F. W. Myers, of psychical research fame. We began by holding a public meeting at St. Mary's Schools, Whitechapel, at which Tom Hughes, Q.C., and author of "Tom Brown's Schooldays," presided. The speakers were Leonard A. Montefiore, a young Jew, and graduate of Balliol College, Oxford; Dr. W. B. Carpenter, the physiologist; Mr. Samuel Morley, M.P.; and the Rev. S. A. Barnett. The crowd came because of the distinguished speakers, and not from any interest in University Extension; but to me the speeches and the ideas they embodied came like a revelation which drew together and synthetized ideas that had been working for years in my imagination. I learnt swiftly enough the catchwords of the political platform, and was a fluent and acceptable political speaker. But I never possessed the political temperament and my heart was not there; it was in the realms of history and in the world of imagination; in these things I was finding my true life. And now had come the new movement which might bring me into touch with all I loved, and to this I resolved to devote myself.

The first University Extension lectures in Whitechapel were given in the Medical College, London Hospital, in October, 1877, and there were four subjects. They were: " Physiology," by Mr. J. McCarthy, M.B.Lond.; " Electricity and Magnetism," by J. E. H. Gordon, the brave young Cambridge scholar before referred to; " Political Economy," by James Bonar, of Balliol College, Oxford; and " Recent English History," by Samuel Rawson Gardiner, of Christ Church, Oxford. They recall curiously mingled memories; the college was used for medical lectures in the day-time, and ladies forming part of our classes at night, I found it necessary to arrive early in order that I might remove diagrams not intended for female view. Gruesome objects were left by lecturers who were not concerned with University Extension, and skulls, bones, and other things had to be got rid of before lectures on History or Political Economy began. The janitor and the medical students made friends with me, as I was secretary of the class, and a wild-headed, warm-hearted youngster who eventually had to be reckoned among life's failures gave me a photograph of a number of skeletons seated round a table, with pots and pipes, as a memento of students' pranks.

The lecturers were of another type to any I had been familiar with, and although I had no particular enthusiasm for science, I attended the lectures on physiology by Mr. McCarthy. Through the good offices of the students I had the run of the museum and the lecture-room, and mastered my subject quickly, and have written once or twice in medical journals during my journalistic career. Leaning on a large pointer, swaying his body to and fro, and speaking in a strange monotonous chant, the teacher of physiology cast a spell over his hearers and compelled their listening. There was no humour in his speech, but he had a curious power of laughing with his eyes while keeping a perfectly grave face. With James Bonar, the political economy teacher, I formed an intimate friendship. I was not many years his senior; we had many things in common, and he was always excellent company. But it was not till I had listened to Samuel Rawson Gardiner that the true value of Unversity Extension came to me. Some one has said that the beauty of oratory is simplicity, and Gardiner illustrated this. Standing quietly before his audience, without note or gesture, he began to talk to them about the nation of which they were a part. It was not his speech—that was only clear, simple, and direct—it was the unrolling of an apparently inexhaustible mind that was the marvel and the charm. I had dreamed of what scholarship might be, and perhaps I had fancied myself a scholar; but now I was face to face with true scholarship, and I sat silent and with bowed head.

All of us who had worked for University Extension

hoped for a large response from the working classes. It did not come. Our four classes brought us a hundred students, and twelve were workmen. In the second year of the movement I, in conjunction with Leonard A. Montefiore, became secretary. He was a scholarly, brilliant young Jew, who seemed to have a great career before him. I wrote of him in the *Progressive Review*:

Among those present was a young Oxford man, full of enthusiasm and exuberant life, whose hearty boyish humour and good-fellowship endeared him to all with whom he came into contact. No kind of work came amiss to Leonard Montefiore. Laughing away doubts and forebodings of failure' writing articles in the Press, canvassing workshops, speaking at public meetings, attending committees, all alike came easy to this bright young spirit.

He, like Bonar, had many aspirations that I shared, and I spent many Sunday nights with him at his house in Portman Square, where we discussed problems of every kind.

He had written in the *Fortnightly Review* on "Liberty in Germany," and in other leading journals on German literature and on various aspects of English social life, and had, he told me, resolved on a political career. But the destinies ordered otherwise, and in 1879, on a visit to America, Leonard Montefiore died.

With his name is linked in mutual work the name of a young artisan, Charles Cannon. Cannon had won his education, as he had his bread, by the sweat of his brow, and our movement appealed to him, as it did to me, as the most important movement we knew. Montefiore was as generous in his friendship to Cannon as he was to me, but Cannon was to follow him into the eternal silence long before our work had reached fruition, though neither saw the shadow that was creeping near to them. But some fruit was ripening as a result of our work, and University Extension was breaking through the worm-eaten barriers of class and prejudice.

It did not do this, however, without meeting its critics. Popular education of a secondary kind, in London and elsewhere, had always adopted " bread-winning subjects," as they were called—subjects, that is to say, that helped a man to better his condition in life and put so much more a year on his income. The accepted theory was that a higher education ought to have a money value or it was of no value at all, and the criticism that was presently brought against University Extension came in the form of an old question, *Cui bono?* " To whom advantage ? " University Extension never ignored the utilitarian side of things, but it took for its motto a sentence from a speech by the Right Hon. G. J. Goschen, M.P., who was the president of the movement : " A man needs knowledge not only as a means of livelihood, but as a means of life." A long correspondence took place in the *East London Observer*, a leading local journal, as to whether we were doing any good at all by our work. I took my share in the letter-writing, and the upshot of my arguing was that an educated man was a better citizen than a half-educated man, and better citizens made a better State. Our correspondence did not convince many who were not convinced before it began, but it attracted notice to our work, and finally new men and women to our classes.

Constant and strenuous work was needed if University

Extension was to continue, as well as money. Of the first there was no lack, especially among the artisan members of our committee, but the second was not so easily reached. In 1879 two changes occurred which were important. McCarthy had ceased to lecture for us, and his place was taken by Thomas Dunman, a teacher who held no university degree, but who had great popular gifts. His engagement was regarded by university men as a lowering of our standard, but his lecture-room was crowded. His treatment of physiology was on a level with the minds of his audience; they had few difficulties, they learned their subject swiftly, and, if university men shook their heads at his style and methods, his students were more than satisfied. He had been a successful science teacher in the Working Men's College before coming to Whitechapel, and with his genius for teaching a bright future seemed before him, for he was but a young man; but before his course of lectures was over Dunman was dead.

The other change was the introduction of literature as a class subject, its teacher being W. R. Morfill, of Balliol College. It was made at my suggestion, and I made it because I had long been conscious of the muddled and desultory reading among the reading people whom I knew. The place of literature in the life of a nation dawned dimly on me, and I resolved to have literature in our classes. No better teacher could have been chosen than W. R. Morfill. He gossiped and told anecdotes about English literature, and joked and laughed about it, but knew it from top to bottom, and it was impossible to listen to him and not to learn. He and Samuel Rawson Gardiner, the historian, were opening new worlds to others besides myself. I had read a great deal of popular history issued by religious and educational publishers, and had long seen that the writers of it set out to prove a case. William Cobbett's blundering "History of the Protestant Reformation" showed me conclusively that there was another side to the story of the Reformation, but no writer that I had seen seemed to have the courage to face it, or even pretended there was anything to be said for the believers in the Ancient Faith in England. James Allanson Picton's "Life of Cromwell" was a book I read with pleasure; it was a good piece of literary work; but it was strictly partial, and the Puritans were saints and the Cavaliers devils or else fools. But listening to Gardiner I realized that here was a man who knew as much as any of the popular writers did about England, and he was weighing with scrupulous care both sides of the question, and trying to get at the truth. And when later I heard some wonderful lectures by Mandell Creighton on the Middle Ages I realized that the temper of the sect or the political party was not the temper in which to write true history.

It was at this time I met a young Oxford man in James Bonar's rooms at Stepney who was introduced to me as Arnold Toynbee. To those who knew him at Oxford he had an abiding charm, but I only remember a wonderful courtesy of manner, and nothing more. My impression of the interview is that we neither of us cared for each other, and perhaps because of this the greatness others saw in him was veiled from me. But he was destined to exercise a far-reaching influence on the thought of his time, and I was to become intellectually and spiritually the richer because of it.

IX

A CITY TRADESMAN

In the winter of 1879 changes were made in the firm where I worked, and my evenings were no longer my own in consequence of overtime. I always hated overtime, and only stood it as long as I was unable to shift my quarters. In 1880 I left my situation for one where the salary was larger, the work less, and where overtime never happened. The firm I obtained employment in was of a kind that was dying out in London, but while there I probably spent some of the happiest years of my life. It was an old-fashioned law stationer's in High Holborn, the head of which was a Mr. James Sloper, an aged gentleman in his seventies, who wanted a binder who knew all the details of his art, and whom he could trust with special work which had to be done in his house and with great care and skill. We suited each other admirably. He and his two elderly daughters carried on the business, and I and two lads were the only persons he employed. He lived over the shop, and had done so since 1846; was highly respected by every one who knew him through his long business life; went regularly to his parish church—St. Andrew's, Holborn—on Sundays; and cherished, among his life's memories, an invitation to a Lord Mayor's dinner many years before. He wanted a quiet workman; and I a quiet place where there was no overtime, and both of us got what we desired.

In the whole course of my career, I think, I never met a man more just than James Sloper. Full of fads and crotchets, and autocratic always, he nevertheless aimed at scrupulous justice, even when it was against his own interests. His Christianity was of the simple unquestioning order, but it was real. He was loyal to his church; disliked Liberals, but never let his dislike interfere with his business. An instance of his strict sense of justice made a strong impression on me soon after I entered his employ. An order had come in for a couple of reams of very costly paper which we scarcely ever used, and which was to be cut to a certain size. By a mistake on his part it was cut three inches smaller than the order. The paper was, for that order, spoiled, and had to be bought over again. It was clearly his fault, and the paper was put away until it might be wanted again. About a year after the incident an entire stranger came into the shop and ordered a couple of reams of the same paper. He was delighted to hear that he need not wait, as we had it in stock. He knew nothing of the price, the size as we had cut it suited him exactly, and he was ready to pay what we charged. Mr. Sloper could have charged him the original price, and so recouped himself for the loss his old error had brought upon him. But he went carefully into the cost of the mutilated ream, and with mathematical honesty reduced the cost accordingly, and took no advantage of his customer. I often reflected that if all his business transactions were as honest as that one, my old master need not fear if his books were brought up at the Day of Judgment.

My shortened hours gave a new zest to my University Extension work, and I was constantly in touch with the varied activities which clustered round the Church work of the Rev. S. A. Barnett. I lectured often at workmen's clubs all over London, usually on Sunday night, and have had many inspirations from his sermons at St. Jude's, which an hour later I carried on to the platform of some well-filled workmen's hall. I left off talking politics and discussed education, history, and literature, and soon found eager listeners. It was at this time that a desire, which afterwards became a passion, shaped itself in my mind of connecting, if I could, the various Labour movements which I instinctively saw were presently to mould the life of the nation, with the finer elements in our national life—with religion, education, art, and literature—and to that end I gradually worked. The idea at first was vague; but it was nevertheless the propelling force in all I did and have since done. My work was confined to London, and I knew little more of England than can be learned in two or three days' holiday, though I made the most of that to see as much of historic England as I could reach. Devoting myself to the work of education meant always that I was not on the popular line—for education has never really been a popular subject among English people. With all our talk about it, it has been the work of a small number of persons among us; but I did not mind, I kept on.

I had to keep all knowledge of my public work from my good old master, and as he had few interests outside his business and his parish church, and read only Conservative newspapers, this was easy. Generous as he always was in his treatment of me, he would have been afraid of a platform orator who spoke at Radical clubs on Sunday nights, whatever his theme. But he found me out at last, though fortunately for me it was under circumstances of unimpeachable respectability. I had been asked to speak one afternoon at the Mansion House on behalf of University Extension. A Cabinet Minister— the Right Hon. W. E. Forster—was among the speakers, and the Lord Mayor was in the chair. I asked his permission to go out for a couple of hours to attend the meeting, without telling him where I was going to; but the *Standard*, his favourite paper, gave a good report of the meeting the next morning, and mentioned my name, so concealment was impossible. He asked no questions, merely remarking in a hesitating way, " So you were speaking at the Mansion House yesterday, Rogers ? " He was always courteous to me in an old-fashioned way, although he was master and I servant; but his courtesy was more elaborate after the Mansion House episode : it was an incident he could not quarrel with me over, but which he did not in the least understand.

Within a few doors of Mr. Sloper's shop stood the last of the Elizabethan inns in the city—the Old Bell, Holborn. I had hardly begun to study the Elizabethan period when I went to work for him, and had not noticed the place. But its picturesque charm soon asserted itself over me, and I probably drank more beer there than I should have done if it had been, as it is now, a showy, attractice, modern tavern. The hostess was a friend of my employer's, and was a stately, ladylike person who would have been at home in a West End drawing-room. The inn, however, had no attraction for my employer, and he would probably have been considerably puzzled, and have suspected my general sobriety, had he known the attraction it had for me.

Once, indeed, I fancied his mind sometimes got outside his business after all, for in discussing matters with his daughter he referred twice, as I thought, to the "first century." My bench was close to his desk, and I pricked up my ears in amazement. What in the world had he and his daughter been reading that related to the first century? But, alas! for my ears, or my imagination! What they had been talking about was the *first entry* in the weekly ledger! The life lived by my old master and his two daughters must have been drab and monotonous enough, but they were happy in it. And now that it is only an episode in social life, forgotten probably by all but me, it is pleasant to recall the old-world courtesy and kindness, and the simple honesty of character, that I met with among the dusty reams and folios in the house of James Sloper in Holborn.

X

JOURNALISM

My connection with the University Extension Committee meant a closer connection with St. Jude's Vicarage and with the Rev. S. A. Barnett and his wife. The aim of Mr. Barnett in Whitechapel was expressed in a sentence I often heard—" to bring the people together; to get them to know one another." I was not impressed by the formula, but I admired the man who uttered it. It was a great idea put into simple words, and it had within it the breaking-down of class prejudices and the widening and humanizing of our whole social outlook; but I saw nothing of that then. But happy hours and a full share of intellectual wealth came to me in working with the Vicar of St. Jude's to carry the idea out. In his " at homes " at the Vicarage and the schools I met and conversed with Herbert Spencer, W. B. Carpenter, Norman Lockyer, Rev. J. Estlin Carpenter, and many other intellectual leaders of that day—men whom my old friend Edward Baker used to speak of with an awe well nigh as great as a good Romanist might speak of the occupant of St. Peter's chair. And I visited the studios of Watts and Leighton, and saw many rare and curious collections of pictures with Mr. Barnett's help, and the leisure which the shorter hours at Mr. Sloper's gave me was bearing rich fruit, and by and by there came the desire to write.

The sole motive that moved me at first was the desire to get a larger platform from which to put forth my educational ideas, and the platform I resolved to reach was that of the newspaper world. I was absolutely untrained, had never really learned grammar, and had only my instinctive love of what was best in literature to guide me; but it proved an excellent guide. In June, 1876, I published in the *Paper and Printing Trades Journal* an essay on the influence of cheap literature on the working classes. It was first blood, and I wanted another taste. In August, 1881, I wrote in the *Women's Journal* my first article on trade-union matters—an article on factory inspection entitled " Hot Weather in the Workshop." It was based on my own experience of factory life in London, and reads crudely enough now, but it was—up to its lights—an honest piece of work.

This serves to recall my connection with the women's trade unions and my friendship with the only great woman the English Labour movement has produced—Mrs. Emma Paterson. My serious trade-union work did not begin till my educational work had ended, but I gave for several years help to the women's unions. The helplessness of the woman in the industrial world always made a strong appeal to me. She was a pathetic, and sometimes a tragic, social fact, and as the trade unions seemed likely to help her, I worked with them, and so made the acquaintance of Emma Paterson. She began her public career in the Workmen's Club movement, and passed from that to the organization of trade unions. Happily married, but childless, she devoted her life to the service of her sisters, and found a staunch ally in her husband. Without either physical attraction or charm, the quiet, shrewd little woman exercised an influence on the Labour movement which no other woman has equalled since her day, and its secret lay in her entire sincerity and absence of pose. She never cared for the limelight, and never thought herself great; but she was great in the truest sense of the word. She came nearer to being elected to the Parliamentary Committee of that very conservative body the Trade Union Congress than any woman did in her generation, and this was due to her fine instincts and her power to gauge with accuracy the mind of the Congress, and to make Congress understand that she did so.

Of an entirely different type to Mrs. Paterson was Jeanette G. Wilkinson. Small of stature, dressy and aggressive in appearance, shrewish and sharp-tongued in conversation, she was, nevertheless, splendidly loyal to the causes she championed, which were women's trade unions and woman suffrage. It must have been heartbreaking work to these two devoted souls. Working women did not respond to their efforts, and at one of her lectures poor Miss Wilkinson was interrupted by a rosy-cheeked matron shouting out, " 'Ere, shut up, do; this is what I call woman's rights," holding up before the amused audience an exceedingly fine specimen of a baby. The women's movements could not have lived in their early years, if they had not been financed by kind-hearted people among the wealthy classes. The Church was a tower of strength to them. It lent its schoolrooms free of charge, and the Chapter House of St. Paul's Cathedral and the Jerusalem Chamber at

Westminster were equally at their service, and Church dignitaries were often bled for their funds. I know of one case of a cleric who is now a distinguished member of the episcopal bench, who had spent all his salary before it became due, and who pawned his watch and chain in order to send a subscription to a movement against lead poisoning in the potteries. Many were the meetings I attended at saint this and that schoolroom, and more and more was it borne in upon me that a few devoted women and one little journal could not make a great movement if the rank and file did not care. But the little journal had taken my first trade-union article, and Emma Paterson, its founder and editor, understood my aims, and my gratitude went out to both.

Emma Paterson died in December, 1886, worn out by her strenuous labours on behalf of her not particularly grateful sisters. It was written of her in the journal she founded:—

She loved work better than talk, and seldom cared to speak in public unless there was something to be said that she alone could say. She never aimed at eloquence, but said straightforwardly what was needed, and had always such a clear understanding of her hearers' point of view that her speeches never failed to be well received. From a girl, her work had brought her in contact with "all sorts and conditions of men," and her tact and sobriety of judgment enabled her to enlist support for her favourite objects in very various quarters. No Parliamentary Whip ever knew better "who was who," in the political world, who would help a cause for love, and who for popularity or other secondary reasons, and few parliamentary personages are as well informed as she was as to the not less important questions connected with the prominent characters among the working classes, who is honest, who is both honest and influential, who is only influential, and who is neither one nor the other. "So and so," she would write of a colleague, "wants watching over, he is too good natured," and, without ceasing to be good natured herself, she always remained too wary to allow a good cause to be compromised by a false step taken in ignorance.

Jeanette G. Wilkinson, less known and less lovable, died practically of starvation. Single-minded, self-sacrificing, and sincere, she never saw how little response her work received, and a handful of elderly women mildly anxious about a vote seemed to her the dawn of a red revolution. A pioneer with all the enthusiasm and passionate energy of a pioneer, she met with a pioneer's fate. Ill-health destroyed her capacity for work; Women's Suffrage societies only cared for her while she was able to draw audiences; friends fell off, and the last days of the poor woman who had lived so nobly and so unselfishly were days of privation and suffering, relieved at last by death.

The first article by me on a labour question outside trade unionism appeared in the *Pall Mall Gazette* in June, 1883, and was a description of a Sunday morning at the Tower Hamlets Radical Club—the same club as that pictured by Sir Walter Besant in his novel "All Sorts and Conditions of Men." I still did occasional work in the clubs, and my lectures on English history and literature on Sunday mornings were getting to be marked features in East London club life. At the Commonwealth Club, Bethnal Green, in February, 1884, I gave a series of four lectures on "Charles I. and the English Commonwealth," and these lectures were afterwards published in the *Club and Institute Journal,* and I count among my treasures a beautiful volume of Tennyson, given me by the club at the close of the series. But I was losing my illusions as to the possibilities of the club movement. Its social value I saw, but I was seeking other values, and when one morning, in the midst of a lecture on Shakespeare, I was asked to make a break to let the man come round with the beer, I knew my work at the clubs was drawing to an end. Both the clubs referred to here have long ceased to exist, and I wrote of the Tower Hamlets Radical Club in 1883 as follows :—

The church bells were clamouring loudly, if not very musically, as I turned my face eastward in search of a certain prominent Radical club, at which I meant to spend my Sunday morning. The club I sought for is one of the largest of its kind in East London, and is situated in a back street on the south side of Mile End Road. "The great joyless city of two millions," said Mr. Walter Besant, writing in a popular magazine about the East End. But the "joylessness" was not very apparent on the faces of those who were walking leisurely along Whitechapel Road, albeit the Sunday was a very dull one. Some vigorous hymn-singing saluted my ears as I passed the "barracks" of the Salvation Army, and now and again little groups of people went along, carrying very conspicuously gilt-edged books, and sometimes wearing an air of smug self-satisfaction, as if conscious that they were spending the Sunday in an orthodox fashion, let who would spend it otherwise. But the large majority were simply taking their Sunday morning's walk and enjoying it, heedless alike of church or conventicle, and laughing with equal good humour at the shouting of the revivalist preacher or at the chattering of the street urchin who endeavoured to imitate his eloquence. The street in which the club is situated is a respectable but somewhat old-fashioned thoroughfare, filled with dwelling-houses, which might be inhabited by the better-paid artisans of the East End. In one of these houses the club in question holds its meetings. The house is distinguished from those on either side of it by its being more dilapidated and less cleanly in appearance. Over the gateway is a lamp, on which is painted in red letters T.H.R. Club; while on the window which faces the street the same initials appear in black. On entering I found myself in close proximity to what seemed to be the reading-room, some ten or fifteen men being seated round a table smoking and reading newspapers. The walls of the room were ornamented with portraits of various political leaders, conspicuous among them being Lord Palmerston. Beyond the reading-room was the bar, at which a brisk trade was being done; the bar is a tolerably large one, but it was nevertheless crowded. Outside the bar, at the bottom of a short flight of steps, was a stall for the sale of literature; on it I saw the *Dispatch*, the *Referee*, the *Stage*, the *Freethinker*, and various cheap political pamphlets. Passing the stall and opening a door which faced me, I entered the great hall of the club. The hall into which I entered was crowded to the doors with an audience composed entirely of men. At the upper end of the hall was a platform, in the centre of which was placed a table covered with red baize. On the left of the table was a gaily painted screen, on the right a large piano. The platform was empty when I entered, so I had leisure to examine the hall and its occupants. It is capable of seating about five hundred people, and was built, I was told, entirely by the co-operation of the members of the club. The panels were gaily painted with alternate landscapes and festoons of flowers, and the screen and platform are painted to harmonize with the walls. The roof is supported by strong wooden beams, which are brightly coloured likewise, and the general appearance of the room on entering it is bright and attractive, though certainly not artistic. Round the walls, in easy reach of a person seated, were narrow shelves, the use of which was plainly apparent.

The audience was of a mixed character; many were decent-looking workmen of respectable appearance, but many were dirty, unshaven, and, if appearances might be trusted, would by the time the meeting was ended be none too sober, and these last did their best to festoon the lower part of the walls, by the aid of the shelves aforementioned, with glasses of beer. But now from behind the screen there came the chairman and a middle-aged man in a frock-coat, whom I took to be a lecturer. I was, however, mistaken, for he came to the front of the platform and commenced to recite from memory a play. I could not catch the title owing to the noise in the room, but a miser and his hungry servant figured prominently in the recital, which was not badly given, and seemed to be enjoyed by the audience. After an interval, which seemed to be for the purpose of a further consumption of beer, another recital was given; and by a programme which I purchased of a decent-looking elderly gentleman at the door I saw that an entertainment of a similar kind was to be given in the evening. As I walked away after the meeting was over, I could not help asking myself the question what influence an association like that which I had just visited would have upon the character of its members if this was the highest it could offer them. There was nothing coarse or low in the recital I had listened to. It was simply an average melodrama, such as may be seen on the stage of any minor theatre; but the conditions under which it was delivered were the reverse of elevating—the atmosphere reeking with the smoke of a hundred pipes, the tremendous consumption of beer, the " beery " look that was gradually creeping over the faces of a large portion of the audience, the noise of pots and glasses, the unwashed and unshaven men—all combined to make a scene at once depressing and saddening. There were many whom I saw there who must recognize these evils. Can they do nothing to alter them? The power to organize may be a great good to the artisan class if they use it wisely; but it will be a curse to them if they can do no more with it than may be done by any ordinary public-house. I was informed that political lectures were given on alternate mornings, and this is so far good; but a lecture under such conditions could not be of much value. Until the potent sway of the brewer be removed it is scarcely possible that much good, social or political, can come from such an institution. Let those who wish to serve the organization to which they belong make a strong effort to remove this evil; they will have the sympathy of all who wish well to the artisan class. Until this is done the more intellectual among workmen will avoid the clubs, and those who remain in them will simply play into the hands of their worst foes.

In the 'eighties one of the most popular Sunday newspapers among London workmen was the *Weekly Dispatch* —it used to be called the " Bible of the working classes." It was edited by Mr. H. R. Fox Bourne, and my great ambition was to give expression to my views about secondary education in its columns. I wrote several articles in the *Pall Mall Gazette* after my description of the Radical club, but the paper was not read by workmen, and I wanted to reach my own class. The *Pall Mall* then held a much higher place in the journalistic world than did the *Dispatch*, and friends told me if I wanted to get on in journalism I had better stick to the *Pall Mall* and let the *Dispatch* alone. But I was not troubling much about getting on in journalism: what I wanted was to get at the working classes, and imbue them, if I could, with my own ideas as to the value of education. And at length I succeeded, and after a few unimportant articles

I wrote for the *Dispatch*, in January, 1884, three articles on "Education and Working Men." I wrote them over the signature of "An Artisan," and used this signature for many years for my newspaper work. In them I called myself a Radical, scoffed with a workman's narrowness at ideals, and urged on my readers the inestimable value of fact. But I had not been inspired by Mr. Gradgrind, and was an idealist without knowing it, as the following quotation will show. I knew nothing in those days of the larger trade unions or of their activities, but my imagination had been stirred by reading what was being done for University Extension by the Northumberland miners, and by reading an appeal written by Samuel Neil, a Northumberland coal-hewer, on behalf of higher education, and at the close of my third article I wrote :—

It is, however, among the Northumberland miners that the most determined attitude is shown, as the following extracts from a circular issued by Mr. S. Neil, secretary of the University Extension Committee at Seaton Delaval, will prove. . . . He thus addresses the members of the Northumberland Miners' Association :

"The promoters of the University Extension scheme ask your pecuniary assistance towards this system of higher education. You are now asked to say whether the education which has hitherto been the monopoly of the wealthy classes shall be brought within the reach of your own class. Will you aid in closing the intellectual gaps which separate the various classes of society, and in repelling the charge of ignorance which is ever being hurled against the working classes? You, on whose shoulders the drudgery of the world falls—you, whose physical energies are taxed to the utmost—you are asked to make possible the cultivation of those moral and intellectual faculties which you in common with all men possess. It need not be said that these are the faculties which raise man above the brute creation, and that it is only by their cultivation that he can enjoy his life thoroughly. The works of our great poets, painters, and sculptors are still the monopoly of those who are rich enough to purchase a high-class education. Will you aid in making the enjoyment of these pleasures by your class possible ? Do you desire that the working man should attain intellectual manhood, and walk through the world without any sense of intellectual infirmity ? "

Eloquent words are these, London workman, that are spoken by our brother in the North. And in the last sentence there lies a prophecy which the young manhood of England may, if it will, make a fact. Intellectual infirmity is no more Nature's law than is physical infirmity. Very clearly the miner sees what it is that divides class from class. If Radicals look with contempt on all false class distinctions—and he is no true Radical who does not—then the Radical pitmen will give a hearty support to his appeal: for if progress means anything it means the destruction of all sham divisions of class. Real divisions there always will exist while men are what they are. It is a real class division that divides the sober man from the sot, or the hypocrite from the honest man, or him whose life is foul from him whose life is manly. These things always will and always ought to divide men; other things than these are but the survivals of our social fetish worship, and all true lovers of progress should aid in sweeping them away.

The pitmen responded to Samuel Neil only slightly, and to me the London workmen responded not at all. We were as voices crying in the wilderness, so far as the large majority of the working classes were concerned, and I know now it could not be otherwise, but did not know it then. The seed we were sowing bore rich and abundant fruit in later generations. At the time the workmen I knew smiled—but always with respect— at my enthusiasm for education, and went on enjoying life in their own way. It was neither ignorance, nor vice, nor drunkenness that prevented them from taking up the movement which was fraught with such great possibilities: it was simply that they were interested in other things, and remained so for the next quarter of a century or more.

Without giving up my trade, I made my way more and more into journalism, and wrote for some years for the *Dispatch*, as well as for some of the religious magazines. Always with an eye to educational ideas, but gradually broadening my basis, I dealt with such subjects as popular amusements, cheap facilities for swimming, the good and evil of cheap literature, and various aspects of the social problems that were rising on all sides. A popular pamphlet which sold by millions was the "Bitter Cry of Outcast London." It stirred the public conscience to consider the housing and other conditions of the poor, and Walter Besant's "All Sorts and Conditions of Men" drew attention to the squalor and poverty in East London. The Marquis of Salisbury and Mr. George R. Sims took part in the discussion, and both did good work on behalf of better social conditions. I had lived there all my life, and had got solid happiness out of the conditions; some of which to them were terrible. They were not terrible to me. Poverty there was, and I had shared it; but I knew—even though a thin wall stood between them and the workhouse—there was often happiness and upright, honourable lives among the poor. I had seen how the noblest woman I ever knew—my mother—could battle with poverty and overcome it, could create a clean, happy, righteous home on an income that often did not exceed twenty-five shillings a week, and could bring up her children with a knowledge of God and of righteousness with a husband opposing her beliefs. And she was in no sense an educated woman. She was the daughter of an agricultural labourer, and walked up from the village where she was born—Broxted, in Essex—in 1837 to find a situation in London. It was a forty-mile walk, and she was friendless when she got to the great city. But she found a situation, and in 1840 joined herself to a Baptist chapel in Great Alie Street, Goodman's Fields, and remained a member till her death in 1907. Religion was woven into the texture of her life, and whatever there may have been of religion in my own life has come from her. Zoar Chapel, as it was called, was built for Elias Keach, son of Benjamin Keach, a famous Puritan divine, in 1698. It had little history, and was a centre of the most arid Calvinism; but one pure and noble soul was nourished through a long and righteous life on the spiritual food she found therein. It has long since disappeared, but it was—as Alexander Philip points out in his Dickens Dictionary—the original of "Little Bethel," the chapel to which Mr. Quilp went in Dickens' novel of the "Old Curiosity Shop." He speaks of the minister as being a shoemaker, and there was a shoemaker who was an occasional preacher at Zoar at the time when Dickens wrote that book.

It is probable that he borrowed the name from Bethel Chapel, Rochester, a one-time famous temple of worship in that city, though Bethel was a common name for dissenting conventicles, and he used it in the "Sketches by Boz" as well as in the "Old Curiosity Shop." Zoar stood at no great distance from Mr. Quilp's residence on Tower Hill, though there is nothing to show where the residence of Kit's mother was, and she, it will be remembered, was a member of the congregation. Dickens had probably gone into Zoar, heard the shoemaker preach, and made use of the chapel and its phraseology in his own inimitable way. And there is really not much exaggeration in his description of that phraseology. As a little child, I was taken often by my mother, and sat on a hassock at her feet and trembled at the descriptions of Hell and the Devil that I listened to. But it was not little. It probably held some eight or nine hundred people, though it was never full. And it had a fine pulpit of carved oak, and its interior was a typical seventeenth-century tabernacle.

It was at the time of the publication of Besant's "All Sorts and Conditions of Men" in the early 'eighties that I first made acquaintance with a sect in Whitechapel called the Seventh Day Baptists. They are described in this novel, but Edward Baker had told me of them years before. Accident brought me into contact with their minister, the Rev. William Jones, in curious fashion. We met on the roof of King's College Chapel in Cambridge, at one of the excursions to the University which the Rev. S. A. Barnett was fond of organizing. Mr. Jones was an American by birth, and was the original of the Rev. Mr. Armitage in Besant's novel. He was a scholarly, kindly gentleman, who made friends with me at once. I learned from him that Seventh Day Adventism was one of the myriad sects which came into existence at the close of the Civil War two hundred years before; that its members believed Saturday to be the true Sunday, and did not worship on the orthodox Sabbath. They were a mere handful of people, exercising no influence, making no converts, and living in loyalty to ideas which interested no one but themselves. There were scholars among them, and well-to-do folk, and they were good, narrow souls of the most unimpeachable respectability.

But it was not their religion that interested me: it was the old-world atmosphere that enfolded everything at Mill Yard, and the pleasant, beautiful home-life of the minister and his family. I became a frequent visitor to the house, which adjoined the chapel, and house, chapel, and graveyard between them formed an entirely interesting picture of a world long since passed away. They were seventeenth-century buildings, and were surrounded by warehouses, but they formed as it were an oasis of repose and peace amid a babel of business noises. The interior of the chapel was naked of everything approaching to ornament with a bleak Puritan nakedness; and the thinly scattered congregation only added to its general dreariness. Good sermons were preached from the pulpit now and then. Once, indeed, I heard a sermon in which the ancient and beautiful story of Christmas was explained away to nothingness, and this set me analyzing for the first time the tendencies of Puritanism, for I saw in the preacher the spirit against which Dickens was fighting. He was a distinguished professor from an American university, and he was also a living embodiment of Ebenezer Scrooge.

Beyond the chapel was an ancient graveyard, where there had been no funerals for many a long day, and in the graveyard stood the minister's house, a gabled building that had been partly modernized. Except where it had been laid out in flower-beds, the graveyard was covered with long, rich grass, which had more beauty from being left to grow wild. Here in the soft summer afternoons the minister studied his sermons, his wife did her needlework, and his sons, growing to manhood when I knew them, amused themselves on a gymnasium. The quaint old picture has gone for ever, but its memory is fragrant and sweet.

XI

"TIME AND CHANGE ARE BUSY EVER"

Those of us who worked for education in East London through the University Extension Movement were finding out, as Frederick Denison Maurice had found out twenty years before, that the young men and women of the middle classes responded to our efforts rather than those of the working classes. But they did not on that account regard their efforts as thrown away. Enough of the working classes came to prove that their judgments of a social need were not all ill-founded, and they were pioneers and had to till the ground. Ideas about education were of a crude and half-developed kind, and rarely went beyond a training of the intellect. Nobody outside religious circles, and only a few people inside them, ever thought of education as a training of the whole man, and the earlier educationalists of London—those who created the London Institution in Finsbury and the Beaumont Institution in Stepney—probably did believe that a man was "morally better for knowing all about the anatomy of the megatherium," though Newman had not then written this magnificent jibe.

A tattered and time-stained programme of a concert given at the Beaumont Institution in the year 1867 is something of a landmark in this educational history of

East London. The Beaumont Institution was founded in 1840 by John Barber Beaumont under the title of the "New Philosophical Institute." He was a pioneer in the work of insurance societies, and an able and high-minded man, who believed philosophy would redeem East London. In many ways and for many years good work was done at the Beaumont Institution, but in 1867 the only classes on the programme were a class in French and one to teach fencing. The concert, which I attended, preserves on its programme some interesting names. One is that of Miss Louisa Pyne, a singer famous in her day and bearing a curious likeness to Queen Victoria; another, Mr. W. H. Weiss, the first singer of the now well-known song, "The Village Blacksmith." On the back of the programme is a list of the officers of the Institute, and among them are the Rev. T. J. Rowsell, then Vicar of St. Peter's, Stepney, and who, from 1881 to 1894, the year of his death, was a Canon of Westminster; Frederick Charrington, a popular brewer in Mile End; and Henry Wainwright, who in 1875 was hanged at Newgate for the murder of Harriet Lane. He was an excellent reciter, and among his successes was "The Dream of Eugene Aram." I used to recite that poem, and on one occasion gave it when a good-hearted muddle-headed parson was in the chair, who assured his audience he had not heard it done so well since he heard Henry Wainwright. As it was only a few months after Wainwright's execution, I was not flattered by the comparison.

As our classes grew in influence an effort was made to get possession of the old endowment of the Beaumont Trust for the purposes of University Extension. The place was doing nothing in 1883 and ours was the chief educational movement in East London, but we failed. It was, perhaps, well we did. Work of a larger kind was preparing for us, and the old bottles at Beaumont Square would not have held the new wine of social enthusiasm which later was to be poured forth at Toynbee Hall.

It was in 1883 that Arnold Toynbee died. His mark on the life of his time was that of personality. The Rev. S. A. Barnett and Mrs. Barnett brought him into touch with the social activities of London, but the impression he made on the men who knew him at Oxford was curiously like that made by Henry Hallam at his university fifty years before. The publication in that year of a now forgotten book—"Progress and Poverty"—by an American writer, Mr. Henry George, may be said to have brought about Toynbee's death. As he saw the book it was full of economic heresies, and he resolved to answer them. Of weak physique, but full of a passionate spiritual enthusiasm, he gave two lectures at St. Andrew's Hall, Oxford Street, against the book, and the effort ended his career. He died for truth as he knew it, and those who knew him felt that his death was a national loss, and resolved that his memory should not die with his life. Toynbee Hall, the first of the university settlements, was named after him, and its wide and far-reaching influence is among the fruits of his life.

In 1884 I gave up my trade as a vellum-binder, and entered the educational department of a large publishing firm as commercial traveller. It was a curious change to make; commercial travelling was not in my line, but I was introduced through it into new phases of life, and I enjoyed the change. From a pecuniary point of view

I soon found I was not very much better off than with Mr. Sloper, but I moved about England and Scotland, got into touch with our great industrial towns, and got a further insight into our great educational system, and learnt many things I was ignorant of. The firm in question had a series of school readers, and my business was to push them in the schools at the proper times, and I swiftly learned the educational Blue-book, containing the list of the various schools of England and Scotland—a knowledge I soon used to advantage in my journalistic work.

I did not find in the commercial room, when I knew it, the same variety of character that I found in the workshop. There was the same geniality and sense of comradeship, but the intellectual level of the commercial room was lower than that of the workshop. And yet the workman was often very narrow-minded, and knew far less than the commercial man; but the workman, within his narrower intellectual limits, thought a great deal more than the man who was devoted to the art of getting orders, and whose most brilliant flights of conversation never went beyond his financial successes. Many commercials I met were profoundly religious, and usually Nonconformists, but the tendency of the commercial room was in the direction of averages, and a crowd of commercials in the early 'eighties always suggested to me men who might have been made by the yard and cut off in lengths.

My occasional journalism went on and proved an acceptable addition to my income as a commercial traveller, and my subjects broadened out from articles on education to articles on subjects of social interest,

They were chiefly contributed to the *Weekly Dispatch*, over my usual signature, "An Artisan," but some were written for the *Pall Mall Gazette*, and one or two for the *Christian World*. I wrote a few political leaders in the *Dispatch*, and they were full of the partisan vigour which that paper delighted in. Its editor, H. R. Fox Bourne, was a kind-hearted journalist with a wide experience, from whom I learned and to whom I owed much. He was the author of an excellent history of journalism, from which, however, he reaped little pecuniary gain. He gave me my knowledge of the inside of a newspaper office, and I have memories of the dark little editorial office in Wine Office Court, where, amid a litter of "copy," magazines, and cuttings from newspapers, sat the genial editor, with a teapot eternally ready for those who cared. What was known as the "Coffee Palace" movement began in 1882, and in 1884 its shortcomings were criticized by me in an article on "The Faults and Merits of London Coffee Taverns." The following passage expresses very clearly the defects of the tavern methods as they were then. There was a meeting of directors of the coffee tavern companies in Birmingham, and of these gentlemen I asked answers to the following questions :—

Why is it that those whose aim it is to wean men from strong drink vend in the place of it such an atrocious mixture as that which is called tea at many coffee bars ? Why is it that the coffee tastes like anything but coffee ? Why is it that they, with presumably all the latest improvements in the way of apparatus for cooking food, cook, on the whole, rather worse than the dirty little coffee shops we may find down bye-streets yet ? . . . It is a good thing to be able to sit down in well-lighted well-ventilated places and get one's meals, but the meals you get are not up to the building you get them in. It is a good thing for the hungry errand boy to be able to get a thick slice of bread for his halfpenny; but why, oh why, is his "doorstep," as he poetically calls it, spread over with such vile butter?

May I respectfully ask those gentlemen, who I doubt not are enjoying their share of the profits of the concern, to consider these things? I may be told that the fact of the coffee taverns usually being full at the workmen's dinner hour is sufficient evidence of their goodness, but to this I must demur. Dinner is an all-important meal, and must be got somewhere, and Englishmen are long-suffering and slow to wrath, and, even though their discomfort be very great, they will, like the scalded monkey in the legend, "grin and bear it." Let those who meet to sing the praises of the coffee tavern movement remember that there is another side to the movement besides theirs. No doubt they will be able to point to some improvements in the art of supplying the public with cheap food, but I would respectfully urge that doughy puddings, stale pastry, and leathery beef still show we are a long way off perfection.

My remarks as to profits were premature; they were never very considerable in those days; but my criticisms were unanswerable, and my articles on this—as on other subjects—hit the mark. Public catering has improved immensely since those days, and it has done so because it has shifted from a philanthropic to a business basis. Philanthropy and business, "like oil and vinegar, won't mix."

Another subject which I continually attacked was the unclean side of journalism, but I have sorrowfully to acknowledge that the filth and garbage which in the early 'eighties was only to be had in the gutter, or from shops existing to purvey obscene literature, is now flaunted openly in shops which are called respectable, and may be had on railway bookstalls.

I wrote, in 1884, in an article in the *Dispatch*, the following words:—

But there are papers which fall to a lower depth still. Even the brothel has its literature and its organ in the weekly Press. Putting on the semblance of morality, these papers deliberately advertise vice and its haunts. Affecting an indignation at impurity, they pander to the prurient and bid for the suffrages of the obscene. Fouler than the gutter in which it is hawked, this vile trash escapes by a devilish ingenuity the action of a law which reaches less harmful publications. Men have suffered cruel imprisonment for publishing journals which, however, wretched from a literary point of view, were at least free from uncleanness and vice. Men and women are not likely to be harmed by these papers: the harm comes when they fall into the hands of youth. Lads who are not yet men have their minds made familiar with vice, and their moral natures poisoned at its very source. Clinging about the young imagination like foul weeds about the limbs of a swimmer, the influence of these periodicals, if not cast off in time, will render the moral nature helpless, and drag down intellect and character to a degradation that is worse than death.

I kept for a long time as curiosities of obscenity the columns of filthy abuse that were launched at my head for that article. There is a strange irony in our boastings about progress. I knew only one paper of the filthy and degrading kind in circulation in 1884; their name is legion now.

In a remarkable volume of sermons, published in 1911 by the Rev. F. B. Mackay, and preached at All Saints', Margaret Street, entitled "The Religion of the Englishman," is the following passage :—

Shops of a cynical shamelessness now plant themselves in the main thoroughfares, untouched by law. The education of the masses has borne evil fruit in a crop of gutter journals which cater for the lowest tastes, and in an epidemic of cheap impure literature which we have seen for some time on the bookstalls, and against which so far we have made no effective protest.

Every word of this passage is true, and the preacher might have added that some of the worse of these bibles of the bawdy house are written by women.

An article on cheap swimming-baths in the same year placed the whole swimming fraternity of London on my side. Every locality may have its swimming-baths now, supported out of the rates. But then baths were few and dirty. There were practically only three open-air bathing-places in London—Victoria Park Lakes, the Serpentine, and the Highgate Ponds—and I advocated greater facilities. They exist now; people have learned to think about such necessities as bathing, and to endeavour by collective effort to satisfy them. But only the swimmers had given any thought to the subject then.

Mr. H. R. Fox Bourne used to boast that the editorial office of the *Dispatch* was always open to new ideas, and certainly I found it so. Social ideas rather than political stirred my imagination. I had long ago seen through the fallacies of popular Radicalism without knowing it, and—echoing a phrase of Picton's before referred to—I proclaimed from many a club platform that if Throne, Church, and Peerage were swept away at once the working classes would benefit as little by the change as they did by the destruction of the monasteries at the Reformation. But my proclamation was not made to admiring crowds. The Radical clubs saw the change that had come over me, if I was not conscious of it myself, and my audiences fell off. I had read no Socialism then, but had read, and was always reading, history. The few Socialists I knew I had little fellowship with; they and I were thinking of different things.

But I did take up Labour representation. Studying the political evolution of our nation, I saw a period of aristocratic government, followed by government by the middle classes, and it seemed to me inevitable that the working classes would sooner or later find their chance at hand. But up to the time when I wrote my articles only a few workmen sat in Parliament. They were chiefly miners, and were not much more than old-fashioned Liberals; but in ability and character they were an honour to the House. In 1885 and 1886 I wrote two articles in the *Dispatch* on the subject of "Labou Representation in Parliament," and threw out, what seemed to me then, some sound suggestions of how this form of political idealism might be arrived at. The articles were rather superficial than sound; at that time I had not come into touch with the trade union movement, and in fact was drifting away from it, though still remaining a member of my own union, the Vellum Binders. The *Dispatch* then had the reputation of being the most widely read paper by the working classes but one, and

I was accustomed to correspondence on what I wrote in its columns. But the letters on this subject were few enough, and it seemed as though, in Labour representation as in Education, I was a voice crying in the wilderness. A workman of the Liberal type wrote deploring the fact that what I was doing would " destroy the unity of the Liberal party." I did not care two pins about the unity of the Liberal party, and told him so. A young man who was not a workman, but a member of the advertisement department of the *Times*, came to see me and propounded some ideas which in his judgment would realize the thing I was aiming at. An old High-Church clergyman wrote commending what I had written, and he had thought a scheme out which was entirely symmetrical and complete. It was also quite academic, but I thought it better than mine. Nothing came of all this, and for all I saw then my labour was thrown away.

In 1885 James Allanson Picton became a member of the House of Commons, and remained so for ten years. He was highly respected there, but made no particular mark in politics. I saw a great deal of him in those years, and used to tell him that in giving up religion for politics he had given up the greater for the less, and he received my comment with a kindly smile. He did not illustrate the French jibe, " in England the failures of the pulpit drift into Parliament," he was not a failure in the pulpit, for moral enthusiasm remained even when he had given up his faith. But he preached sermons in Parliament; he could not help doing so, and there is nothing the House hates more than that. And he was fond of big words and swelling phrases, and Lord Randolph Churchill convulsed the House by a parody of him on an occasion when he thus inflicted himself on it. He perhaps grew a little cynical as he knew the House better, and said once, "If you wish to lose all your idealism, come into this place." There were men who kept their idealism while still working the Parliamentary machine, but they were not those who entered it, as he did, in the meridian of life, and with another training than a political one behind them. He was always on the side of freedom and justice as he understood them. Scotch crofters, Irish peasants, and persecuted European nationalities commanded his sympathy and help, and an expression applied to him by an Irish member, "a little man with a big heart," fitted him exactly. His pulpit eloquence never left him, and the House of Commons style never reached him. Socialistic ideas came to the front long before he left Parliament, but he was untouched by them, and remained an Individualist to the last. He supported loyally and worked strenuously for Gladstone's Home Rule Bill, and was a staunch supporter of the Liberal party. But he never met with any acknowledgment from it, and it always seemed as though Liberals were half afraid of their somewhat untractable follower. He wrote books on Pantheism, and was a fervent admirer of Benedict Spinoza. I had read Spinoza when I heard him preach about him, and introduced a translation of the "Tractatus Theologico Politicus" into the St. Thomas's Square Book Society. But I found it deadly dull, and the good people of the chapel heartily agreed with me. Picton never lost his enthusiasm for the great Jew of Amsterdam, or his Pantheistic theories, but I, as I read onward, saw that "Pantheism was only materialism grown sentimental." He was a Nonconformist to the end, but in his later years frequently wrote letters to the *Church Times*, in which he lashed without mercy his Nonconformist friends for their inconsistency and injustice in their educational policy. They never forgave him, and his death in 1910 attracted little notice from their papers.

As a commercial traveller I failed. It was not my line, and I was mistaken in choosing it; but I saw England, and not only England, but something of Europe too, during my two or three years on the road. And I enjoyed the life, with its variety and good fellowship, and the sense of failure when it came was galling to me. At about this time, too, Mr. H. R. Fox Bourne ceased his editorship of the *Dispatch*, and my work there ended I rapidly found other activities—some remunerative, some distinctly not—and my life became more varied and strenuous, and less happy than hitherto. And among the ideas to which I turned my mind was that of co-operation. I had read the story of co-operation in Lancashire among the working classes, and knew how vigorously it flourished in various parts of Great Britain, and I had listened to the eloquence of Thomas Hughes, Q.C., George Jacob Holyoake, Lloyd Jones (for many years editor of a paper I was fond of in my boyhood's days, the *London Journal*), and to Edward Owen Greening, but I had never seen their ideas in practice.

A correspondence, started in the *Co-operative News* and *Pall Mall Gazette* in April, 1885, on the possibility of a co-operative bookbinding society appealed to me strongly, and I became a member of the committee started to found it. Bookbinders did not take it up, nor were London workmen as I knew them co-operators. If co-operation would assure them a comfortable situation, they were ready to support it; but not otherwise. A new society was of the nature of an experiment, and a comfortable job could not be guaranteed. In 1886 I took the management of the new society, which began its work in Tottenham Court Road, but I resigned it at the end of six months. I was not a bookbinder, but a vellum-binder, and that fact was discrediting it in the bookbinding trade. But it was a fruitful six months. I realized what a force co-operation might become if the working classes would take it up. But I saw also that the man of strong individualist proclivities never would take it up—it gave him few chances—and that the weak man, who might take it up, would be slow in developing it, though he might and often did, put it finally on a solid basis. Young men were not attracted by it; its leaders were men of years and experience. To the Socialist workman, on fire with a new idealism, and who often told me—and believed his own words—that presently men would agree in politics and all vote one way, and capitalism would perish in a night, co-operation was half wasted time He would not work for it, although I never knew him averse to sharing its advantages. And the Bookbinders' Society, which after I left it migrated to Bloomsbury, where it still flourishes and has done excellent work, began its career chiefly by the support of middle-class people, who were able to send it books to bind, and did so.

The development of the co-operative idea has been slow, but its possibilities are immense. I once gave a definition of Socialism at a University Extension examination as "co-operation writ large." Mr. Asquith, the present Prime Minister, who was then a University Extension examiner, only awarded me a second-class certificate at that examination, and probably that was all I earned. But I have always regarded that epigram as sound. You cannot have any kind of successful Socialism without the true co-operative spirit, and the great lesson taught by co-operation is the need for the unity of the spirit. The co-operative idea, great as are its possibilities, would not solve all our social problems, even though the world adopted it; there is no single idea in human thought which will do that, and there is no single idea which will ever possess the world. Co-operation appeals to a certain order of mind, and can be made a success by a certain type of ability. But nothing could be better for the commercial life of England than the steady development of the co-operative idea among the now better-educated democracy. Wherever it flourishes there is a thrifty population, and from its ranks have come men and women who, because of its freedom and its teaching, have been able to take a worthy share in the work of the world.

Falling out of regular employment, I remained for a year or two at a loose end, and on the whole rather enjoyed the experience. I became a hack writer for the Press, and I became also an occasional hack for the Liberal party. But nothing could make me happy in political work, and what I did was done purely for pay. I soon found you were regarded entirely as a hired mercenary by those who employed you, and this I was not content to be. The only memory of consequence that remains was that of the number of ex-Nonconformist ministers I met among the political mercenaries, men beyond middle life mostly, who were beginning to lose their chances of success in their calling, and sometimes—though not always—like Mark Rutherford, to lose their faith. Mark Rutherford snivels about it, and I never met a derelict parson who did that, though I met some who had taken to drink and were on the down grade : generally after their belief had gone. Some of them made a very honest try to put politics in the place of religion, but it was a woeful failure, and they soon knew it. And now and then I met a man whose life was full of the " things of the spirit," but who, because he was old, and possibly a little tedious, had no chapel, and had to earn what he could as a political hack, doing anything he was paid to do. Such men as these gave a touch of tragedy to the sordid underworld of politics. When Mr. Gladstone's Home Rule Bill of 1885–6 split his party asunder, all sorts of new schemes were afloat in the political world, and likely men had their chances. Offers came to me, among others, to take a paid office in the then infantile Unionist party. It was exactly what I wanted, for, if my life was interesting, my salary was very uncertain, and although I could never have lived in a Unionist environment, for the first time in my career I could not make up my mind. I had never taken the pains to think out the Home Rule question, and I wanted to be loyal to Mr. Gladstone. But what if he were wrong ? And then came an offer to edit a new Unionist monthly. But I did not accept the secretaryship of the Unionist club, the Unionist journal never got enough capital to put it on its legs, and I remained a little longer in the underside of Fleet Street, and made friends and companions of the hangers-on of the journalist world of the 'eighties. I had the gift of the ready writer, but was otherwise untrained, and had forced myself into the newspaper world by sheer dogged persistency.

I was not, however, able to force myself into a permanent position on the staff of any paper, and became, what I never was as a workman, somewhat impecunious occasionally. To some the life I lived would have been full of hardship, but I found no hardship in it. I could still live the workman's life, but had not his regular wages. It would have been bitter hardship to the gently nurtured, penniless lad from the university, and such I met with now and again. Worse equipped for journalism than I was, in spite of their university training, creatures of feeling and imagination, nervous and highly strung, but with no power of observation and none of the commonplace qualities so necessary to newspapers, they were tragedies in their world as Edward Baker was in his. Of one such tragedy I knew the ending. A sad-faced, delicate youth, he had something of the true literary faculty in him; he wrote exquisite reviews, but never succeeded in anything else. The charm of some of his criticisms lingers in my memory still. Subtle, kindly, and high-minded, it always seemed a wonder to me that he never got his chances on some high-class journal that could appreciate his gifts, but he never did. Once he interviewed me in connection with some public work in which I was engaged, and as I had done one or two interviews myself by that time, I gave him all the help I could. But the interview was a failure; editors did not want men who could not do what they were told, and after a few more months of struggle and poverty he ended his life by his own hands, and rests in a suicide's grave.

A strange, delightful, contradictory personality was a man I met among the older journalists. He was a hack who was never out of work, because he could do anything

—except keep sober when money was to be had for drink. Generous, warm-hearted, with a fund of Falstaffian humour, and incapable of anything mean, I passed many delightful hours in his company. There was a deep vein of religion in him—so deep that I often wondered if his early training had been that of a clergyman. But he was reticent about himself, except about his amours. I made large allowances, however, in listening to these legends, as I knew well the glowing imagination of my friend. He did his work much quicker than I, and once, when I was sitting with him in the taproom of a wretched little Fleet Street beer-shop, finishing some police-court work, he snatched a sheet of my manuscript paper, and before I had finished my task handed me a really powerful little poem entitled " My Life is hid with Christ in God." It was a strange and startling episode which I never forgot, and I saw depths in his nature then I never dreamed of before. I have lost the poem long since, but when I read it I wished I had been its author.

He was in no sense a woman-hater; he had been twice married, and had grown-up sons, but he *did* hate the lady journalist. I had met but few, and those I had met I respected. But he " knew every specimen known to Fleet Street." Of one he said, " Know her ? I should think I did. Gaunt, frowsy, and strident-voiced, and with a standing quarrel with Nature for not having made her a man. Smokes cigarettes, drinks whisky-and-soda, and doesn't mind saying sanguinary in the vernacular." With all my affection for my bibulous friend I did not wish to become like him, and finally came to the conclusion that life in the workshop was a better thing than hack work in Fleet Street, interesting as the latter undoubtedly was, and so in 1888 found myself back in the old familiar environment again.

It was well for myself and for the whole future of my life that I did so. Gradually I found I was drifting away from the old educational work that had been so good, and, because the human side of things was always of supreme interest to me, was making friends with the flotsam and jetsam of the London streets, but nothing was coming of it. It was largely wasted energy, sympathy thrown away. And in the Labour world, to which I belonged by a kinship of blood, forces were seething and struggling that were presently to influence the politics and the social life of the nation from end to end. I cared more always for ideas than action, though I have lived a far more strenuous life than many who are called men of action. It was in the workshop that the new ideas were being born; it was from the workshop that the future political leaders and rulers were to come. The currents of life ran strong there, despite their crossings and confusions, and I knew the men at the bench and in the factory, though I only knew them in London. I learned the life of labour in its larger aspects in after-years, and loved it as I learned it. But when I went back to the workshop after my few years of varied experience in other spheres, it was to see the workmen and labour problems in a different light, and I realized that labour in London, many-coloured and varied as was its life, was only a phase and an aspect of labour as a whole, and my business was to reach and to understand the whole. London was the Microcosm, and the Macrocosm I had yet to learn.

XII

MIND AND CHARACTER IN THE WORKSHOP

THE Right Hon. G. W. E. Russell, in his "Retrospects," quotes the following description of Hyde Park in 1880 from Lord Beaconsfield:—

Is there a more gay and grateful spectacle in the world than Hyde Park at the end of a long summer morning in the merry month of May? Where can we see such beautiful women, such gallant cavaliers, such fine horses, such brilliant equipages? The scene too is worthy of such agreeable accessories—the groves, the glittering waters, and the triumphal arches. In the distance the misty heights of Surrey, and the lovely glades of Kensington.

Commenting on this Mr. Russell says:—"This passage would need some retouching if it were to describe the Park in 1910, but in 1880 it was still a photograph."

On summer Saturday afternoons Hyde Park was a great place of resort for young workmen employed in the City, and in the early 'seventies I was often there, with Edward Baker, or with men of my own age. We enjoyed it as heartily as Lord Beaconsfield, but for other reasons. Our interests were in the flower beds, and the rhododendron bushes, and the great green grassy sward, on which we might lie and rest with no one to call us to order. The aristocratic crowd meant nothing to us, and I do not remember that we even envied them. We were young men, and if pretty women went by we noticed them. But we certainly thought we knew women quite as pretty in the workshop, and for their cavaliers, if we had any words at all, they were largely those of contempt, no matter how handsome or well-groomed they may have been. An old dying stump known as the Reformers' tree, because it was near it that many of the early Hyde Park meetings were held, interested us a little, but the "world was young then," May Day demonstrations had not begun, and our desire was to enjoy. To spend an afternoon strolling idly among the flower-beds, talking and laughing, speculating about the world of which we knew little, and occasionally finishing the day with a dip in the Serpentine, was a delight as great to us as any pleasure the people in the chariots knew.

Roughly my workshop life as a man extended over thirty years, and during that time I was in four workshops where I had comrades, but in the few years I had with Mr. Sloper, I was alone. I entered very fully into all the life of the workshop. My interest was for intellectual things, and I tried to make others care for them too, but I never met anyone who cared so keenly for them as Edward Baker and Edward Roberts of Cardiff, among my workshop friends. The things we discussed most in the workshop were the stage and politics. If we had any ideals at all, they did not get beyond being foremen in our own trade, and some among us used to say, with youthful cynicism, "there wasn't much in that." When I realized that ideal for myself in later years, I entirely agreed with them. On the whole the tone of the workshop in the 'seventies was conservative, except in its politics, and there was a leaven of conservatism even there. Liberalism was the political creed of the majority of the working classes, and they did benefit by the trend of Liberal policy up to a certain point, and the leading Liberals desired that they should. But the attitude of the average Liberal member of Parliament towards Labour was patronage so long as it did not get troublesome, and covert opposition when it did. In 1870 I was working at a leading London firm in my trade, the head of which—Sir Sydney Waterlow—was Liberal candidate for Southwark at a by-election in that year. He was opposed by George Odger, a working shoemaker. It was the first working-man candidature that London had seen, and was not taken seriously. But Odger was an able honest man, and, in addition to being trusted by his fellows, had the support of John Stuart Mill. Waterlow adopted an ingenious method of checkmating Odger. He employed two or three hundred hands, many of whom lived in the constituency he was fighting, and during the election any workman in the firm who would shout at his employer's meetings, might have an evening off and half-a-crown pocket money, on as many nights as there were meetings. He did not win the seat, only polling 2966 votes, against Odger's 4382. The Conservative candidate, however, polled more than either.

XIII

HENRY IRVING AND THE DRAMA

In theatrical matters the mind of the workshop was very conservative indeed, and I shared in its conservatism till the advent of Henry Irving. Edward Baker helped me to my first understanding of the stage. He was able to take a view of dramatic art which was much sounder than that of any man I had met then. But when, in 1871, I saw Irving in "The Bells" I became at once a devout Irvingite, while he remained faithful to old traditions, and to the old school of dramatic art. It was often a very noble school, and it reigned in the workshop long after Irving had dethroned it everywhere else. Baker had memories of Mr. and Mrs. Charles Kean, players whom I never saw. Instinctively I wanted to see the best men on the stage, as—when I began to go to picture galleries—I tried to find out the best pictures. It was my mother's influence that created this spirit in me, only the best was good enough for her. There was a gleam of divine light amid the fogs of Little Bethel, and she saw it, though the great novelist did not who has made the place immortal. High colours and broad outlines were among the predominant characteristics of the old school of actors. Of subtlety there was none, of refinement not too much, but the declamation was often magnificent. The women studied the psychology of shrieking, to its last detail, and a burst of screaming was held to be a fine expression of dramatic passion. There was a tendency with all these actors, except, perhaps, Samuel Phelps, to become stilted and artificial, and as time pressed heavily upon them, their characters went perilously near to being caricatures; but they knew how to declaim blank verse, and could give you its resonant music in a way which neither Irving, nor any of his school, quite succeeded in doing.

Phelps was the man of genius, who stood apart; and he was the idol of the workshop. To the end of his career, which closed in 1878, he was the most polished and perfect speaker of blank verse on the English stage. A certain hardness of voice never detracted from the dignity and melody of his declamation, and there were moments when the rolling lines seemed part of his natural speech. He had given up Sadler's Wells long before my theatrical days; but I saw him at Drury Lane under the management of F. B. Chatterton; who said at the close of his managerial career, that "Shakespeare spelt ruin and Byron bankruptcy." I also saw him within a little while of his death, at the Gaiety, under the management of John Hollingshead.

Creswick stood next in succession to Phelps. He was an actor fond of romantic plays, and during his management of the Surrey Theatre in Blackfriars Road, these were largely the plays he produced. He was a romantic actor first, and Shakespearean actor afterwards. "True to the Core," "The Orange Girl," and the "Idiot of the Mountain" were among the Surrey successes, and of the last of these a good story is told. Creswick played the name part, and when the rehearsals were preparing a

K

young fellow who had been engaged but who had never been in London before, made his appearance at the bar of the adjoining tavern, which happened to be filled by members of the company, manager Creswick among them. Finding himself among his future comrades, he stated who he was, and why he was there. "Oh," said Creswick, with a sly glance at his fellow-actors, "and so you are the countryman who has come to play in the 'Idiot of the Mountain,' and are you the Idiot?" "No," was the prompt reply, "it's the manager who engaged me who is the idiot." Needless to say, that young player was received at once into the good fellowship of his comrades, Creswick included.

The fierce controversy which raged round the acting of Henry Irving found its full echo in the workshop, and I was in a minority of one in defending the new actor. He was making a revolution in dramatic art, and the workshop wanted no revolution there. It held certain stereotyped ideas as to Shakespeare's conception of his own characters, and these ideas were represented by the men and women it was used to—or it thought they were— and Irving's wonderful psychological studies of passion or crime were things it could not understand, and would not accept. But Irving stirred my emotions and gripped my imagination as no actor has done before or since. I differed keenly from some of his conceptions, but their artistic wonder was a new fact in my theatrical experience which I could not explain. What Clement Scott wrote of Irving's wonderful personal magnetism in Hamlet, in 1875, exactly expresses the influence his acting had on me from the beginning. "Over all, disputants or enthusiasts, has already been thrown an indescribable spell. None can explain it; but all are spellbound." No such influence came from the older school, not even from Phelps, as came with Irving. When I tried to analyze his acting, it all seemed made up of little things, but they were like the last chippings of the sculptor's chisel. Collected together they were but a little heap of dust, but they made the statue perfect. My first experience of the greatest acting then on the stage was in the days of my boyhood, when, in the year 1865, I went to Drury Lane Theatre, to a performance given in aid of the actors at the Surrey Theatre, which had just been destroyed by fire. The play was "The School for Scandal," and the cast included Phelps, Creswick, James Anderson, Amy Sedgwick, Mrs. Stirling, and all the minor parts were filled by distinguished men and women. It was a great event, and my enthusiasm knew no bounds, but Irving introduced me into a world of art of which these actors had no glimpse.

His appeal to the imagination was direct, and he disregarded entirely the ordinary stage accessories and traditions. He was not an elocutionist in the old actor's sense of the word; and this was a defect which many people never quite got over. But there was a compelling power in the strange and wonderful voice, and a mobility in the beautiful face, which the old actors could not compass and did not possess. The controversy about him began—or at all events reached the workshop—when, in 1873, he produced Bulwer Lytton's play of "Richelieu." Bulwer Lytton's plays were never much more than dramatic surprises, fustian and fine sentiment, but "Richelieu" was almost great, and stood out from among the rest as a play for great actors to win triumphs in. Macready, Phelps, and Creswick had all won success in the name part, and a great stage tradition surrounded it. It had a famous catch phrase, "and all in spite of my Lord Cardinal," which always won applause. Catchwords have gone from the stage now, and only remain in politics, and they were going when Irving put on "Richelieu" at the Lyceum. He dressed for the part from the picture of Richelieu in the Louvre; Phelps and Creswick according to the stage view of a Cardinal. Three episodes in the play indicate the traditions which Irving, with marked success, abolished. Young De Mauprat, the lover of play, is secretly plighted to Richelieu's niece, Julie. The cardinal is ready to sanction the marriage, but persuades the young noble that he desires him to marry someone else. De Mauprat declines marriage under such conditions, with the remark that marriage "asks the courage of a lion." When he finds out that Richelieu wants him to marry the girl he loves, he is as willing to marry, as before he was averse, and the Cardinal, with a chuckle, gives him his own words back. The stage tradition made the Cardinal accompany this with a decidedly vulgar dig in the ribs with his elbow; this Creswick and Phelps followed. Another episode was when Richelieu tried to lift the two-handed sword of his soldier years, and finds that age prevents him. Phelps and Creswick accompanied this with a burst of rather aggressive sobbing. In the great scene where the Cardinal protects his niece from the emissaries of the king by the threat of the thunders of the Church, Phelps and Creswick held above the trembling girl a great glittering cross.

The workshop was entirely on the side of the nudge in the ribs, and the sobbing, and the glittering cross, but Irving swept them all away, and reached a much finer dramatic effect without them. Fierce and long sustained were the arguments which I waged on behalf of the new actor and his methods, and they continued with his Hamlet. Here he showed his perfect artistic instincts in a similar way. In the scene with his mother when he uttered the words, " Look on this picture: and on this," the usual plan was either for Hamlet to have his father's portrait on his neck, or else to have it painted on a panel, while his uncle's portrait glowered on him from the opposite wall. Irving had neither. He simply indicated by a wave of the hand the two pictures which he was calling up in his mind's eye; they were not in the room at all. The workshop rose in furious revolt at this innovation, but the new actor was purging his art of the meretricious and the commonplace, and was lifting it to levels it had perhaps never before occupied. I have seen many Hamlets: some of them great. Miss Marriott made a great Hamlet. Barry Sullivan and T. C. King were actors whose artistic ideas were conscientious and commanded respect, and the Hamlets of Forbes Robertson and the younger Irving dwell long in the memory. But no Hamlet I ever saw left in my mind such a sense of intellectual greatness, and of artistic completeness, as did the Hamlet of Henry Irving. The art of a departed actor cannot be estimated like that of a departed painter or sculptor, and we have little to go upon but impressions. But they have a value, however incomplete they may be, and the impression he made upon the dramatic imagination of his time, combined with the magnificent services he rendered to dramatic art, mark out Henry Irving as the greatest personality that ever trod the English stage.

The workmen's club movement developed a certain

type of dramatic art which was of interest, because, in the majority of cases, the actors were workmen or women, who were employed at their ordinary labour in the day-time, and acted on their club stage at night. Not every night, often not more than two nights a week, but what they did represented their dramatic ideals. Occasionally there was very good acting on the club stage, and actors made their first bow to audiences there who afterwards found positions in the ordinary theatrical world. But it was not the club actor who left his environment—and after a time forgot it—but the club actor who remained, whom I found most interesting. A handsome young workman actor—I think a compositor by trade—who was known as Mr. Byron Ballard, never went on the regular stage, but would in all probability have achieved success there had he done so. He had a company of his own, and went about the clubs with it, and really made an excellent Hamlet, and appeared in other Shakespearean parts. Shakespeare is always honoured by the working classes, and is much more studied now than when I was a young man. But Byron Ballard was always a popular Shakespearean actor, quite conventional, but within his conventionality entirely good.

Domestic and romantic drama used to be the most popular form of dramatic entertainment in the workmen's clubs in the 'seventies and 'eighties, though now I am told the frivolities of farce and musical comedy delight most. It was a characteristic of the clubs as I knew them that the unclean was always the unpopular. In the art of acting, so far as the clubs were concerned, the women were greatly inferior to the men, but there was one actress whom I remember in the clubs who possessed both originality and dramatic power. She was in her forties, comely in appearance, and a widow with three or four children to bring up, and was glad of the ten-shilling fee she received each night she played. She was a good elocutionist of the popular type, but possessed a decidedly raucous voice. Her friends on the female side used to explain this by pointing out that she got her living by selling cats' meat during the day, adding to her income by acting at night. It was a perfectly honourable calling if it was so, and I always respected the hard-working humble woman whom the theatrical critics knew nothing of, even though her delivery of Shakespearean blank verse was sometimes rather an infliction. She made some success in a version of a play in which Madame Celeste used to act, the " Woman in Red." It was only popular melodrama, but there was plenty of declamation and noise in it, and it had a long lease of popularity. Apropos of Madame Celeste in this play, there used to be a wicked story current that when Madame was on tour with it, her advance agent, either through spite or bad penmanship, posted her to appear in a particular town in the " soul-thrilling drama " of the " Woman in Bed." She was furious when she reached the town and saw the bills, but there was not even standing room in the theatre.

A workman with strongly marked characteristics and many abilities was Richard Gaston, a club actor and reciter; and, as editor of the Club and Institute Journal, he was perhaps the first club journalist. He was a shrewd, amusing bachelor, who said and wrote caustic things about women, but quietly befriended many of them. His line was old men's parts chiefly, and one of his successes was Chrysos in " Pygmalion and Galatea." The part was one of J. B. Buckstone's successes, when the play—which was written by W. S. Gilbert—was produced at the Haymarket in 1871; but it was not till 1891 that Gaston played the part. He was in his way a trainer of young actors and actresses, and a lady who is now acting old women's parts with much success on the West End stage, owed her first training and introduction to theatrical life to Richard Gaston. The *Club and Institute Journal*, which he edited for a few years, but which finally collapsed for want of support, represented the mind of the clubs—which was also the mind of the workshop—very accurately. I wrote articles in it on the drama, and on literature, and he wrote the "leaders." The rest of the paper was filled with accounts of club entertainments and other functions, written by the members of the clubs themselves, and they were often a sad spectacle; not so much from the point of view of mere composition as from that of intellectual outlook. I often used to wonder as I read them whether our quarter of a century of educational work (it was in the 'nineties that the magazine was published, and in 1891 that I made my first contribution to it) had done much good after all. But I did realize then that the club movement was only a part of the life of labour, and that there were other phases of that life much larger and of farther-reaching importance.

XIV

SOCIAL IDEALS

AMONG the popular writers who, in days now entirely passed, have exercised a great influence on the mind of the working classes is Mr. George R. Sims. In 1877, when the *Referee* first appeared, his column "Mustard and Cress," and his "Dagonet Ballads" took working-class readers by storm. Not because he had any knowledge of working-class life, but because he was a live, original journalist, who reflected all their prejudices against the aristocracy, as well as some of their principles, and struck out a new line in journalism. His gift of humour was spontaneous, abounding, and clean, and he was full of a manly straightforwardness which went right home to the heart of the workshop. The simple vigour and picturesque description of the "Dagonet Ballads" made them immensely popular on the platforms of workmen's clubs, and I was probably one of the first to recite "Christmas Day in the Workhouse," since I committed it to memory and recited it at the Dublin Castle Club, in East London, within a week of its appearance in the *Referee*. It was a harrowing, powerful story, and it became immensely popular among reciters of every kind. I have always believed that it had its influence in moulding and educating public opinion in the direction of other work which became mine in after years—Old-Age Pensions. Equally powerful was the influence of some early stories of his—the "Social Kaleidoscope." There was always a foundation of truth in his most extreme utterances, but it was not the truth so much as the denunciations that appealed to us in the 'seventies. His pictures of the life of the aristocracy were always vivid and highly coloured, and to us they were entirely true. In style he resembled Dickens, but the literary traditions he carried on in his early stories were those of G. W. M. Reynolds, except that he avoided mediæval romance, and was never morbid or sensual. One of my most successful lectures during those years was "George R. Sims as a public teacher." It drew crowds.

The average workman, as I knew him, was not capable of sustained reading, and the short story and crisp paragraph inaugurated by G. R. Sims were much more to his palate than the long stories I loved. "Romola," "Felix Holt," the stories of older authors, and the sketches of Washington Irving, filled me with delight, but not even the latter—short though they were—could I make popular in the workshop. It was not from dislike of literature, or lack of intellectual energy, it was rather custom and habit, which might be and was broken down when the time came to do so. Meanwhile the things of immediate and pressing interest came first. Domestic life, with its anxieties and its responsibilities, was for workmen—and rightly and naturally so—a more important matter than books.

The intellectual awakening of the workshop came with the spread of Socialism. Liberalism was a salt that had lost its savour, though the working classes of the 'eighties and 'nineties hardly knew that; they only knew it was different to the taste. The younger generation of workmen saw no outlook along its lines, and to them the platform orator of the Liberal party was a vendor of commonplaces, and Liberalism itself little more than a note of interrogation. But the new gospel of the collective ownership of the means of production, distribution, and exchange flashed like a bright bewildering vision into the mind of Labour, and it seemed as though the seeds of revolution were being sown. It was, however, the kind of revolution that went at a measured pace, and the "capture of the machinery of the State" was a bigger thing than workmen knew.

It was not in the mind of Labour only that the new ideas grew. In January, 1882, Alfred Milner, my fellow-secretary in the University Extension movement, who is now the Viscount Milner, delivered a series of four lectures at St. Jude's Schools, Whitechapel, which lectures were entitled "An Examination of Socialism"; and from October to December of that year he delivered another series on "The Laws of Wages and Rent." In these two series he certainly laid the foundations of a scheme of scientific Socialism, but the men who talked Socialism at workmen's clubs did not come to University Extension classes, and the excellent lectures were condemned to be delivered largely to a middle-class audience.

Socialism never gripped my imagination as it did that of my shop-mates. This was because, when it arose as a new gospel of Labour, my mind was passing into a critical stage. I had tried, and had seen, the trial of many social experiments, a critical habit of mind had grown up within me, and I had begun to look at social problems from the human side, rather than from that of machinery. I was greatly attracted by the early activities of the Fabian Society, but the reasons which prevented me joining it were practical and not theoretical. They met at Willis's Rooms, at St. James' Street, and I dwelt at Mile End, and between the two and quite close to me stood Toynbee Hall. Fabianism on its intellectual side, its able men and its carefully thought out theories, made a strong appeal to me, but the pull of Toynbee Hall was stronger. There I carried on the earlier traditions of my life, and saw later on that I was entirely right in so doing.

There was a good deal in Socialism that commanded my sympathies, if my reason was not convinced, and Mr. Harold Cox, then one of its shining lights, wooed me earnestly to join the Fabian Society. I did not know then that I was destined to bring about what Mr. Ben Tillett called "the first bit of Socialism that England had entered upon"—Old-Age Pensions. I felt a horrible sense of repulsion at one of the first Socialist meetings I attended, when I heard a speaker say, "It does not matter if a man is a thief and a murderer; if he believes in Socialism he is a comrade," and denounced him vigorously; but I did not credit the whole movement with the utterance of this fool. William Morris, artist and poet, was among its leaders, and if Mr. H. M. Hyndman had little enough of the true qualities of leadership, he won a loyalty and devotion from his followers, and those who knew him best, that was a beautiful thing to see. There was an immense pathos in the early Socialist ideals of the working classes, and Canon Scott-Holland said they were the only people with any touch of the prophetic spirit, though they were probably frightfully wrong in matters of detail. The most complete parallel I could find to their idealism was in the " Glory " of the Salvationist. The same vagueness, the same self-sacrificing enthusiasm, the same devotion, was found in Socialist and Salvationist alike. But socialists have had sufficient force to stamp themselves on legislation, and the influence of Toynbee Hall was—*plus* a strongly critical element which was entirely to the good—on their side. But Toynbee Hall, and what grew out of it, belong to another chapter.

XV

TOYNBEE HALL

MEMORIES of my visit to Oxford ten years before came back on me like a flood, when, in 1883, I was asked to go to Oxford and read a paper before a society of graduates at St. John's College. I had spent one week-end there in the intervening ten years, as guest of Claude E. Montefiore, younger brother to my friend Leonard A. Montefiore, but Oxford for me was still Oxford the historic, Oxford the romantic, Oxford of the glamour and the charm, and I had never really touched its life. I had got to know pretty well, through my University Extension experiences, the average 'varsity man as he was when he came to London, full of enthusiasms, and raw from his university, but that was not the same thing as knowing the life of the university itself.

The swift changes that were taking place in social life, and the easy facilities of travel which could be availed of by the well-to-do, were bringing about a class separation in all our great towns, and were fraught with many social dangers. The recognition of this fact by the Rev. S. A. Barnett was the recognition of a principle that went deep, and the remedies for it went no less deep also.

His desire that people "should get to know one another" was a bigger idea than I realized, and the destinies had chosen me to take some part in carrying it out. His first steps in "bringing the people together" were to interest the men in the universities in the people outside their charmed circle, and to this end people of all ranks in life were asked down to Oxford and Cambridge to give expression to their ideas. The custom is common now; then it was a new departure, to be praised or blamed by the Press, according to the party to which the particular paper happened to belong.

I was the first workman who had been asked, and those who asked me knew nothing of that visit of mine ten years before, and how it lingered in my memory, and I found out in conversation with the dons and the undergraduates in my two days' stay, that Oxford meant more to me than it did to a good many who were sharing its advantages to the full. I have no memory of anything in that paper. I only remember a crowded college hall, genial hosts, discussion and invitations of all kinds for the next day. Mackarness, Bishop of Oxford, met me at one college, and Edward Stuart Talbot, Warden of Keble, and now Bishop of Winchester, invited me to see the Holman Hunt picture, and he was a helpful, pleasant companion in the days of that visit. And Sidney Ball, of St. John's, then a kind-hearted young graduate, full of ideas and enthusiasms, showed me the treasures of his college, and my heart warmed at the sight of a Caxton Chaucer, which, I was told, was the most perfect in existence, and the illuminated missals and old vestments I saw were a very pleasant study for a Sunday afternoon. Laud's hat and stick were also there, but although Laud was a brave and loyal-hearted Churchman, he was not one of my heroes.

Efforts were made in all directions to interest university men in the new movement, which really meant inviting those who wished to do so, to learn social problems at first hand. I remember telling an audience at Cambridge that trying to learn social problems merely from books was like trying to learn to be a doctor without walking the hospitals, and the sentence was much commented on at the time. Among the things published during the shaping of Toynbee Hall was a leaflet by myself, in which I put the settlement idea as it presented itself to me then. It was originally framed as an article for the *Pall Mall Gazette*, but it was rejected, and in an amended form saw the light as a settlement leaflet. In its concluding paragraph I said :—

Let those who take part in this work lose sight of self if they would do it successfully. They will find many among the artizans who, by their sincerity of purpose and integrity of character, are worthy of the friendship of any man. If they seek to make friends among their poorer neighbours they will find the same differences of temperament and character as exist among their own class. They will find high and noble lives, lives as full of chivalrous manhood as the life of any knight of old. They will find others whose thoughts never rise above the commonplace, and whose lives have little enough of the ideal in them.

The type of man who is most likely to succeed is the man who does not hope to achieve miracles, who is willing to work and learn while he works, in the faith that no sincere and wise effort for human good was ever in vain. He must forget class and think only of humanity. He must forget creeds and think of that which in the last result is the inspiration of all creeds, the desire to purify and ennoble human life. He must not think that social diseases are to be cured in a moment, any more than physical diseases. He will find dull heads sometimes; but he will find, too, that they often have warm hearts to balance them. He must have faith in the power of high principle, in the force of noble example, faith in his fellows, faith in the English character, belief that in the majority of human hearts there will be an answering echo to every inspiring cry. With these things and with steadiness of purpose that is not turned aside by difficulties or failures, those who cast in their lot with this scheme may help forward the march of human progress.

It was written for young men, and what the young 'varsity man had to learn first of all in those days was that human nature was pretty much the same all round. They were amiable, friendly, charming, and entirely well-meaning young fellows, but they surveyed life from a pinnacle, and needed to come down to earth. But I knew that coming from theory to fact, while it usually meant the dispelling of illusions, sometimes meant, too, the loss of ideals and inspirations, and perhaps I helped to guard against that in the leaflet.

Toynbee Hall began its work in 1883, but I did not take a large share in its activities till 1886. I wrote for the *Toynbee Journal*, a pleasant little periodical, edited by E. T. Cook, which, however, had only one year of life, served on committees, and did what I could for the new cause. But the three years between 1884 and 1886 were the years of my commercial travelling, of founding the Co-operative Bookbinders' Society, of journalism and political hack work. In 1887 I became foreman of a department of the Co-operative Printing Society, and in January, 1888, was elected as one of the delegates of the Tower Hamlets Liberal and Radical Association to visit Ireland, and report on the condition of the Irish peasantry, and on the question of Home Rule.

XVI

IRISH EXPERIENCES

I was by this time a Home Ruler, but had never seen Ireland. There were some twenty delegates, and Mr. George Lansbury, who for a time was M.P. for Bow and Bromley, was one of them. I was in bad health, and elected to go to the south of Ireland, where the climate is mild, and was leader of the South of Ireland party. We made up our minds to see things as thoroughly as we could, and to avoid the popular sensationalism which, while it made copy for the Press, represented no real principle. I put myself in communication with the then Marquis of Ripon and other leaders of opinion to achieve this aim. We were told that if we desired to fix public attention on our work we should have to do something which would get us sent to gaol. I have always believed in the disgracefulness of gaol, and to go there for the sake of advertisement was a form of political humbug which I would not lend myself to, and which, to me, savoured strongly of comic opera. It was done, however, to a large extent, but it did not bring Home Rule a day nearer. One political enthusiast—I think he was a milk salesman —went out frankly stating it was his intention to get into gaol. He got a month's imprisonment, and two or three lines in the daily press as a compensation. The man was sincere and thought he was helping Ireland; really he was only making himself ridiculous. He wanted to "touch the heart of the nation," but as much of the nation as noticed him laughed and called him a fool. There was much more than he knew in the old-fashioned English belief in the disgracefulness of gaol.

The sufferings of the simple-natured Irish peasants under the rule of absentee landlords touched us to the quick. The mud huts and the strange, but very real, home life within them in the villages among the Galty Mountains, the close bonds that united priests and people, and the hold of their ancient faith upon them, I had read of, but had never seen at first hand before. On the slope of Galty More I went into a hut standing by itself, some three-quarters of a mile from any other house, in which dwelt an old woman and her donkey. Half the hut was the donkey's stable, the other half the woman's dwelling. It was a capacious hut, and the half the woman lived in was wonderfully clean. A turf fire burned fragrantly in the grate, a crucifix hung above the mantelshelf, and the old woman herself was delightfully prim and neat. Not always, however, did I meet such pictures as that of the clean old woman on the side of the Galty More. My companions were quite horrified that a Christian should live in the same house as a donkey, but I was not. I remembered Donkey Row, at the back of Stepney Church, and as a child had seen on Sunday afternoon the donkeys looking out of the ground-floor windows. It was certainly not an ideal way to live, but I knew some of the costers who lived thus, and knew them sometimes as kindly men and women, who would have liked another place for their animals no doubt, but who were not greatly spoiled by their company. And there are always crowds of men and women in the world, and probably always will be, who make far less respectable company than donkeys. And the old Irishwoman frankly said to us, " Shure, he's a faithful baste, and I couldn't get me livin' without him, and he's company, too, on long cold nights."

A picture that Rembrandt might have painted was presented in one of the cottages. Everything was squalid and wretched enough, and the dark of the January afternoon was faintly lightened by a wretched tallow dip that burned on the mantelpiece. A man and his wife occupied the mud cottage, and crouching on a heap of dirty straw by the fire was a creature who, at first glance, might have been taken for a gigantic ape. But it was a woman, clothed in rags, with unkempt grey hair, backward sloping forehead, and eyes that had an almost wolfish glare. A rope about her waist fastened her to a staple driven in the ground, and it was easy to see the poor creature was an idiot, whom it was regarded as unwise to give freedom to. The woman who dwelt in the hut had an intelligent, kindly face for all her squalor, and I asked why she kept the idiot there, and whether it would not be better to send her to an asylum, and so avoid the care and responsibility which her presence in the cottage needs must involve. " And who minds the trouble, and what for should I send her away; isn't she my own sister ? " was the touching reply.

An aged village priest of magnificent personality remains vividly among my Irish memories. He was nearing his eightieth year, he told me, but his tall form was upright as a pine, and his eyes as clear as they might have been in his youth. He had a reverential way of lifting his velvet skull cap whenever he uttered the name of God, which was very beautiful. Garrulous, as an old man is, his talk was, all the same, delightful to listen to. He was full of stories and legends of the kind that are found among those who live close to Nature, and whose characters are formed by Nature rather than by what is called civilization. He had lived fifty years in the mountain village where I found him, and his cottage was only just a little better than those of the peasants around him. But he had more than a peasant's mind, and yet seemed to express entirely their simple, unquestioning faith. I had slept among the mountains the night before, and the wind howling among the trees and the hills, with almost a human note in its wailing, set me thinking of the Irish belief in the Banshee. The old man was full of folk-lore stories, and, perhaps a little flippantly, I said to him: " And doubtless there are plenty in these districts who still believe in the Banshee." Pausing for a moment and fixing his eyes upon me, he replied, in a voice that had conviction in every note: " Sir, *I have heard the Banshee*."

Humour and pathos were blended in the old man's talk, touched now and then with a beautiful religious faith.

" Oh yes; it's the lake in the mountains that St. Patrick drove the last sarpint into, and he's there till the day o' judgment, and if you'll go there at midnight, and he hears you, he'll put his head out of the water and ask you if the day of judgment has come yet; " and the sparkling old eyes gleamed with mirth as he told the story. It was with an almost terrible aspect, however, that he told the story of the " cry of the hounds." " It was long ago, when I was a young priest, and the people were hearing mass in the open under the sky. And the landlord came by with a hunting party, and he whipped the hounds, and made them cry so that you could neither hear the prayer of the people nor the word of the priest, and so he made them cry till the mass was over, for he was a Protestant landlord, and hated the Faith. And old Bridget, leaning on her staff, her grey hair loose in the wind, said: 'The hounds you make cry now shall cry at your burying. And it's near, it's near.' With a curse and a laugh he rode away, and within a week lay dead, thrown from his horse as he rode. They gave him a great funeral, for he was a wealthy man, and while they were lowering his body in the earth, another hunting party whom none could see went by in the distance, and mingled with the words of the burial service rang out clear on the afternoon silence the cry of the hounds."

We were received with enthusiasm everywhere, and probably our speeches were partisan enough; although, so far as my group was concerned, we resolved if we could to get at both sides of the question. It was the fact that the wretched peasantry had no semblance of security of tenure even when they had put up their mud shanties themselves, but might be evicted and their houses pulled about their ears, that was such a horrible element in the peasant life we saw. On the Ponsonby Estate bedridden old women had been cast out on the roadside, and their houses burnt before their eyes, and such things as these were common episodes—everyday incidents in the Ireland of that time. It was impossible for any one with ordinary human feelings to go among these poor people and see their wretchedness without his nature going out in sympathy toward them. The Egans with their idiot sister, and the old woman with her donkey, probably found some touch of contentment amid their miseries, but even that little fraction of human joy was at the mercy of the landlord or his agent, and could disappear at the notice of an hour.

At Youghal I visited the house of Sir Walter Raleigh, and was shown the tree under which he sat and smoked the historic pipe and his servant poured a bucket of water over him, thinking he was on fire. But I had begun to read the Elizabethan period now, and scepticism about that tobacco story had set in.

The great power in Ireland then was the Irish National League, and its permit carried us about, and afforded us introductions to all sorts of society. My credential is dated from the offices of the League in Dublin, on January 19, 1888. It is signed by Mr. Timothy Harrington, M.P., and says that:—

> Mr. Frederic Rogers and friends have come to Ireland for the purpose of making personal inquiries into the present condition of the country, and I shall take it as an especial favour, if our friends among the clergy, and any officers of branches of the National League, to whom they present this note of introduction, will kindly do all in their power to facilitate their inquiries.

On our return to London I used both platform and Press to make public our experiences, and for a long time was in touch with Irish politics, and matters relating to Home Rule. But Home Rule was killed for a generation by the tragic downfall of Mr. Parnell, a year or two later. He was a great leader, but he threw away a career for the sake of a worthless woman. Those of us who were supporting him in his desire for Home Rule for Ireland were struck with dismay on the appearance of Mr. Parnell as co-respondent in the O'Shea divorce case. We did not express any opinion on the moral aspect of the affair, but we knew how it would be regarded by the English people. I thought it possible to save the position if he had resigned the leadership of his party, and give them the chance to choose another leader if they would, and wrote in the *Pall Mall Gazette*:

Unless the Liberals are prepared to lose the General Election Mr. Parnell must resign. The matter rests with him, and he must be appealed to. He has sacrificed much for the cause, let him now sacrifice himself. The Irish people may elect him again as their leader, and if they do we must treat with him as their leader, but this will be so much the worse for them, and so much the harder for us. Let him put it out of their power to do so by giving up his leadership, and his cause will win; let him do otherwise, and think that the English people will condone his offence because his own supporters do, and his cause may be put back another generation.

He did not resign, he did not take the heroic course, and all happened as I said. He died a year after the tragedy, and twenty-five years later Home Rule was still among the unachieved ideals of politics.

XVII

THE CO-OPERATIVE MOVEMENT

New developments were taking place in the Labour movement, and the great Dock Strike of 1889 was one of them, and it marked a new departure, not only in the Labour movement, but in the political life of the nation. I was active then in the co-operative movement, and did not want to have too many irons in the fire, and was not identified with the dock strike beyond assisting in helping the women and children who were hit by it. There was much activity in the co-operative movement in those years, and it strongly appealed to me. The first Co-operative Festival at the Crystal Palace took place in 1889, and these annual festivals continued many years, and have made a deep impression on social and philanthropic work by what they have done. And the Guild of Co-operators, an organization which existed to make popular the doctrines of co-operation, was in full swing. I was active in both of them. The inspiration of the co-operative festivals came from Edward Owen Greening, a man who gave his life to the co-operative idea, and an altogether fine type of Englishman. At the festivals I played many parts. At the first one I superintended the exhibits of the Co-operative Printing Society, and at others I made speeches, read papers, and wrote articles in the Press on behalf of the cause in which I believed. Really the success of the co-operative movement depends now on the possession by its leaders of business instincts as well as ideals. Character—and all that is involved in that word—can make, and has made, the co-operative movement a mighty force in our social life. I have taken my share of the militant movements of Labour, and am glad to have done so, but perhaps that which has been—to me—the most entirely satisfactory part of my work in the Labour movement was connected with co-operation.

The men whom I met in connection with it, who were leaders in its councils, were often not workmen; they were men of the middle classes who were inspired with a sincere desire to help the working classes out of the industrial slough in which they found themselves. But the working classes in London responded very little to their appeals. In Lancashire and Yorkshire, in the North and in the Midlands, co-operation showed itself a power to be reckoned with : in London it was very largely a middle-class thing. But I learned how self-sacrificing middle-class people could be, for ideas that were not for their own benefit but for that of their fellow-men, when I worked among the co-operators. Edward Vansittart Neale, who was nearing fourscore when I knew him, spent a fortune, and gave his life, to co-operation, because he believed it would solve the problems presented by the industrial system. Thomas Hughes, author of "Tom Brown's Schooldays," worked long and loyally, and faced many bitter disappointments in the same cause, inspired by the teaching of Kingsley and Maurice; and with him worked John Malcolm Ludlow, on behalf of the Friendly Societies, as well as of co-operation. But

I learned nothing of these things from the Labour movements of those days, and Edward Baker, with all his intellectual activity, knew nothing of them either. The admiration he gave to one distinguished co-operator, George Jacob Holyoake, did not come from any knowledge of his work for co-operation, but was given to him because he was a Freethinker. Looking back at that early work in the world of Labour, I realize now that one of the most pathetic facts in it was, that large numbers of men from all classes of society were willing to help in the emancipation of Labour, but we of the working classes mistook our friends for our enemies, and shouted empty words on platforms and believed we were working for social reform.

Toynbee Hall gave hospitality to every idea that seemed to make for human well-being, and, among its university extension lectures and classes to further the education of the working classes, found room for many discussions on co-operation. Drawn there by these interests, and finding myself among old friends, I was again filled with my old passion for study and was once more in touch with that for which I cared more than for anything else in life—the Literature and History of the country to which I belonged. The Shakespeare class under the direction of Sidney Lee gave me new inspirations, but I had already a reputation for Shakespeare lectures in the workmen's clubs. And round about the Shakespeare class lingered a group of intellectual lads who were reading Elizabethan literature, but they were without a leader. I remarked to the Rev. S. A. Barnett that it seemed a pity no one among the university men would take the leadership of such a promising group. "Well, then, why don't you do it?" was his reply. Thus was born the Elizabethan Society.

XVIII

THE ELIZABETHAN SOCIETY

I cannot recollect the time when I did not know something of Shakespeare. He has been part of my intellectual life ever since I had an intellectual life. I lectured on him as soon as I took to lecturing, and gained a reputation for Shakespearean scholarship far beyond my deserts. I had no theories about him, and snorted scornfully at the Baconians and their theories of authorship when they came my way. I enjoyed his verse as I enjoyed the sunshine and the trees, and no higher enjoyment can be got out of poetry than that. Lord Milner, in the days when we were both young men, tried to prove to me that Shakespeare was not the greatest poet of the world, and that the melody of Goethe's verse in German was equal to that of Shakespeare's in English. I could not argue the point—I do not know German—but I repudiated utterly such an appalling heresy. I knew Goethe, but only through translation: I loved him, but he was not Shakespeare.

Robert Browning wrote in "Christmas Eve":—

> "A thousand poets pried at life
> And only one amid the strife,
> Rose to be Shakespeare."

Shakespeare brings with him the sense of an exhaustless capacity, a limitless freedom. He is the complete expression of the idealism and the life of a great England. It is a full-blooded and impetuous life, daring and dreaming nobly, but in fierce revolt against all that would tame or curb the hot passions of the flesh, or check the dancing, bubbling fountains of human joy. "Dost thou think, because thou art virtuous, there shall be no more cakes and ale?" was not only the utterance of a drunken roysterer; it was an attitude of mind, a shout of defiance to the preachers of self-restraint. And there was justification for the shout when those preachers so interpreted their gospel as to make it suppress every warm and generous impulse, and in the name of virtue turn to sourness all that was sweet in life. Men with fire in their blood turned in scorn from such a gospel, resolving to gather in the joy of living while it was near:

> "For never-resting time leads summer on
>   To hideous winter, and confounds him there
> Sap choked with frost, and lusty leaves quite gone,
>   Beauty o'er-snowed, and bareness everywhere."

Authority had fallen, and men held themselves free, alike from the restraints of morals and of faith. Intoxicated with the new wine of national liberty, they hated fiercely, revelled gloriously, and loved and died in heroic fashion, and if there was no pity in their hate neither was there any stinting in the passion of their love. The restraining spirit of chivalry had passed with the social life which gave it birth, and the energies of the "spacious times" were at once greater and less than those of mediæval days. The outbreathing of a new spirit, filled with vision and with purpose, and struggling towards creative power, passes over even the follies and the littlenesses of life, as we see them in Shakespeare's world, and when that life in its greater aspect meets our eyes there are regal virtues and gigantic sins. But they never transcend the human; they are the sins and virtues of men, and not of devils or of demi-gods.

He knew with a perfect knowledge that the world of imagination is greater than the world of reality only while it keeps touch with nature's meanings. For him nature is the supreme fact, out of whose beauty and mystery art is born. Art in its highest reaches can transfigure Nature and clothe her with a glory than is an inspiration, but if it passes beyond her sphere in search of that she does not know it enters the realm of chaos and old night.

The Elizabethan Society was founded on March 8, 1884, and I took charge of it as Vice-President in 1886. We met every week to read the works of Christopher Marlowe, and were about a dozen in number, working-class and middle-class lads combined. The first secretary when I came to the Society was Bertram Dyer, who afterwards became the librarian of the public library at Kimberley in South Africa, edited a paper, and had a short but quite distinguished career in that colony. While he was with the Society he did much to shape its early policy, and his death in the colony which he had made his home was greatly lamented.

I laid down a principle in our Elizabethan studies which experience had shown me to be perfectly sound, and the following of which gave the Society the influence which it attained in literature. The principle was that we were to read the Elizabethan authors themselves first, and what other people had said about them after. We gathered a delight from Marlowe's verse by this method which we should have missed if we had followed commentators before reading the poetry, and if we were wrong in our judgments, as probably we sometimes were, we knew all the joys of first love. And I suggested that if our Society would justify its existence we must do some practical work for literature. We could not publish old editions or reprint scarce works as the New Shakespeare Society did; we had no money, and we had not arrived at the stage of writing books. But our discussions as to what to achieve were to have larger results than we knew, and among them was the erection of the Marlowe Memorial at Canterbury.

The second secretary of the Society was a London errand boy, who had been a choir boy at St. Peter's, London Docks, and received an intellectual stimulus there which set him reading poetry, and writing in a minor way, and finally sent him to us. His name was James Ernest Baker, and in those days he was a strange, delightful creature who learned things quickly, was full of enthusiasm, but fundamentally weak in character and with insanity in his blood. I found a use for his enthusiasm in the fact that there had never been any public and national recognition of Marlowe as a poet, and suggested that the Elizabethan Society might bring it about. Baker had shown considerable ability in arranging the series of monthly papers which have formed so marked a feature of the Society's work; and altogether he was quite the person to stir up the enthusiasm required.

On July 26, 1888, he wrote to the *Standard* a letter drawing attention to Marlowe's work, and claiming that Marlowe " laid the foundation of English blank verse, which, in its more developed form through the medium of Shakespeare and Milton, has become the life-blood of English literature, and the supreme instrument of tragic poetry." The letter attracted much notice, and the result was the formation of the "Marlowe Memorial" Committee. Sidney Lee, now Sir Sidney Lee, who had been a member of the Elizabethan Society since its beginning, and became President in 1890, was treasurer of the memorial; Lord Coleridge, Lord Chief Justice of England, was its Chairman; and among the members were Robert Browning, Lord Tennyson, James Russell Lowell, Edmund Gosse, A. H. Bullen, A. C. Swinburne, Rev. A. B. Grosart, John Addington Symonds, Henry Irving, Leslie Stephen, Andrew Lang, Dr. Richard Garnett, Alfred Austin, the Rev. H. C. Beeching, now Dean of Norwich, and among American scholars, Horace Howard Furness and Professor Child. I was secretary and young Baker assistant secretary.

In the beginning of our work we had to face obloquy. Marlowe had the reputation of being an atheist, and the anti-religious party claimed our work as a victory for their principles, though we never identified ourselves with them in any way. Bradlaugh, their great leader, was dead; Annie Besant, their second in command, had ceased to believe in their principles, and lesser men ruled in the Hall of Science. But they did to some extent care for literature. They studied it as the historians of my youth time studied history—to prove a foregone conclusion. Marlowe was only interesting to them because he was a reputed atheist, and it never occurred to them that he had written the last of our religious plays.

It was the kind of reasoning and of admiration common

enough then, common in the conventicle, in the club, and in the workshop, and it was, practically, admiring a man for his second-rate qualities. Unitarian writers issued pamphlets to prove Milton a Unitarian, Baptist writers grew eloquent over the fact that Bunyan was a Baptist, but showed not the slightest knowledge of his place in literature, and listening to lectures on Marlowe or Shelley at the Hall of Science, the impression was that the lecturers regarded them as better poets because they probably did not believe in God. It all led to a general lowering of both literary and moral values.

We were only concerned with Marlowe's poetry, and meant to draw public attention to the work of a great literary genius, who had hitherto been misunderstood, and was known only to the few, and in the correspondence which took place about Marlowe, Sidney Lee wrote in the *Pall Mall Gazette* of him:

He created tragic drama in England. The first to apply blank verse to stage uses, he revolutionized dramatic method and made great drama in England possible. As the author of "Hero and Leander," he takes rank with the author of "Venus and Adonis." Shakespeare's acknowledged indebtedness to him constitutes in itself a sufficient claim to the veneration of all literary students. It is very late in the day to recapitulate such facts—facts familiar to every educated Englishman. . . . It is not probable that Marlowe's life was particularly saintly, but that his character was specially vile is conclusively disproved by the frank testimony of his eminently honourable friend and publisher, Edward Blount, who wrote of "the impression of the man that hath been dear unto us (Marlowe) living an after-life in our memory." Drayton and

Chapman were among Marlowe's eulogists in his own generation, and their evidence is of more value than that of the anonymous slanderer on whom your religious correspondent exclusively pins his faith. Surely men, whether religious or irreligious, ordinarily have the charity to recognize the great and lasting good work of departed heroes, especially when nearly three centuries have elapsed since they were laid to rest in their graves.

The Lord Chief Justice Coleridge, our chairman, was a man of fine personality, and our meetings occasionally took place in his rooms at the Law Courts. Literature with him was a means of intellectual recreation, and he was altogether modest in talking about it, and made no claim to knowing more than the ordinary reader might know. In his letter to me, written on August 24, 1888, in which he accepted the chairmanship, he said :

I am really hardly enough of a literary man to accept the office of chairman, even if the committee desire it. But as I suppose, with the exception of Mr. Browning, I am at least the *oldest* admirer of Christopher Marlowe amongst those you mention, I will do what I can, if you desire, supposing the committee should choose me.

Robert Browning's age prevented him coming to committee meetings, and he died before the memorial was complete, but he wrote from De Vere Gardens on August 3, 1888 :—

I can have no possible objection in lending my name for whatever may be its worth, to co-operate in honouring the memory of a glorious poet such as was Marlowe of the mighty line.

He had only another year of life before him when he

wrote, but the handwriting is firm and clear as the handwriting of a young man. Henry Irving and Ellen Terry gave a reading at St James's Hall, which resulted in a profit of a hundred pounds, and Wilson Barrett and others distinguished in the dramatic world were among our subscribers, and the Marlowe Memorial was erected in the old Butter Market in Canterbury, and was unveiled on December 16, 1891.

Henry Irving was asked to unveil it, and it was there I met him for the first time. It was a memorable occasion, but the good citizens of Canterbury, beyond the Mayor and some of the chief officials, were not interested, and the crowd came largely from the outside. In the course of his speech Irving said:

It was Marlowe who first wedded the harmonies of the great organ of blank verse which peals through the centuries in the music of Shakespeare. It was Marlowe who first captured the majestic rhythms of our tongue, and whose " mighty line " is the most resounding note in England's literature. Whatever may be thought of his qualities as a dramatist, and whatever place he may hold amongst the great writers who framed the models of English tragedy, he stands foremost and apart as the poet who gave us, with a rare measure of richness, the literary form which is the highest achievement of poetic expression.

In my own speech I said:

Of the man Christopher Marlowe we know little enough, and what is most remembered is what his enemies have said. But we do not judge a man, and we should not condemn him, upon the statement of his enemies. Son of one of your city's handicraftsmen, born at a time when in this England of ours there was an awakening of national life, and when the hearts of Englishmen were stirring with strange and wondrous visions of their country's glory and her place among the nations of the world, Kit Marlowe had, within his passionate poetic soul, all the strange longings and hopes that were the offspring of that bygone time. Educated at your King's School yonder, brought up under the shadow of your stately cathedral, surrounded all through the most impressionable period of his life with places that linked him with his country's past, what wonder was it that his young pulse kept time with hers, that all her strange unequal longings in him found voice? She had broken with the fetters of old traditions. She felt within her the consciousness of a mighty strength; even the very winds of heaven had seemed to help her to scatter the pride of her foes in the dust. Every son of England felt that he had his work to do, not for himself, but for his country, and through his country for the world. To Kit Marlowe, King's scholar of Canterbury, there was given to do a work which would presently make England's literature great as that of the older nations of the earth. He, too, would break with old forms, and would show men what a wonderful instrument their language might become. With all a young man's glorious consciousness of strength, with all a young man's unconsciousness of weakness, with strange and subtle yearnings after higher things, and with an animalism that was ever dragging at the spiritual and trying to pull it down—in the short spell of his strange brief life he infused a new spirit into English poetry, he inaugurated a new departure in English literary art.

No portrait of Marlowe exists, and the memorial took an allegorical form. The artist was Onslow Ford, R.A., and its design is a muse on a stone pedestal, playing a musical instrument. On the front of the pedestal is a statuette of Irving, as Tamburlaine the Great, and it was intended to have on the other three sides of the pedestal three more of the characters of Marlowe's plays, Sir

George Alexander as Faustus, Sir Herbert Tree as Barabbas, and W. S. Willard as Edward II. The necessary funds for the additional figures were not, however, forthcoming, and only the great actor who unveiled the memorial remains in effigy on the pedestal on which it stands.

During our visits to Onslow Ford's studio to discuss the form of the Marlowe Memorial, we saw much of another piece of sculpture there in progress, the monument to the poet Shelley. It is now at Oxford, but, as originally projected, was to have been placed over Shelley's grave. Its design is a bronze pedestal consisting of four allegorical figures supporting a platform of rock upon which is stretched the dead figure of the poet as he was washed up from the sea. The position is that of helpless death, and no living body could maintain such a position long. But a model was needed, and about the model the sculptor told me the following story. He was seeking vainly for one among the professional models when a handsome young pupil who was studying under him offered himself, filled with enthusiasm at the idea of posing for the dead poet. So loyal was he to his ideal that he lay in the cramped and strained position required till he suffered from bed sores. It is a beautiful human figure, and fine sculpture, but family disputes with the then living members of the Shelley family prevented its erection in the Protestant cemetery at Rome, and it never left England, but is hidden away in a dark corner of Shelley's old college: University College, Oxford.

The result of the Marlowe Memorial was to awaken a new interest in Elizabethan literature, and the stimulus given to its study and to its publications by the direct and indirect results of our work has never ceased. To quote a passage from Edmund Gosse after "Marlowe had been successfully neglected for three hundred years," he became suddenly the subject of leading articles in the chief papers and magazines, and of paragraphs and leaderettes in the minor ones. The Elizabethan Society would have justified its existence if it had ceased work then, but more was before it.

In December, 1889, Robert Browning died. He was a member of the Marlowe Memorial Committee at the time of his death, and in the closing years of his life obtained the public recognition denied him in the earlier ones, though it is right to say that he was always appreciated by "those who knew." But his works were expensive and difficult of access, and Dr. F. J. Furnival, the distinguished English scholar, who had been a personal friend of the poet's, wrote to us suggesting that the moment was opportune for obtaining from his son or his publishers a shilling selection of his poems for popular circulation. The Elizabethan Society set to work. I drew up the following memorial to Robert Barrett Browning, which was extensively signed by students and persons connected with educational institutes all over England :—

Sir,—
The undersigned, being a few among the many who have gathered knowledge, and hope, and inspiration from your father's poems, venture to ask you to publish a selection of them at a price that will place them within the reach and ownership of all. They are emboldened to ask this because they believe there are thousands who would profit by their perusal, who are unable to do so now because of their high price. They would respectfully suggest to you

the issue of one or two shilling volumes containing such of the shorter poems, from the earliest to the latest, as best illustrate the special characteristics of your father's genius and teaching. They do not suggest any mutilation of the longer poems, for the sake of "extracts," regarding this course as bad in itself and harmful to genuine students. They know that such volumes would be welcomed by many to whom Robert Browning is an illustrious name, honoured from afar, but not yet known as a friend and guide. Believing that he has made the world so much the richer by his life's work, they ask that some share of the wealth of wisdom and poetry he so freely bestowed, shall be placed within the reach of all who are able to appreciate its value. And the number of these is growing greater every day.

Mr. Howard Pearson, of the Midland Institute, undertook to get signatures for the Midlands, Mrs. Ireland for the North, while the Elizabethans made themselves responsible for the London area. Robert Barrett Browning agreed to our suggestion, and the result of our labours was the issue by Smith and Elder, at the close of 1890, of what was known for a long time as the "Shilling Browning." There are many shilling volumes of Browning now, but the thanks and congratulations which came to the Elizabethans for the first one were pleasant to receive.

The historian, whoever he may be, who writes the story of our stage between 1890 and 1910, must give an important place to the work of William Poel and the Elizabethan Stage Society. He has stood consistently, and in the face of adverse and sometimes spiteful criticism, for sound learning in dramatic art. His performances of old dramas in old costumes, and without scenery; his careful research into the history of stagecraft, and the stimulus he has given to its study, have had an influence on English drama which has never received its full appreciation. Of a performance of "Measure for Measure," given by Mr. Poel and his company at the Royalty Theatre in London in 1893, I wrote:

You did not get reminded every now and then of the ways of the modern drawing-room, as you so often do on the modern stage. It was Shakespeare in his own clothing, and it had a strange and beautiful witchery about it all that was delightful to those who knew the life of that wonderful time. It was a daring act to close the play by a prayer for Queen Elizabeth, but it was in keeping with the whole performance. It was what they did then, and the custom survives in an occasional "God Save the Queen" at Drury Lane Theatre to-day. The prayer was that given at the end of "Ralph Roister Doister," and it was repeated by the actors kneeling, the "Amen" being chanted as it is in church. It was a fitting close. The charm was wound up as it should have been, and one left the theatre with a sense of having passed for a time into a land of romance, and of having caught a glimpse of a world of which we can now only dream.

The above words expressed accurately my sense of the value of Mr. Poel's work in 1893, and they express it still. His society was called the Shakespeare Reading Society then; in the year following he explained to us his plan for forming an Elizabethan Stage Society, and courteously asked our sanction for the use of the name. We cordially agreed, and there was always community of action between us. His two best productions were Marlowe's "Faustus," given at St. George's Hall, London, in 1896, and the play of "Everyman." The average playgoer did not understand "Faustus"; he is rather worse than the average churchgoer in not understanding what he is not used to, but "Everyman" made its place in the popular imagination at once. Perhaps it was not the playgoers so much as the religious world, and the intellectuals, that made the success of "Everyman," but it was a great thing to make popular this noble play among the playgoers of our time.

The commemoration of Philip Massinger was the next piece of public work undertaken by the Elizabethans. The restoration of the ancient church of St. Saviour's, Southwark, preparatory to its conversion into Southwark Cathedral, had been going on for some years, under the direction of its vicar, the Rev. W. Thompson, D.D., and he desired to put into the church a number of stained-glass windows, in memory of the various men of letters, who were connected with the church. Probably no church in England has had a closer connection with literature than St. Saviour's. Gower lies within its walls; the pilgrims to the shrine of Becket, the murdered Archbishop, heard mass there before starting on their journey; Shakespeare was one of its parishioners; his brother Edmond and the dramatists John Fletcher and Philip Massinger lie buried within its walls. The Massinger window was the gift of the Elizabethan Society to Southwark Cathedral. A committee was formed, of which Sir Walter Besant was chairman and myself vice-chairman. Among its members were Augustine Birrell, M.P., not then a Minister; Sir Henry Irving, Edmund Gosse, Sidney Lee, Sir Alfred Milner, C.B., K.C.B., Richard le Galliene, Mrs. Lynn Linton, Miss Braddon, Mr. Wilson Barrett, and Mr. H. Beerbohm Tree. It was in May 1895 that we started the Massinger Window Committee, and on Saturday afternoon, July 11, 1896, it was unveiled before a very distinguished audience by Sir Walter Besant.

Once again the Elizabethans had the satisfaction of seeing references to the " spacious times " and of Massinger as one of the dramatists of those days in every front rank paper in the English Press. They increased their numbers considerably, but were never a large or a moneyed Society. They could not publish scarce books or pamphlets; a good many of them were just workmen, and those who belonged to the middle classes were quite poor. But the scholar's instinct was strong within them all; their studies were systematic and regular, and what they did stimulated the study of literature elsewhere, and brought together classes of society which otherwise would have remained far as the poles asunder.

My speech on Marlowe made Henry Irving my friend, and when he learned that all my life I had been a devout Irvingite he bade me welcome to the Lyceum. On the production of Tennyson's " Becket " on the evening of February 6, 1893, I, in company with my friend George B. Burgin, the novelist, was invited to the supper behind the scenes when the curtain fell. First night suppers at the Lyceum were great functions during the Irving management. It was all so swiftly done. Becket lay dead on the stage, amid the flashing of lightning and the rolls of thunder, the curtain fell, and the invited ones filed out at once to the stage. By the time they got there it was transformed into a great supper room, in which was a great table built into a half-circle, like that in an ancient Eastern dining-hall, and a magnificent stand-up supper was laid for those who cared to partake. Politicians in evening dress mingled picturesquely with actors in mediæval costume. Asquith, then, I think, Home Secretary, was there, and Onslow Ford, the sculptor, and George Alexander hurried over from the St. James's Theatre, and moving in and out among them all, courtly and dignified as a prince, was the Becket of the play. A little while before he had been the austere monk of the Middle Ages, stern, strong, and fighting to the death for principle. Then he had stood on the stage in front of the curtain, the public man, talking in a popular way to a popular audience, responding as readily to their sympathetic shouts as they did to the points in his wonderful acting. In a real and living sense he loved his audiences, and was their servant while they gave him sympathy and applause. And to the end of his supremely great dramatic life he never lost the mysterious, half-hypnotic power of touching their feelings and swaying their emotions as he pleased.

Once I took the daughter of a distinguished poet, the Hon. Roden Noel, in to see him after the play was over— a charming girl, who was anxious to shake hands with the great actor. He was geniality itself. "Glad to see you, glad to see you young ladies; your father wrote a sonnet on my 'Lear,' did he not? Now what will you have by way of refreshment: tea, apollinaris, or wine?" Ellen Terry I never really knew, though I had talked with her now and then, and remember a charming episode in Irving's room one night. I forget what we were discussing, but he had given me permission to see a play from behind the scenes, and it was an interesting experience. While there Miss Terry came in, and presently entered two little girls, the children of some one there. The great actress was not interested in our talk, but on the entry of the children she sat down flat on the floor, and, placing her arms around them, drew them towards her and became a child at once in companionship to them. It was a delightful Lyceum episode.

Another personality who came in touch with the Elizabethan Society was Richard le Gallienne. He came first in 1893 to read a paper on William Chamberlayne, and again in February 1895 to discourse on John Cleveland. Young, handsome, fragile in appearance, affected, refined, and with flashes of fine manliness now and again, it was impossible to know him and not to like him. His young wife accompanied him, and their devotion to each other was a pleasant thing to see. But in 1894 she died, and for the young author the world was never the same again. We knew her well, and I sent him words of sympathy. "Such sympathy as yours *does* help," he wrote sadly in reply, and then he left us. Three years later he came again, but life and thought had changed with him, and he moved now in another orbit than ours.

In October 1889 I became a member of a famous literary club, the "Vagabonds," and attained to the dignity of "an old Vagabond" long years ago. Something of pathos and of romance is found in its origin. A few young literary men and others met in the rooms of Philip Bourke Marston, the young blind poet, and cheered the darkness of his life by their friendship. He was a son of Westland Marston, the dramatic author, and his life was a tragic and heroic struggle against physical misfortune. In playful humour he called the friends who met in his room his " vagabonds." Marston died in 1887 at the age of thirty-six, and his friends who met in his rooms resolved to continue their meetings, and call themselves the " Vagabonds Club."

I was not one of Marston's friends, but Charles Whibley had introduced me, a year or two previously, to Milnes Patmore. Captain Milnes Patmore was the son of Coventry Patmore, the poet, and was known among his intimates as the " child of the toys." Readers of Coventry Patmore will remember his charming and pathetic poem " The Toys," which begins:

> " My little son, who looked from thoughtful eyes
> And moved and spoke in quiet grown-up wise."

But Milnes Patmore, when I knew him, was a frank, cheery sailor, well on toward middle life, making no pretence to literary powers, but with a crowd of literary friends. I found him excellent company, and we spent many pleasant hours together, and he it was who introduced me to the " Vagabonds," and they duly made me one of themselves. They met in those days in quiet old-fashioned taverns round Fleet Street way, the Mitre in Chancery Lane being one of the taverns, and eschewed evening dress and the company of ladies. I was soon able to fit in with their methods, for I made speeches, recited poetry to any extent, told stories, and thoroughly enjoyed the evenings and the company.

Evening dress and the company of ladies had not been reached by the vagabonds of those days, and the atmosphere of the old Fleet Street clubs hung about them: freedom and careless unconventionality, as men interpret those terms, and a genial Bohemian spirit, which seemed to me to fade away as they grew more dignified, and artificial, and polite. The men one met were not all of them in the beginning of their career. F. W. Robinson, the novelist, who had begun his career by making the acquaintance of Archbishop Whately, and who when I knew him reminded me always of Robert Browning, was among our most respected members. He attracted Whately's attention by a series of journalistic letters purporting to be written by a hospital nurse, and used to tell a story of how the acquaintance began by the Archbishop addressing a letter to him beginning "My dear Madam." Jerome K. Jerome, Coulson Kernahan, George B. Burgin, and Israel Zangwill were among the younger men, and Albert Chevalier sang "My old Dutch" at a Vagabond meeting before he had made it famous at the Halls, and Fred Terry recited "Sal Grogan's Face" one night, I having recited the same poem at the previous meeting. There were comparisons of course, and I, naturally, preferred my own reading. Cynicus, whose quaint amusing drawings were just then taking people by storm, and who had a studio in Drury Lane where he carried on the vagabond traditions, was among our members, and the strange, half-crazy genius, Aubrey Beardsley, came now and then, repelling and attracting by turns.

Among the curious and striking personalities whom I met there from time to time was a man whom I knew in the political movements in East London, Edward B. Aveling. He was the son of a Congregational minister in London, and had many brilliant qualifications which fitted him for public life. He attained a certain notoriety by publicly joining the atheistic party at the Hall of

Science. I had been to the Hall of Science a great deal with Edward Baker, but after his death I ceased going, for the place never attracted me, and I was always in revolt at what I listened to. It gave me, however, an intellectual stimulus, and sent my mind in an opposite direction, and this was good for me.

But I wanted to know Aveling: the man interested me, and I found him a strong personality when I made his acquaintance at the "Vagabonds Club." The first advice given me by the friend who introduced me was, "Don't on any account lend him any money." The advice was quite unnecessary. I knew the workshop borrower too well, the man who, no matter how high his wages, "wanted to borrow sixpence" about the middle of the week, and I carried out literally the idea of Polonius, and was neither borrower nor lender. Aveling proved a charming companion, and we had many things in common. He had been a member of the London School Board, had made his mark as author, science lecturer, and political speaker, could be when he chose a man of refined manners, but it did not take me long to find out that he was utterly without principle and that morally he was a wastrel.

He had a handsome, intellectual face, but there was always a touch of the diabolic in it, and when I knew him he was living with Eleanor Marx, the daughter of Karl Marx, his first wife having separated from him because of his cruelty years before. I never knew Eleanor Marx, but those who did said her devotion to him went to the verge of slavery. Marriage was impossible for her, as his first wife was living, but on the death of that lady he treated Eleanor Marx as a *roué* treats a cast-off mistress, and was married to Eva Frye. The alleged suicide of Eleanor Marx, which followed soon after the marriage, was among the tragedies of Socialism. Aveling died by his own hand soon after the death of his unhappy mistress; it was said that had he lived he might have been charged with her death. The facts are known, and some day perhaps the story will be told in its completeness. Eleanor Marx was a deluded, weak, but loyal-hearted woman, and Aveling was a villain, all unworthy of such foolish but faithful love.

XIX

THE BOOKBINDERS' STRIKE, 1891–1892

It was during the agitation on behalf of the Marlowe memorial in 1891 that the bookbinders' strike for an eight hours' day broke out, and I was dragged into its vortex. The full history of that strike is found in Mr. Vaughan Nash's paper, the *Trade Unionist*, which lived during the years 1891–2, and in the volumes of the " British Bookmaker " for 1891–2–3. In the first-named journal the story is written by myself; in the second by W. H. Edmunds of the London Bookbinders. When it began my friends of the trade union world resolved, in their own phrase, " to dig me out of my books." But I was not buried in them. My life was full of active work, although it did not specially interest trade unionists. I was a constant speaker for the Guild of Co-operators all over the home counties. This was an organization which existed for helping and advising co-operative societies in the South of England, where they always needed much advice. I was also on the Education Committee of the Co-operative Wholesale Society, and among my colleagues were Vaughan Nash and his wife, then Miss Rosalind Shore Smith. Vaughan Nash in those days worked with me at the Co-operative Printing Society, where for ten years I was foreman of the binding department. He was afterwards a journalist, and then became secretary to Sir H. Campbell-Bannerman, and to Mr. Asquith. And my leisure was devoted to the Elizabethan Society and to literature.

I was entirely happy in my work, but the appeal of my trade union I could not disregard. I knew a movement was on foot to get an eight hours' day, but foremen do not take part in trade union debates, and if this relieved me from a duty I was not perhaps burning to fulfil, it also prevented me from getting any facts. But I was in a position to help my colleagues if I decided to do so. The directors of the Co-operative Printing Society took a sane view of the workman's duties, and never interfered with what I did after hours so long as I did my work satisfactorily while I was employed by the firm, and when therefore my old shopmates waited on me and asked me to speak at the great meeting of all the trade societies of the bookbinding trade on July 14, 1891, I consented, informed my generous-hearted manager, John Bradley, who told me to do as I liked, and flung myself into the fray.

I was thus in the unique position of being a leader of a strike and of working at my trade at the same time. I allowed none of my other activities to stop, and the physical strain was terrific, but I stood it and went on. I resolved—if I could—to get public opinion on the side of my trade, and to this end sought the assistance of the Press. I was well known in the journalistic world, and it was a time when the Press was beginning to look favourably on the Labour movement, and to realize that the workman had a case. Journalists were then usually pretty ill informed, and, moreover, looked at our fight purely from the middle-class standpoint. But Toynbee Hall was influencing journalism; Vaughan Nash was a resident of Toynbee Hall, and the younger men of the Press tried to make themselves well informed on labour matters, and sometimes succeeded.

Sir E. T. Cook, who was then editor of the *Pall Mall Gazette* though not then knighted, and I had worked together in University extension matters years before, and I obtained an interview in the *Pall Mall Gazette* of November 20, 1891, in which I laid the case of our men before a class of readers who would have been unlikely to have known it in any other way. An incident in connection with the interview illustrated—for me—very exactly indeed the attitude of the journalistic mind towards labour. The interview was described by the journalist who interviewed me, a pleasant, well-meaning youngster enough, as with an "intelligent" member of the craft, the implication being that the rest of the members were not intelligent. I promptly had the word altered to "well-known" before the interview was printed, and we laughed hugely over the journalistic mind in the trade.

No man who cares for public well-being wants to see a strike, and no trade union leader who cares for his fellows wants to see more than one. But the majority of strikes have been revolts against industrial tyranny, endured till it could be endured no longer. All the forces of society have been arrayed against the workman, and he has sometimes had to endure a slavery which did not differ in its essential qualities from that which existed in the plantation of Simon Legree, except that it did not include the lash. The terms "freedom of contract" were sheer cant when applied to agreements between masters and workmen of fifty years ago : the freedom was all on one side. It is a principle of ethics that it is as culpable to endure wrong when you can resist it as it is to commit wrong, and we are all quite ready to applaud those who are fighting against wrong provided they are not at the same time fighting against our own interests and ideas. It is the custom—a very English one—to estimate a strike purely by its money value, but the strike, even when it may be entered upon for insufficient reasons, has its roots in deep and abiding human instincts, the instincts which prompt men always and everywhere to resist injustice, and these cannot be estimated in pounds, shillings, and pence.

The bookbinders' strike was forced on the trade unions by certain employers in the book-binding trade. An eight hours' day for the trade had long been under discussion between workmen and employers, and that it was a practical and workable idea was proved by the fact that, as a result of some six months of conferences between the members of the London Chamber of Commerce and the members of the Bookbinders' Unions some seventy London firms employing about two thousand workmen agreed to begin the year 1892 with an eight hours' day. Certain firms, however, held out, and against them the men were forced to strike if an agreement was to be come to in the London trade which would secure uniformity of hours all round. The strike was not entered upon till every resource of diplomacy was exhausted. The question had been discussed on its merits inside the Chamber of Commerce, but we could never get it so discussed by the dissentients outside, who refused to be bound by the decisions of the Chamber, and the strike began.

Just about this time Mr. Vaughan Nash started the *Trade Unionist*, and gave me a free hand in its columns. All through the strike I was flooding the Press with letters, paragraphs, and articles on behalf of the men, and, as I often attacked firms and employers by name, I signed every article that appeared in the *Trade Unionist* and most that appeared elsewhere. The *Daily Chronicle*, the *Sun* (now dead), the *Star*, any and every paper that I could press into my service I did. At night I made speeches at meetings and rushed hither and thither, until at last I broke down. But before long I was in the fray again, cheered and helped by my friends in the Co-operative Printing Society, and by its manager. That I was a marked man in the London trade goes without saying, but the fact did not disturb me in the least.

The heroisms of a strike are often among its most remarkable characteristics, and also among its least noticed ones, but they quickly manifested themselves to me. For young men a strike may mean no more than a temporary loss of wages, and—this always—a pretty considerable demoralization. But for older men it means little positive benefit, be its success never so brilliant, and if it fails they stand a chance of going under, so far as their trade is concerned, for the rest of their lives. For a man past middle life to give up a good situation, well knowing that every day that passes will make it more difficult for him to get another, and to do this not for his own benefit, but for that of his trade and for the men that come after him, is heroism of the highest kind, and akin to that which has made martyrs and saints and created the glory of history. From the point of reason, logic, and worldly wisdom generally it can all be shown to be stupid, no doubt, but then how dreadfully stupid all martyrs have been from those points of view! It was much wiser to burn a spoonful of incense before an image of Jupiter in ancient Rome than to go to the lions, and a large number of people burnt the incense. But some chose the arena and the beasts, and their cause triumphed and shaped the destinies of the world.

But the bookbinders were not shaping the destinies of a world; they were fighting a very humble industrial battle, and trying to get better conditions of labour for their trade, but brave men and fine qualities manifested themselves as they have done in the struggles which have made the history of mankind. Among the most striking characters in our fight was a young workman named Frank Dleny. Handsome, pale faced, frail of form, but with deep burning eyes and an eloquent tongue, Dleny's influence among the strike leaders was unique. He was a member of one of the religious bodies, by temperament he was a mystic and full of poetic idealism, and it seemed strange to find him leading a strike. He had about him that exalted personal magnetism which somehow commands respect by its mere presence, whether it is given expression to or not, and, no matter how coarse a man might be in his ordinary talk, he stopped his ribaldry when Dleny came into the room. And by-and-by his speeches were full of a strange power to me, for I realized that the young trade-union leader was cast for death. He died before the strike was half over, he and his mother dying within a few hours of each other, and within a few hours also of the man who would have been King of England, and whom I met during his University career at Cambridge—the Duke of Clarence, son to King Edward VII.

Another man of fine character and personality was Thomas Sims. We had been friends of many years, and he laughed always and mercilessly at my enthusiasms for education and literature. He had no enthusiasm of his own of any kind. Happily married and in regular employment, he enjoyed life sanely and in a workman's way, and never understood why I should waste my spare time over " such a stupid business as schools, which could not be of any use to me." But the death of his wife when he was nearing middle-age shattered his happiness, and, with a nature empty of love and aching for sympathy, he plunged into public work. The preaching of Socialism came across his path, and his first enthusiasm was for Mr. Hyndman and Mr. Quelch. Enthusiasm, like love, is a dangerous passion to attack a man for the first time late in life, but with Sims the inherent manliness of his character came out. He was absolutely unselfish in putting his new faith into practice. He believed he saw in Socialism the means of creating better conditions of life for the class to which he belonged. His own position was a good one in his trade, but he ventured it, and lost. The idea of an eight hours' day appealed to him much as a religious principle appeals to a devout soul. A craftsman of sufficient ability to make it worth the while of employers to come to terms with him if he would have sold his comrades, he steadily withstood every temptation, although he was losing all chances of a livelihood, and knew it. The simple words " I am a man, sir," uttered to an old employer who would have given him his place again if he would have given up his fellow-craftsmen, summed up for him the whole position, and left nothing else to say. It was a sentence that revealed a soul, and it was remembered by those who stood around his grave.

The strike was only a partial success, with all its heroisms, its tragedy, and its farce. We were not able to get a uniform eight hours' day, but we did make a revolution in the trade, and revolutions are always a balance of loss and gain, and it takes a long while to see which kicks the beam. They are made by passion, pain stretched to the last endurance, idealism sound or unsound, as it happens, and not by reason. They are made when the blood is hot and reason is not listened to, and it is because of this that they are full of burning lights and lurid shadows, glorious visions, and will-o'-the-wisps that lead into heaven knows what quagmires. Men are winnowed out in their fierce winds, and the straw and the chaff are blown into space and lost. But the wheat remains, the men of solid character justify themselves, and, even though it takes long days to bear fruit, the fruit comes.

When the strike was over in 1892 I took the Presidency of the Vellum Binders' Society, and held it till 1898, and we set about reorganizing the trade. In the vellum-binding industry a large amount of the London work was done for the Government Stationery Office, and this had been for many years a monopoly of two firms. I was determined to smash that monopoly, and did so. When the three years' contract of the Stationery Office expired in 1893 I drew attention, in a letter in the *Daily Chronicle* of March 6, 1893, to the fact that a statement had been made in the offices of the Vellum Binders' Society that week that a man who had been recently employed by a firm working for the Stationery Office, had worked all one Sunday on piecework for this firm for 4s. 6d. On the same day I got Mr. Henry Dalziel, M.P., as he was then, to ask a question on the letter in the House of Commons. My facts were incontrovertible, and Sir John T. Hibbert, Secretary to the Treasury, had to admit them. Deputations to Government followed, and an agitation, in which I, being then the only man in the trade whom the employers could not touch, was the central figure. I ran no risk, and I revelled in the fight, and the whole trade was solid at my back. The result of it all was that the contract was removed from one of the two firms referred to, and a monopoly of many years—as many as I could remember—was broken. The effect on the trade was magical, and there came times when my trade society had absolutely no men out of work, the kind of triumph that few trade union leaders achieve.

In 1892 I went for the first time as a delegate to the Trade Union Congress. It met in Glasgow; it took a week out of the fortnight's holiday allowed me by the firm, and in the week following I paid my first visit to the Lake district and the Wordsworth country. The poets had long been my own familiar friends, and Southey and Wordsworth had made their country familiar and dear to me, and it was a delightful and refreshing episode after my week at Glasgow. The Congress itself captured my imagination at once. The keen, intellectual pleasure which had been born in me by the study of history and literature had made me look at things in many aspects, and while I realized the value of the Congress in helping forward the cause of labour, and helping also to educate public opinion as to the facts of its conditions, I saw in a flash that it was going to be a training-ground for Labour politicians, and that it might become a larger and more enlightened ground than that which had trained Liberalism and developed the democratic idea generally.

National development was of keen interest to me. I read a great deal of what philosophers and politicians had written about the science of government, and had come to the conclusion that there was very little science in it, and that accident had quite as much to do with it as science. I had never known anything in politics that was discussed purely on its merits; it was always discussed in reference to the exigencies of a particular party. Liberalism was born out of English Dissent, all but a few of its supporters were Dissenters, and when a great Churchman like Gladstone sought for support for his measures he got most of it, not from his Church, but from Dissent. And it was because of this that Liberalism never really developed a national temper. My sympathies went naturally with Liberalism, but I could not shut my eyes to the fact that the temper of the sect was everywhere manifested in it. I could recognize the honesty of purpose, but could never love the man who was the friend of every country but his own, and Liberalism did undoubtedly produce this man. My reading of history had made me love my country, and my lectures on history were my methods of making other people love it if I could. But the Trade Union Congress stirred new ideas in my mind; my week at Glasgow in 1892 was a week of vision, as well as of practical work, and of my first Congress I wrote on my return:

The Parliament of Labour, like the Parliament at Westminster, has its faddists and its bores, and its gassy talkers, but questions were discussed there with as much acumen and as much fairness of judgment as in the House of Commons. Why should they not be? The Trade Unionist, like the cooperator, is getting educated in the duties of citizenship through the organization to which he belongs. Underneath all the talk there was seen to be an earnest, honest purpose, that of helping Labour to get its fair share of the fruits of its work. Regarded as a phase in the development of the Democratic idea, the Congress was in every way hopeful and encouraging. It was dominated by a high ideal of justice; it endeavoured to be just even to its fools, and there is no more difficult task in existence than that. Its practical side was as well developed as its ethical side, and its windbags were mercilessly pricked when they stopped useful work.

I was there on the eve of great constitutional changes, in the life of the congress, and this I did not know. My trade had not been represented at Congresses for many years, and I had everything to learn at the Congress of 1892. The old trade unionism and the new were in sharp conflict. Labour movements have often had a larger outlook than the sects, but they stiffen and grow conservative quite as rapidly. But they are class movements, and the nation is larger than any class within its borders, and will live when they have passed into forgetfulness and dusty oblivion.

And amid all these trade-union activities the Marlowe and Massinger memorials and the shilling Browning were born. But I owed much to the band of young literary enthusiasts whom I gathered round me at Toynbee Hall. Warm-hearted, brilliant, eloquent of tongue, and quick to acquire any knowledge that he desired, William Henry Cowham and I formed a close friendship, and his abounding vitality and youth made me forget my own middle age and the dust of small detail which I breathed in the Labour world. Death claimed him in 1898, when life and domestic happiness were opening out before him. William Hutchinson, who was with us on the committee of the Massinger memorial, died at about the same age as Cowham, and left behind in his short and strenuous life quite a large body of literary work in the way of editing and translating. Arthur Hayward, scholar and man of culture and refinement, and my successor in the active work of the Elizabethan Society, and Otto Sallmann, best of dramatic readers, all helped in the work, and one there was to whom I have before alluded, a pathetic failure in life's battle, James Ernest Baker. His love for good literature was keen, his instinct for it true and sure. For some years he was secretary of the Elizabethan Society; and his pleasant, cheery ways made him welcome everywhere. He had poetic gifts of a minor order, and several of his poems appeared in the *National Reformer*, then under the editorship of John M. Robertson, and for some period of his life he professed the opinions of the *National Reformer*.

But the early aspirations of Ernest Baker found no realization. As manhood came on it was apparent that, even with all the help that friendship could give, nothing would save him from the downward path. Vice gripped him in her hideous claw, and he had no strength of character to stand against it. Those who knew him best knew the good there was in the strange and stumbling soul, and tried again and again to save him from himself. It was in vain. "Let me alone, do not trouble about me; I am not worth your trouble," he said to one who tried to help him in his degradation. The end was near when he spoke the words, but before it came there came back to him the faith of his childhood which he had cast aside, and perhaps it came back to him with those words. Like the earlier Baker whose story I have told, Ernest Baker died in a workhouse and rests in a pauper's grave. During the last weeks of his life he gathered much pleasure and some spiritual help from the religious essays of Coulson Kernahan, and of George Macdonald. Peace came at last, and his death was the passing of a penitent soul. "I fear nothing: I have cast myself at the feet of Christ" were the words with which his life went forth.

XX

BLACKLEGS AND A PARSON

A STRIKE creates a tradition and a moral standard among the men of a trade, which last a generation and sometimes longer. With all the newspaper talk about trade union tyranny, no man has ever been prevented from earning his living by his fellow-workmen, in the way which he has been when he has been black-listed by employers. But what a man does during the progress of a strike, and whether his actions have been mean or honourable, is usually remembered by his fellows, and determines their attitude towards him for the rest of his life.

Happily for the general well being, the virtue of loyalty is more common than most people suppose, and it commands admiration by its beauty, wherever it is seen. And a man who has been loyal to his fellow-craftsmen in a time of crisis, wins a place in their hearts which he rarely loses again. But the blackleg in a trade dispute finds his parallel in the sneak at a public school. He may get forgiven when the storm has passed, but he is never respected or trusted. And yet: although there is no room for pity or compromise in a time of strike, which is a time of war, there is something to be said for the blackleg when all is done.

The blackleg that comes to the front in a strike is

usually a kind of labour parasite, living on the body of labour as vermin live on the body of a man, and showing by his presence that there is foulness somewhere or he would have no place. He can be classified, and when this is done he becomes interesting. Sometimes he is a poor creature who has never had his chances in life, a failure whether by his own fault or not. He has never properly learned his trade, and is looked down on and kicked by his little world, and he takes the opportunity which a strike gives him of revenging himself. Sometimes he is a skilled artisan who has lost his character by crime, with whom his fellows will have no more to do than they can help. Sometimes, too, he is a man of a different type to either of the two described: a quite decent type of young man, who has perhaps been occupied with activities outside the labour world, does not understand it, and not infrequently thinks himself a little above it. He wants to get on: naturally enough, and is not particular about standing by his fellows, and sees no reason for fighting for anything but his own hand. But men of this class learn by experience and usually their experience leads them to become good trade unionists.

Among the notable characters of the Bookbinders' Strike, outside the ranks of the strikers, was the Rev. Freeman C. Wills. He was vicar of St. Agatha's, Finsbury, during the strike, and died at Eastbourne in May, 1913. It was round about his parish that most of the important activities of the strike raged. A strange eccentric creature; threadbare and poverty-stricken, and for whom his clerical brethren had never a good word, the Bookbinders found in him a kindly and generous friend. He never expressed any opinion as to the merits of the strike: it was human sympathy and kind heartedness that were the forces which prompted his actions. He saw men fighting honourably for a principle, and came and offered them help. He placed at their disposal the schoolroom of St. Agatha's: from which the school had long since departed, and found coals for two great fires which were kept alight during the time they were there. The strike was in the depth of winter, there was no meeting-place for the strikers but the public house, and the value of a service like this was simply inestimable.

He was obnoxious to many people because of his religious views. He identified himself strongly with the Catholic party in the English Church, but the men on strike cared nothing for this; they only knew that in the shabby and eccentric priest they had found a friend when they needed one. I knew him first on his business side, and this is often a better index to a man's character than his religious opinions are. He was a journalist as well as a parson, and was brother to the one time rather famous dramatist, W. G. Wills. The plays of W. G. Wills usually excited furious controversy, as he had a way of putting the ugly side of popular leaders like Knox and Cromwell, which did not appeal to the gallery. When first I met Freeman Wills he was editing a magazine called *Eastward Ho*: the title being borrowed from the famous Elizabethan play of that name. To this journal I was an occasional contributor, and—although the journal could not have been a financial success—he was prompt and regular in his payments. Many magazines with a much better financial backing than he had did not possess the same virtue of prompt payment, as I knew from experience.

He wrote plays himself, but had not the gifts of his

o

brother. His great success was the play in which the celebrated actor, Mr. Martin Harvey, achieved such fame, "The Only Way." No Dickens' play ever achieved the long and continuous success which this play did. Our associations were chiefly literary, but during the strike he made a suggestion of a startling character to me. He asked me if I had ever looked at Labour problems from the religious standpoint, and on my replying in the negative suggested that I should do so, and said farther that if I would give an address on them from that point of view one mid-day when the strikers were all about, the pulpit of his church was open to me. I was distinctly frightened at appearing in the pulpit, told him I knew nothing of theology, and was quite certain that the Bishop of London would never grant me permission to speak in a church. He replied that he knew quite well that I knew nothing of theology, and he did not want me to talk any, he wanted me to talk about the problems of industrial life, and that Bishop Temple's consent was unnecessary as the church of St. Agatha was a mission church and unconsecrated.

I consented, and the day on which I was to make my first appearance in the pulpit was the day after the Duke of Clarence and Frank Dleny died. A short service was held in the church, four members of the Vellum Binders' Society gave the quartette, "God is a Spirit," by Mendelssohn, as an anthem, and I entered the pulpit and—entirely contrary to my custom—read a carefully written address which I entitled "Christ and Commercialism." And when the benediction had been pronounced, and the service had ended, the memories of the dead prince and the dead workmen were honoured together in the " Dead

March from Saul," which was played on the organ as the congregation dispersed.

What I said in that address seems now, in the light of the utterances on religion made by leading members of the Labour Party during the last four years at Browning Hall, to have anticipated many later developments. But I had no idea of anticipating anything when I wrote it out: I simply followed my reasoning whithersoever it led. But because of its interest in connection with later developments in the world of Labour, it is given here.*

---

* "My friends and comrades, I often feel very sick at heart with politics and all that pertains thereto. If I were a thirty years younger man, with the experience I have gained during the past thirty-five years, I would, methinks, abandon house and home and wife and child if need be, to go forth amongst the people to proclaim afresh and anew the full message of the Gospel of Jesus of Nazareth. We are, all of us, somehow or another off the track. What is wanted is a fresh inspiration, a fresh vision of the great truth which Christ gave His life to proclaim, that not only have we individual souls to be saved, but the individual soul cannot be saved unless the collective soul be saved likewise."—J. Keir Hardie, M.P., at Browning Hall, May 5, 1913.

XXI

CHRIST AND MODERN COMMERCIALISM

THE remark likely to be made by the ordinary business man, on first seeing the title of this address, would be, "Christ and Modern Commercialism, what on earth have they to do with each other?" Truly, little enough, I reply; and yet it is not without a reason that I link them together. For Christ is the world's ideal, and modern commercialism the world's fact. The ideal is divine, the fact hideous; let us place them side by side, and see what each can say of the other. And when we do this, we find that the ideal helps us to face the fact; that the wondrous personality of Jesus of Nazareth, which has stamped itself on the heart of the world as no merely human personality could have done, as no personality has done before or since, is as full of inspiration for us, who are fighting the battle of labour to-day, as it was for those who were fighting the battle of faith eighteen centuries ago. It is an often-made speculation—made so often as to almost be commonplace—If Christ came back to earth again, how would the men of this nineteenth century receive Him? what would He think of those who now speak in His Name? Look for a moment at the great commercial chaos in which we dwell; this crowd of struggling men and women made in the image of God, but transformed by competition into images of the devil. Think of the palace of the capitalist, and the garret, or the cellar, of the poverty-stricken wretches out of whose misery he makes his wealth; think that this is the present outcome, the flower and the crown of our boasted civilization; think that after centuries of religious teaching and preaching, after generations of scientific culture and training, the last utterance of modern thought to weary and heavy laden humanity is the doctrine of the survival of the fittest, which, being interpreted by modern commercialism, means that the weakest shall go to the wall; and then look back through the mists of time to that strange divine Figure that walked the streets of Galilee, and uttered words that are full of music yet: "Come unto Me, all ye that are weary and heavy laden, and I will give you rest," and say what link there is that shall connect the two.

Modern commercialism is dominated only by one principle: Get as much as you can, and give as little as you can for it. In this doctrine does the capitalist find all his law and his prophets. What matters if my brother is crushed in the struggle—it is the law of nature that crushes him, not I; am I my brother's keeper? Is it fault of mine that bread shall be so dear, and flesh and blood so cheap? Nay, am I not one of the world's benefactors in what I do? It is better that I should buy this flesh and blood, and feed it at a cheaper rate than I do my dogs and horses, than that it should rot in the streets. At least, I give it its market value, and this I do not determine; it is determined for me by the inexorable law of supply and demand. Why should I reduce my profits, or lower my balance at the bank, because people are starving? what is it to me that so many men and women are unemployed? I give employment to as many as I can, and have done all that can fairly be asked of me.

So might Dives argue to-day, and in many a public assembly in our land there would arise an applauding Hear! hear! But who determines the market value of a fellow-creature? Is "the inexorable law of supply and demand" the final standard of appeal? If there is no demand for a man's labour, is it an inexorable law that he shall starve? The logical outcome of the teaching of modern commercialism brings us only one answer: Yes! And when that is uttered, there creeps in upon our hearts the chill and deadly thought that after all this may be true; and if it be, what matters all our struggling? Why, why should we sacrifice ourselves for others? Let us be content with our own success. What matters who falls, so that we can hold our own in the fight?

> "Let us alone. What pleasure can we have
> To war with evil? Is there any peace
> In ever climbing up the climbing wave?"

And again there comes the Christ voice, like a strain of heavenly music: "All things whatsoever ye would that men should do to you, do ye also unto them, for this is the law and the prophets." And there rises in our hearts a feeling of strength and hope, and every good instinct within us is in revolt against the doctrine that there is no higher law in the world than that which is taught in the commercialism of to-day; and we ask by what right society dooms men to starve. Who are we that we shall decide that there is no demand for our brothers' existence? Is it true that the law of supply and demand is an inexorable law of nature, or is it we who have as yet only half learned Nature's laws?

Bold questions these, some will say, and who shall answer them? The answer will come out of the warfare that labour is waging with the evil elements that are in modern commercialism; and in that warfare labour will do its best and most lasting work when it is filled with the spirit and inspired by the example of Jesus Christ. What do I mean by these words? Am I merely talking the rhetoric of commonplace theology now, or is there definite and tangible meaning in what I say? I should be wasting your time and mine if I were to utter only meaningless phrases for the sake of seeming to square with popular orthodoxy, or of producing effect, knowing as I do the battle that labour is fighting to-day, and the work it has got to do before it can take its proper position in our social life. We are beginning to see that the system, the habit of mind, which regards the worker as the slave of the capitalist, as simply the creature whose mission it is to produce, while others consume, is wrong; and when this idea has grown fully upon the national conscience, then will the transformation of modern commercialism begin, and the power that will transform it, I repeat the words again, will be the Spirit of Jesus Christ.

For the central idea of Christ's life is that of sacrifice. A life given—not a life sold for a money sum. It is only by sacrifice that anything worth winning in the world's battle can be won. "The cross" is worked into the very texture of human life, and you cannot escape it, if you would live at all. You may deny the beautiful story as an old wife's fable, if you will. You may say Christ is a myth, the incidents of His life only the episodes in a religious romance, the cross simply an accidental element in the story; but you will not alter the fact that you will have to bear your cross if you want to live any life at all that is other than that of the brute. You may not see in your honest blindness, you may not acknowledge in your intellectual pride, that the cross you bear, the tribulation that is searching your character and purifying your heart, is verily the cross of the Christ Himself; but you must bear it, you must learn its lesson, because that lesson is part of the eternal law of the world. Only when you fall below the man; only when you come to be so debased and degraded as to be akin to the brute; only when in very truth you are as soulless as he, shall you escape the working of this law. Both the glory and the anguish of this law of sacrifice are pearls, and they may not be cast before us if we convert ourselves into swine.

Labour to-day is realizing, slowly and brokenly, but still realizing, the influence and the power of sacrifice. Out of the blood of the martyrs came the seed of the Church; out of the sacrifices that labour is making in its warfare with capital, the new social order shall grow. Do you feel too weary and depressed to fight and to endure for that which seems so far away? Think, then, of the weariness of that Divine Soul, when all the wise men of the world were arrayed against Him and His work. What a failure, what a mistake, what a wretched ending to a great idea, must have seemed the tragedy that took place on the summit of Mount Calvary nineteen hundred years ago! Poor foolish Hebrew artisan, He went preaching about the villages to ignorant fisher folk, giving them ideas that never could be realized; and this is the end of all His talk. So might an intelligent Sadducee have reasoned, never dreaming that the hour of Christ's despair was, in fact, the very hour of His triumph; that out of the darkness of that death was shining the brightness of an everlasting life.

Slowly and surely there will come a reaction against the iron materialism of our commercial world. Not the inexorable law of supply and demand, but the needs of a man's life will be the standard by which the wages of a man's labour shall be fixed. The doctrine that the weakest shall go to the wall may be all that science can tell us, when we ask her to help us to solve the problems that face us now; but we shall move onward till we find a higher law, and we shall find that law, not in the selfish spirit of modern commercialism, but in the self-sacrificing spirit that is in Jesus Christ. Labour has its face turned upward in its onward journey now. Once it was bowed and bent and brutish, its face fixed earthwards, and with no ray of hope in its heart. But in the light of its new hopes, the strings of its burden are loosened, and it gathers strength and courage as it sees the brightness that is shining at the head of the way. There are quagmires to struggle through, there are difficult hills to climb, there are dark valleys to pass. But if it keep its face upward, its aims high; if it resolve that it will make no terms with the forces of evil, forces that tell it of speedy remedy, then the promise of the future is for it. Not for it the triumphs of the sword; not for it the conquests of the warrior; not for it peoples oppressed by peoples; its hopes lie otherwhere. A society from which the demons of poverty and starvation shall be cast out. A nation wherein the bond of brotherhood shall break down the walls of class. A people whose desire shall be, not for warfare with their brothers, but only with the dark forces of the world, with which all must fight. Conquest, not of our brothers' household, but of Nature's secrets, for the bountiful Mother has more to tell us yet than we dream of now, only we cannot understand her words. All these things lie hidden in labour's half-conceived ideals : and who can touch them with a living inspiration, but He in whose face a divine glory is shining still—Jesus Christ the Carpenter, Jesus the eternal Son of God ?

XXII

BROWNING HALL AND OLD AGE PENSIONS

It was the surplus millions of the Co-operative Movement that first set me thinking of Old Age Pensions, and it was accident that brought me into touch with Browning Hall, but the two were to have a close connection with each other, though I knew nothing of this at first. It was at a Saturday afternoon meeting at the Co-operative Wholesale Society that the delegates from the various co-operative societies were discussing what might be done with their surplus capital, which amounted, I think, to six millions then, when I flung out the idea that they could use it for creating pensions for old workpeople in their movement. It was a new idea, I had not thought it out any more than any one else, but it started there, and caused much discussion. The year was 1895. A year after that I met, at a public meeting in Finsbury, a young man who was speaking on the same platform as myself, a Mr. Tom Bryan. He had been a stockinger at Leicester, and claimed to be one of the founders of the Independent Labour Party; he is now at the head of one of the social organizations at Bournville, near Birmingham. We took to one another at once, and, through him, I was introduced to Mr. F. Herbert Stead, who was warden of Browning Hall. The introduction began a friendship between Mr. Stead and myself which has been one of the most valued friendships of my life.

He was brother to the great journalist who perished in the *Titanic* disaster, Mr. W. T. Stead, and had been working several years at the old conventicle where Browning was baptized and which, at that time, was called Locks Fields' Chapel, but which Mr. Stead had re-christened Browning Hall. It was a centre of many activities, not a university settlement like Toynbee Hall, but—what Mr. Stead called—a "social settlement." The building was put up in the year of the French Revolution, and this, added to its connection with Browning, made it the sort of place which attracted many people, myself among the number. I often spoke on its platforms, and gradually realized that the work being done there was among the most remarkable of any work in London of the same kind, and—as usual—London did not care twopence about it. It was a dead Congregational church when Mr. Stead took it on in 1895, and the Congregational Union of that day wanted to pull it down on the ground that there "was no one in Walworth." There was no one from the Union's point of view, there were only about a million people, and they were all poor, and there had been a flourishing and well-to-do congregation at the chapel when Browning was baptized there in 1812. Mr. Stead, however, found a few of the original members of the congregation still living, took on his duties without salary, set the Congregational Union at defiance, and has done a work in the old chapel that has made its influence felt, not only through the United Kingdom, but through the world.

I had long ago made up my mind as to the place of

Browning in English literature, and had a way of startling literary friends by dogmatically proclaiming that the three greatest English poets were Shakespeare, Milton, Browning. The early environment of Browning was middle-class and decadent Puritanism of Georgian and Victorian days, and because of the influence of Puritan ideals upon his life he never possessed the freedom of spirit and spontaneity of life which characterizes Shakespeare. But in intellectual grasp, in sure and firm insight into the qualities of the soul, in the power to seize on to and depict the distinctive and vital elements in motive and in character, he is the equal of Shakespeare. Catholic ideas and Puritan thought are often in conflict in what he writes, but he never knew the Catholic faith with the intimacy that Shakespeare did. He accepted the conventions that surrounded him as part of the general scheme of things, so far as his own conduct was concerned, and scandal or youthful indiscretion were far from him. But he found no inspiration for his verse in the conventions that guided his conduct. It was impossible that he should do so. Middle-class society, as he knew it, was a thing of narrow ideals and narrower customs. Its highest aim was respectability, its highest achievement mediocrity. The Elizabethan drama was a thing forgotten among the people he knew, Shakespeare an author whom good people should avoid, and the Renaissance an episode in history that was only half understood.

Richly dowered with magnificent imagination, but setting it aside as a secondary thing whenever an intellectual problem arose, it is to the Middle Ages that he turns for the subject of his first great poem, "Paracelsus." In the fascination which thought and its development had for him, rather than action and its results, in his keen and absorbing interest in the spiritual and intellectual problems that belong to man, he stands nearer to the subtle thinkers of the Middle Ages than to the Elizabethans, and certainly nearer than to the men of his own day. That he was entirely able to compass the Elizabethan spirit, and was in a measure master of its form, the story of Ottima and Sebald proves beyond argument. But he has no kinship, conscious or other, with the Dionysian spirit of the Renaissance, the foundations of his nature were Puritan, and if he parted company, as he certainly did, with his Puritan ideals when he reached manhood, some leaven always remained to fetter a soul that apart from them was magnificently free. It is the form only of Browning's poetry that repels. Not because of its obscurity; that charge so often made is not true, his poetry is never obscure to those who realize his methods of expression. It is its ruggedness, its sense of unfamiliarity, its defiance of literary convention which creates the supposed obscurity. Uncouth and careless by turns, he seems at first acquaintance to lack standards, suggests struggle with difficulties of expression; tremendous effort with strangely inadequate results. Some of his noblest thoughts are set to barbaric music, or spoken with a stammering tongue, but it is a Titan that is struggling for speech, and if the melody is barbaric it carries with it the elemental charm that is found in wild music or untutored song, and reaches the deepest depths of the soul.

In the old chapel, associated with the early years of Robert Browning in the year 1898, the committee was formed which was to bring about the establishment of a national system of Old Age Pensions, and in 1899 I was asked to become its secretary. My activities in the larger area of the labour world, the area of the United Kingdom, began with my visit to the Trade Union Congress in 1892, and in that year occurred the first reference at a Trade Union Congress to Old Age Pensions. The work of the Congress appealed to me, and I rapidly became known and found friends among the delegates. I had the same pleasure in the work of the Labour Movement as that which, in earlier years, I found in University Extension. I saw a creative power at work, though what was to be born of it I knew not. Beginning as a congress enthusiast I swiftly developed into a congress critic, and, finally, into a congress journalist, sitting, when my delegate days were over, at the press table some fourteen years, and representing the *Westminster Gazette*, the *Church Times*, and other papers during that period.

The Trade Union Congress was then, and is now, the best expression of the mind of organized labour in England. Scotland has its own Trades' Congress, and that I have visited once; Ireland has its Congress also, but it is a feeble concern. Large sections of English labour stand outside these Congresses, and those not always inferior or unintellectual people, but the English Congress influences legislation, is the driving force of one political party, and gets its will in politics in a way that neither Scotch nor Irish Congresses have ever done. Its mechanism tends, every now and then, to become stiff and old-fashioned, and nothing wants oiling oftener than popular machinery. It represents a portion, a large and determined portion, of the popular will, and the popular will is absolutely feminine in its fickleness and love of change. It is, however, the power we govern by, and as illustrating the possible tendency of future legislation the resolutions of a congress are invaluable. They are often mutually destructive of each other taken as expressions of ideas, they change and vary for no apparent reason whatever, they are crude, prolix, and illogical by turns, but beneath and through them all is an articulate voice, the voice of those who are oppressed seeking to cast off the oppressors' chain.

There was more character in it than in the House of Commons itself because everything was more natural. The ritual of Parliament is highly interesting as a study of political symbolism, and doubtless has its place and value when Parliament is considered from its artistic side, but it can never be other than anathema to the plain man, let him be right or wrong. Ritual is an entirely natural growth, and there is plenty of it in the Labour movement, and a little in the Trade Union Congress, though not enough to check its development. Those who created the congress wanted it to express the ideals of labour, and with no false notes. But as soon as it became a power efforts were made by the middle classes to obtain admission among its delegates, sometimes no doubt with the best possible intentions. In the two other sections of the Labour Movement, co-operation and the Friendly Societies, the middle-class element was useful and helpful. The trade unionists were, however, quite right in refusing to allow middle-class influence to enter their ranks.

The test-case was that of Miss Edith Simcox at Dundee in 1889. Miss Simcox was a lady journalist of much ability who had been sent as a delegate to Congress by one of the women's unions. She was not in any sense recognized by the Congress as a working woman, and had no knowledge of the mind of labour, though she had a reputation for a large knowledge of economics. Her credentials were returned to her and the subscription of her union not accepted. She was entirely sympathetic with the aims and objects of the Congress, and her endeavour to enter Congress was prompted by the best of motives, but Mr. Broadhurst, M.P., gave utterance to a sound principle, and expressed the feeling of Congress, when he said, " Miss Simcox was clearly not the class of person entitled to sit in that Congress as Labour representative." She had been a member of the London School Board, and in 1880 she had delivered a fine address at St. Jude's Schools, Whitechapel, in connection with the University Extension Movement, to which I had listened with delight. But my sympathies were entirely with the Congress which refused to admit her to its membership, although I was not in that year a delegate.

At the Trade Union Congress I took active part in the debates on such subjects as factory inspection and the evasion of the Fair Wage Clause in Government contracts, and before long ran for the Parliamentary Committee of the Congress. I never stood any chance. I represented the Vellum Binders, a trade union which had but 500 members, and the tendency of Congress has always been to give power into the hands of the larger unions. A union was entitled to a delegate for every thousand or under a thousand members, therefore my union was only entitled to one. I had the support of the smaller trades, and polled well, but although I ran several years in succession never attained the object of my ambition.

Meanwhile other developments were taking place among the working classes, and not the least among them was the formation of the Independent Labour Party. I do not venture to give the exact date of its birth, there are as many different statements about that as there are about the birth of Homer, but its first annual conference was held at Bradford in 1893. I disliked it because of the large middle-class element in it, but saw it had possibilities. I was never actively connected with it, but tried to maintain a judicial attitude towards it in my public utterances. Its middle-class element was, to me, a sham, and gave full excuse to those who called it a bogus organization. It had a shibboleth, but no standards, and if my trade unionism had taught me anything it had taught me the value of standards and the danger of lowering them. It called itself socialistic, but its socialism was of the mildest kind as compared with that taught by Mr. Hyndman, and I had long ago made up my mind that if logic was the whole of the business, then Hyndman and the S.D.F. had the best of the argument. But it was not, and the I.L.P. was evidence of the fact. For it represented largely the politics of the younger men, and youth is never logical, though it is usually cocksure. I knew the young man of the Labour world, and knew he must have ideals, a fact which Liberals did not care to recognize. I remember a little group at a Leicester Trade Union Congress, a prominent Liberal politician, and two or three eager-faced youths. The politician was a man of abundant personality, with an enormous white waistcoat and a bland and benevolent smile. "I don't believe in your industrial politics," he said, turning to the young men, "give me liberty and the open road." "But won't you let us see where the road leads to?" was the reply. The open road of Liberalism meant to the young men who flocked into the ranks of the I.L.P. unlimited competition in the industrial world, and they asked themselves the same question that co-operators had asked half a century before, What is the best way to limit it? To them unrestricted competition was an evil which only the strong hand of the State could remedy.

The dynamic force of the Independent Labour Party has always been Mr. Keir Hardie, M.P. He is the idealist rather than the politician. I have by no means always shared his ideals, but I have always admired the selfless sincerity which has enabled him to put on one side all chance of office or political success for the sake of his ideal, and have wished there was more of that rare quality in our public life. It is this steady integrity of purpose, combined perhaps with a touch of old-fashioned Scotch mysticism, which gives him his hold on the working classes. He knows the literature of his country in a way that English Labour leaders do not know theirs, and I have a memory of a morning in Edinburgh when we walked down Princes Street and discussed William Dunbar. I knew him well, but Keir Hardie knew him better, and he did not quarrel with me when I claimed that Dunbar was as great a poet as Burns. There is always arising "a new king in Egypt that knew not Joseph," and he will arise much oftener in a democratic world than in a monarchical. Because of this it seems likely that the influence of the famous Labour leader may be nearing its limits. If it is there will probably be room for much criticism of his career from the purely political points of view. But the political view is always the lower, and he has chosen the higher. He has taught in politics an old truth: that men must believe before they can be saved.

The wave of revolution that was passing over the industrial world did not leave out the Trade Union Congress. Entirely new developments grew out of the influx of new life which came into it after the great dock strike of 1889. Many new unions were formed after that social upheaval, and not many of them were long lived. Largely unions of unskilled men, it was difficult to find among their members men of sufficient ability to become leaders, and through the door of the new and often smaller unions, there was a danger of the adventurer and the political wire-puller getting into the trade union world. It was to prevent this that Miss Simcox had her credentials returned, but the motives of the political adventurer were not so honest as hers. The trade union movement was powerless to prevent this, as it was constituted before 1895, and what was known as the policy of Cardiff made a revolution in the old-fashioned mechanism of Congress. The two valuable things this policy achieved on behalf of purity of representation were these. The conditions of delegacy were altered, and no person was allowed to attend Congress who was not either a paid official of his union or a man working at his trade. This was a change that effectually kept out the political adventurer who was not a workman, and gave full opportunities to the trade unionist who was. Some wise legislation was also inaugurated to prevent dual representation. It was possible for a trade to be represented twice over by being represented through its union, and again through a trades council. The trades councils were never in a logical position in the Trade Union Congress, but they were admitted when congresses were weak, and strength before all things was the necessity. Their anomalous position had long been recognized, and when the policy of Cardiff decided that representation from trades councils should no longer be admitted, they did a sound as well as a popular thing. (A trades council is a body composed of representatives of trades in a particular town or district, and is a local, not a national organization.)

The difference of opinion which—while it lasted—split trade unionism asunder, came with the system of voting which was inaugurated. The smaller unions in the Congress had been largely over-represented because the larger unions would not incur the expense of sending the full number of delegates to which they were entitled. A system of voting by card was therefore adopted which for all practical purposes gave the control of Congress into the hands of the larger trade unions. Every trade society was entitled—after 1895—to one vote for every thousand members or fraction thereof. The methods of voting is by card, one card being issued for every thousand members or fraction thereof, and it is possible for any union to send one delegate with the whole voting power of his union in the shape of the necessary number of cards in his pocket. I am not aware if this has ever been done, but the possibility of it remains in the machinery of the Congress.

There was principle and conflict of principle involved in the policy of Cardiff. "Taxation brings with it representation," said the smaller unions, uttering the old-fashioned democratic shibboleth. "Yes," said the larger unions, echoing the words of Dr. Samuel Johnson, "but the more taxes we pay the more votes we are entitled to have." There was a great deal to be said for the argument of the larger unions, just as there has always been a great deal to be said for the argument of Dr. Johnson. Dr. Johnson's view, however, was never accepted formally in English politics, but the argument of the larger unions was made the law of the Trade Union Congress. They did contribute more money to the Congress exchequer than the smaller unions, but in accepting the principle embodied in the new system of card voting working-class democrats gave away many other principles which they considered vital to true democracy, and what they did at the Cardiff Trade Union Congress in 1895 may have far-reaching consequences in a conservative direction in future years.

The smaller trades were in violent revolt, and I was their champion, and in the battle I had opposed to me as champion of the larger trades, Mr. Burns, M.P., now the Rt. Hon. John Burns, President of the Local Government Board. I had always great admiration for the work he had done in the Labour Movement, and a profound respect for the man. All through his political career he has stood for purity of representation in the industrial world, and those familiar with his public utterances during that career cannot fail to recognize, amid much that seems otherwise, a splendid consistency and sincerity of aim that is rare enough among politicians, and to these lofty qualities the historian of the future will do justice. He was interviewed in the *Daily Chronicle* of September 15, 1895, on the Cardiff policy, and I replied on the 17th in the same paper on behalf of the smaller trades. A reply to me from him on the 18th and to him from me on the 20th finished our battle, and there was good cudgel play on both sides. We were as polite to each other as a couple of French duellists, and each claimed he had won the victory. Our politeness, however, did not detract from our vigour on either one side or the other. We were personally strangers before our conflict, the result of it—after a little previous standoffishness on either side—was to make us fast friends.

Among the various resolutions I brought forward at trade union congresses the one of most importance was that relating to the labour of child-bearing women. I asked Congress to say that no employer of labour should be permitted to employ a women eight weeks before, or six months after, the birth of a child. I knew this question intimately and from the inside, as I had worked all my life in a trade where women were employed, and a woman working ten hours a day at her trade within a day or two of her confinement always seemed to me to outrage the principles of elementary decency, and to carry us back to savage life. It was rare that poverty was the cause of this. The best-paid women were the greatest sinners, and so long as they got the money cared nothing either for decency or for the child they would bring into the world.

The resolution was moved at the Birmingham Trade Union Congress on September 9, 1897, and attracted considerable notice in the medical as well as the Labour Press. In moving it I said :

We shall all agree that the woman with the pains of motherhood before her, or the duties of motherhood upon her, is in the wrong place when she is in the midst of the toil and bustle of the factory, and we shall all know that, in trades where women are employed, the woman working, when health, decency, and humanity alike demand that she shall rest, is one of the commonest and most deplorable pictures of our industrial life. On the surface it is apparent that evil results will come of this, but it is not until we get beneath the surface and find out what health statistics have to say on the subject that we find out what those results are. In the statistics prepared for the Registrar-General, and in the debates of the British Medical Association on infant mortality and female labour in factories, we find evidence so startling that if we care for the future of our own class we are bound to face it. The mortality of infants during the first year of life varies greatly in manufacturing and rural districts, but it is always greater in those districts where mothers work at a trade. If we take the adjoining county of Staffordshire we find North and South Staffordshire manufacturing and Central Staffordshire mainly rural. The towns in North and South Staffordshire are pretty much on a par as regards conditions of health, but in the North the infantile death rate is nearly double that of the South, the reason being that in the North are the potteries and weaving factories, and there the labour of married women during their period of child-bearing is common, while in the South with other industries such a class of labour is relatively small.

In the county of Dorset, almost entirely rural, infant mortality is 83 per 1000; in Lancashire, almost entirely manufacturing, it is 178 per 1000. That these deaths are due to the employment of the mother and her constant divorce from the home is proved by facts of another kind. To this day it is quoted in medical statistics that during the suffering and privation of the Lancashire cotton famine, suffering and privation so nobly borne as to make that period one of the most heroic chapters in English industrial history, the mortality among little children showed a remarkable decrease because the mothers were not in the factory. In the old strike at Coventry in the silk weaving days, in the siege of Paris, among the French working women, with all the suffering, the children did not suffer because their natural food was to hand. Get your statistics from whithersoever you will, they tell the same story. In Norway and Sweden where the employment of married women is far less relatively then in most European countries, infant mortality has been estimated at 10 per cent.; in Western Bavaria, where the large majority of women work, it is 50 per cent.

These facts have but one significance. They are Nature's testimony to the selfishness of modern life. They are not the results of a system, they are not half so often as we think caused by necessity; they are the outcome of a laxity of public opinion, of a moral sluggishness that almost amounts to a moral paralysis on matters relating to women that is shared by all classes alike. They bring to us weaknesses we can never surmount, for children born of the bodies of mothers who are exhausted by undue work are handicapped in the race of life at its very starting-point, and go to make up the weaker elements of our class, which are for ever pulling us down. They give point and truth to the bitter observation of old Bishop South, who, looking with despairing eyes on the children of a great manufacturing town, said: "Poor babies, you are not born, you are damned into the world." Fellow-delegates, by your voice and deliberation lead public opinion to-day; lead it now, and remove this stain and sin from our social life.

The men, with one solitary exception, voted in favour of the resolution, and it was carried. The women—to a woman—voted against it. And the evils against which I protested are as manifest to-day as they were in 1897.

As a Congress delegate I was nearing the end of my

career. I sat at one more Congress, my last being Bristol in 1898; in 1899 I was secretary to the Old Age Pensions Committee, and was neither working at any trade nor was I a paid official of my union, so was no longer eligible. This did not sever me from my old friends, but it made a change in my attitude to trade unionism, and I became a Congress journalist. The change, however, took place with dramatic effects which were not anticipated either by myself or any one else. Bristol became an historic congress from the fact that during its sittings the Colston Hall was burnt to the ground, and the delegates rendered homeless for the time being. Accommodation was found in another hall, and the Congress work went on without very much of a break. The final meeting on the night before the fire was a meeting of the Printing Trades group, and I, as a Vellum Binders' representative, was one of the speakers. It happened, however, that I was speaking at two other meetings on the same night, and reaching the hall a little before ten found the meeting nearing its close. My speech, however, was demanded, and it was short, vigorous, and the last of the evening. Two or three hours later the Colston Hall was in flames, and it is still a legend among older Congress men that the speech of Frederick Rogers set it on fire.

The Trades Congress seen from the Press table took on a colour and a picturesqueness which, as a delegate, I did not see. Of picturesque personalities there was enough and to spare. Of Mrs. Paterson I have spoken in a previous chapter, but I should not include her among them. It is a fact that the woman in the public arena is much oftener grotesque than she is picturesque, except when she is young, and when she is young she lacks experience. One of the most striking of the picturesque personalities was Edward Cowey of the Yorkshire miners. A giant in stature, with a leonine head and face, energy and passion were his chief characteristics, and with these he did all his work. His voice was like a roll of thunder, but in his closing years it became an inarticulate roar. He had little tact but much personal magnetism, and none of the arts of those who could control the Congress without his strength, and he often got himself heartily hated for nothing worse than a blunder. But he was a controlling force when he chose to be so, and although manifestly uneducated, was often a high-minded man. He had been brought up in one of the religious sects, and the poetry of the Old Testament was in his blood. His interests were few; it is the tendency of the mining industry to become as self-centred as it is unique, but one subject always stirred him to poetry and passion, and this was the need for workmen in Parliament. "But the door of the House of Commons can only be opened by a golden key," he would shout in stentorian tones, and the miners found that key before all the other industries. A totally opposite type of character was David Holmes of the weavers—clever, diplomatic, selfish, coldly eloquent, and finding the whole of industrial experience in his own trade, he proved a first-class leader for it, and controlled it, as he controlled the Congress, by sheer intellectual force. His ideals were more often those of the middle class than those of his own order, but he kept his influence in industrial circles until his death.

A man distinguished for the simple honesty of his character was W. C. Steadman. "Billy always runs straight" was a Congress phrase which expressed his character exactly. He was for some years secretary of the Parliamentary Committee of the Trade Union Congress, and was President of the Nottingham Congress in 1908. He used to listen often to my lectures on history at the clubs as a young man, and in his later life sat for a few years in Parliament. He was many years my junior, but I spoke at his grave.

Journalists of every shade of political opinion have prophesied the death of the Trade Union Congress ever since it became large enough to attract public notice, but it has grown larger year by year in spite of the prophets. It has seen the birth and death of many congresses, scientific or other, and its chief rival in length of years is the Church Congress, though there is no other point of resemblance between them. It is likely that we are nearing the limitations of Congresses as an expression of public opinion, but even if so the Trade Union Congress will live as long as any of them, and it is its genuineness and reality that will keep it alive.

When I spoke for the first time on Old Age Pensions at the Co-operative Wholesale Society I had been reading old literature. The contrast between the treatment of the poor in the mediæval monastery and in the modern workhouse appalled me. The monastic methods were crude and unscientific enough, but they had some touch of human kindness in them, and one of the first problems which society had to face after the so-called Reformation was poverty and age in industrial life. Bishop Ridley, preaching at St. Paul's Cross, propounded the first scheme of Old Age Pensions. It was for his own diocese of London only, but if every one of his episcopal brethren had followed his lead the beginnings of a national system of Old Age

OLD AGE PENSIONS 221

Pensions would have been created in the reign of Edward VI. instead of having to wait till that of Edward VII. The other party, however, came into power on the death of the young king, the Bishop was burnt, and his scheme forgotten. It was an incomplete scheme enough, but it and its author deserved a better fate. Daniel Defoe, Sir W. Petty, Thomas Paine, and others played with the idea, but it was not till the 'eighties of the nineteenth century that it really came into the domain of practical politics.

It was the economists that brought it there, however. It was an idea working in the scientific mind many years before it became a subject for the political platform.

Mr. Charles Booth, whose books on the social conditions of London had placed him at once in the front rank of English sociologists, had shown that the only logical system of Old Age Pensions was the universal and non-contributory system, and this view of the problem appealed at once to the working classes.

The Rev. S. A. Barnett and Mrs. Barnett in their book on "Practical Socialism" foreshadowed it as a future social reform, the Fabian Society included it in their programme, and Mr. George Turner's pamphlet did much to popularize the idea among the working classes. In 1892 a pamphlet by Charles Booth, entitled "Pauperism, a Picture ; and Endowment of Old Age, an Argument," was published. It was an epoch-making book, for it put the case for Old Age Pensions with a clearness and a precision which carried conviction to all, and frightened those who manipulated political finance. In 1894 he published a book on the "Condition of the Aged Poor," which contained such a formidable array of facts that some public action became all but imperative, and in 1895 the first Royal Commission to consider the problem presented by the aged poor was appointed. They considered, they reported, and they took no action. Their report, however, proved a valuable document when the time for agitation came. In 1898 another committee was appointed to consider the possibility of Old Age Pensions, and this committee reported that pensions were impossible. To Charles Booth's ideas they would have nothing to say; they held that they did not come within the terms of their references. In 1899 Mr. Booth published for the first time a complete scheme of Old Age Pensions; in the same year there was appointed by the House of Commons a "Select Committee on Aged and Deserving Poor," the chairman of which was the Rt. Hon. Henry Chaplin, M.P., and also in the same year the National Committee of Organized Labour was formed, the object of which was the promotion of a National System of Old Age Pensions.

Its first meetings were held at Browning Hall, Walworth, and were convened by Mr. F. Herbert Stead, who has written a history of the Movement. His object was to focus public opinion and bring about the application of the principles which Mr. Charles Booth had promulgated. Mr. Stead afterwards convened conferences in seven of the chief towns of Great Britain, the conferences consisting of elected delegates from friendly societies, trade unions, and co-operative societies, with occasionally representatives from Boards of Guardians and Poor-Law societies. Mr. Booth attended each of these conferences and explained his theory of a National System of Old

Age Pensions. The time and place of the various conferences were as follows:—

"December 13, 1898.—Browning Hall, Walworth, London.
"January 17, 1899.—Burt Hall, Newcastle-on-Tyne.
"February 23, 1899.—St. James' Hall, Leeds.
"February 25, 1899.—Co-operative Wholesale Society, Manchester.
"March 11, 1899.—Hannah More Hall, Bristol.
"March 14, 1899.—St. Andrews' Hall, Glasgow.
"March 25, 1899.—Technical Schools, Birmingham."

The result of these conferences was a practically unanimous vote in favour of a universal, non-contributory system of Old Age Pensions at sixty-five years of age. Four more committees were afterwards formed at Cardiff, Leicester, Nottingham, and Edinburgh. A central executive, consisting of persons elected from each of the above-mentioned committees was then formed, and in July, 1899, I was appointed secretary.

The business of the committee was to convert the nation to its views, and it decided from the beginning to stand outside all political parties. I was chief missionary, but I had a crowd of willing helpers from the trade unions and friendly societies, and we resolutely avoided all political by-paths, and concentrated ourselves entirely on getting pensions for the aged in place of Poor Law Relief.

Everybody but a few old-fashioned people gradually began to accept pensions in the abstract, but nobody knew exactly what they meant by them except Mr. Charles Booth and our committee. Among my first opponents were the members of the friendly societies.

Not all of them by any means, not the younger men, nor those who had got to close quarters with the problem, but a sufficiently strong number of them to make an opposition which people told me I had to break down or convert. I did neither, for I was tolerably certain that if my cause made headway the friendly societies would come round eventually, and so it proved. In the first year of the agitation, during the sittings of the Trade Union Congress, at Plymouth, I called on a leader of the Friendly Society Movement, and the whole of our interview was spent in an eloquent attempt on his part to convince me that my ideas were wrong. But the whirligig of time, as usual, brought round its revenges, and nine years later, when success was in sight, I read an article by him in (I think) the *Manchester Guardian*, which proved conclusively that my ideas were right. I was always ready to lecture or debate at Friendly Society meetings, and watched with keen interest the influence of our movement upon them, and steadily, slowly, and always things went our way, though the societies often hardly knew it themselves.

An invaluable colleague, inspirer, and friend was Francis Herbert Stead. We usually looked at action, and sometimes ideas, from different points of view. He was full of a fiery, passionate, and high-souled enthusiasm, which he was for applying always and everywhere, and had in him something of the fervour of the Hebrew prophet. I was ardent and enthusiastic too, but King Solomon's "There is a time for all things" was to me as vital as the Athanasian Creed, and I would not use enthusiasm when it seemed to me that a cold and practical policy did the work better. We probably balanced each other very well. He was honorary secretary, I organizing secretary, and with all our differences of temperament there was never even an approach to a breach between us, and my debt to him for inspirations and ideas no one but myself knows. Enthusiasm set the heather on fire in Scotland, when in 1899 I went to the Albion Hall, Glasgow, and addressed the Glasgow trade unionists, and our committee there, under the leadership of their secretary, Mr. B. H. Shaw, proved one of our strongest assets during the ten years of our work. It was at a meeting in Scotland that I nearly had a bad fall in discussing how the money for Old Age Pensions was to be raised. My committee did not express themselves as to the way of raising the money, denying that it was any part of their province to give financial advice to the Chancellor of the Exchequer. This left me free to indicate whatever methods of raising the money I chose. There were several methods propounded by me, and I was quite able to show that it was possible to raise enough for Old Age Pensions by a tax on alcohol. My audience on this occasion was from the middle classes, and many of them looked as though they might have been elders of the kirk, and I concluded that a temperance appeal would not be unacceptable. They listened with most polite attention while I put forth my arguments, they seemed to accept entirely the case I laid before them, they applauded vigorously when I dilated on the evils of drink, but when I proposed to raise a fund for pensions by putting a tax on whisky their jaws dropped. It was a false move, which I saw at once, and never repeated north of the Tweed, though in justice to my dissentient audience I ought to admit that my logic that night was not so good as it was sometimes.

It was in putting the case for pensions that my difficulties arose. I had to put it a hundred ways in my journeyings to and fro in the United Kingdom. There were audiences for whom rhetoric was a condition of success, there were other meetings which were rigorous in their demands for argument and logic. People who had pensions themselves were among my strongest opponents. Pensioned policemen and soldiers, comfortably off civil servants and such like persons were always profoundly conscious of the wickedness of the thriftless poor, and sometimes I met with bitter opposition from a certain highly respectable member of society, the "thrifty working man." I dealt kindly with him because I knew intimately the conditions of his life, and knew there was much to respect in him in spite of his narrow outlook.

That it was a narrow outlook, and that still there were qualities to respect in the narrow persevering mind, is proved by the following bit of real life which I culled from the *Co-operative News* during the Pensions agitation—

A motion was brought up at a meeting of the Eccles Co-operative Society the other evening proposing that the grant to the educational department be reduced, and the difference form an old age pension fund for members. In opposing the motion, an old member, Mr. J. Bradley, chimney sweep, and a considerable property owner, said he was born in a workhouse, and ran away. His mother was thirty years in Lancaster Asylum, and died there, and he had no knowledge of his father. When he got married they had not the price of a chair to sit on, and he took his bride home to a cellar, at 1s. 6d. a week. He had nothing to thank anybody for but himself, but he was now able to walk about with his hands in his pockets. He had brought up nine daughters and a son, and, therefore, could not endorse the remarks of the mover that because a man had had a large family he could not save money in the society. Old age pensions would only cause a deal more laziness. Surely the working men were receiving a big enough wage to set a little by for a rainy day. They ought to remember the three "B's," buy no bikes, take little beer and less tobacco, and go oftener to the bank, then they would not have to ask for old age pensions. The old age pension agitation was the greatest mistake of the present day.

He was better than Dickens's "Mr. Josiah Bounderby," because he was not a humbug, and did not pretend to be other than he was. But his character was built of the same materials, and he represented an aspect of the thrift problem which had its mixture of comedy and pathos, as had been pointed out by many writers on thrift, years before.

The Rev. S. A. Barnett had written in the *Nineteenth Century* of April, 1883, "England is a land of sad monuments. The saddest monument is, perhaps, the respectable working man" who has been erected in honour of Thrift. His brains which might have shown the world how to save men have been spent in saving pennies; his life, which might have been happy and full, has been saddened by "taking thought for the morrow."

And the sadness was as great whether his thrift failed or succeeded. If it succeeded he was able to go his own way through the world without being a burden on his fellows. But his success often made him an unlovely character, and he brought with him the sense that a nation of his type might be a horrible thing. If he failed, as too often he did in spite of all his honest thriftiness, then indeed the tragedy was full and complete, and death was but an angel of mercy if it came quickly and rang down the curtain.

XXIII

MEN AND LOGIC

" You will get plenty of heckling as you go about England preaching pensions, and if you stand a heckling from the Northumberland miners you can stand anything," said an old trade unionist to me when I began my propaganda work in 1899. I stood it and enjoyed it. But I liked the miners of Durham and Northumberland, both for their personal qualities and their unique position in the labour world. I did not find the young miner particularly interesting, but the men reaching middle life, with their experience, their intellectuality, and occasionally their superstitions, and their grim rugged humour, interested me at once.

A life lived always close to the mighty and mysterious forces of nature, and touched often with profound religious feeling, becomes finer in its texture and its qualities than a life lived in the factory, surrounded with an eternal whirl of machinery and in constant contact with the decadent elements of civilization. The vivid imagination of so many of the older miners—an imagination which was in no way detrimental to their vigorous powers of reasoning—found no parallel in the factory and the workshop, and—although I liked expounding my thesis— I liked a great deal better the Sunday morning walks about the mining districts, which were by no means always ugly, and the talks with the men about their life and ideals. They accepted the principle of pensions, but argued that five shillings a week "was not enough for a man's meat." This I could not dispute, and would have agitated for ten shillings if I had thought there was the slightest chance of getting it. But I knew the working of the political machine too well to expect anything of the kind, and meant to get the five-shilling pension as a beginning, leaving the future on the knees of the gods.

However religious the miner might be, he did not go to church, and was often desultory enough in his attendance at chapel. There were Catholics among the mining population, but the influence of John Wesley was writ large in all the mining districts of England, though at the period of which I write old men were talking of its decay. I was more attracted by its poetry than by any of its other qualities, and never objected to going to a Wesleyan meeting if any one asked me. One Sunday night I went to a little Wesleyan chapel in a Tyneside village at which a trade union secretary was to preach, whom I knew. He was a man of probity and character, but had not had much education. His reading of the Scriptures was something of an infliction, but his prayer was a wrestle with God, and I thought I understood then the secret of the popularity of Charles Wesley's great poem—

"Come, O thou traveller unknown,"

among men of the Wesleyan denomination. "Come to us, Lord, on the side we need Thee most," he cried in a voice full of a passionate energy. His sermon fell to a very much lower level than his prayer, and the suggestion that the woman of Samaria had come to draw water to make her tea caused a small titter to pass over the younger portion of his audience.

Now and again among highly imaginative miners old superstitious and strange beliefs would manifest themselves in conversation. Half laughed at, half believed in, the men who worked beneath the earth would tell stories, never about themselves, but about friends or acquaintances who had been in out-of-the-way corners of the mine, and had been conscious of something other than themselves near them which had given then a touch of fear, and, if they were religious, would perchance cause them to mutter a hasty prayer. Nothing had ever been seen, and the shamefacedness with which the story was told would be apparent. One aged miner whom I knew in Blyth, a Wesleyan who seemed to know all Wesley's hymns by heart, was wont to check youthful profanity beneath the earth with " Hold thy tongue, lad. Who knows who listens down here ? " Not all miners, however, were of his type. Hard men, grim, determined, and with a touch of the primitive savage in their natures, were created by the conditions of the miner's life, redeemed sometimes from complete hardness by the saving grace of humour. " Yes, you *do* get all sorts of temperatures down these mines," said a man in answer to a question from me. " Sometimes it's cold as winter, and sometimes it's hot as hell." And once a genial old man, about whose health I was inquiring, said, " Ah, man, but I was bad ; I nearly smelt brimstone that time."

A miners' leader of a highly intellectual type, well read and much given to the study of philosophy, was Ralph Young. He enjoyed the friendship of Herbert

Spencer, and it was easy to understand that the two men had much in common. An old-fashioned Radical and individualist, a materialist and an ardent admirer of Mr. Bradlaugh, he was in deadly opposition to the Socialist developments among the trade unions. He told me once when I was his guest at Newcastle, that he did not allow his daughter to "take Scripture" in her school; but individualist though he was, he was a staunch supporter of Old Age Pensions, and likewise an admirer of Westcott, Bishop of Durham, who was not. But Westcott won the hearts of the miners, though it is likely that his preaching was over their heads: as his portrait is in the Miners' Hall at Durham.

A leader of a different type to Ralph Young, though they were friends and fellow-workers, was Hugh Boyle, a Catholic. Young was a reasoner; Boyle was a fighter, and in his day a force at trade congress debates. It was Hugh Boyle who accompanied me one night from Newcastle to a village some distance off, where I was to lecture on pensions. It was in the depth of winter; we had nearly a mile to walk from the station, and we had not proceeded far along the road before we both went headlong into a gully full of snow. But I reached the hall, gave my lecture, and, as I was not returning to Newcastle, arranged to stay in the village, Boyle leaving me at the close of the lecture to go back to the town. "No, we don't have hotels in mining villages, but I can give you a clean bed and a comfortable one," said the miners' secretary, of whom I inquired as to sleeping. He kept his word. It was an old-fashioned mining village with houses perhaps nearing a century old, with the sanitary conveniences horrible, and there was no door to my bedroom; to which I ascended by a ladder through the ceiling of the lower room. But cleanliness and comfort were all there, and I slept the sleep of a tired man, passing on the next morning in spite of the snow to Jarrow and to the church of Bede, and wondering what manner of man he was who, in the beginning of English history, spent his long and useful life on that bleak and desolate spot.

The heckling of the miners did me good, not harm; and I had no falls with them, but I did nearly have a bad fall at the Church Congress at the Albert Hall in the year 1899. I was asked to read a paper on the subject of Old Age Pensions by Bishop Creighton, who, as Bishop of London, was chairman of that congress. The request came when I was out of London, and the paper was hurriedly written within a day or so of delivery. Its facts and logic were unassailable, but its figures, relating to possible cost, etc., with which I proposed to conclude the paper, were worked out in mental arithmetic and put down in pencil as I went to Kensington. I was timed, the chairman was a stern disciplinarian, and as I approached within a few sentences of the figures, ping! went his bell. I turned to argue with him and to plead for a few moments more, but he was inexorable, and when I got home at night and went carefully over those figures again before printing, they were all hopelessly wrong.

Among my opponents on that occasion was the celebrated Canon Blackley. He did good work both by speech and pen in bringing the pensions question to the front, and all his contributions to the discussion were of value, but they never appealed to the popular imagination as Charles Booth's ideas did. His scheme was to compel all persons between the ages of eighteen and twenty to subscribe ten pounds to a national fund, receiving in return eight shillings a week during sickness and four shillings a week pension at the age of seventy. He never faced the initial difficulty of his scheme, which was that the large majority of persons of those ages did not possess the ten pounds, nor the second difficulty, that it left out of calculation existing old people and only dealt with the young. The friendly societies opposed the scheme, and a committee of the House of Commons regarded it as unworkable; but it had stimulated discussion and had focussed public attention on the subject. I had a high respect for Canon Blackley, but my scheme was the opposite of his. He made a slashing attack on me, and I had no right of reply, but Canon Scott Holland stepped into the breach, and replied splendidly to my opponent. It was the kind of incident which calls forth gratitude, and mine went out to my doughty champion.

If Charles Booth gave me the facts for my pensions' campaign, it was in the writings of Edmund Burke that I found my inspirations. I was not pleading for State help on behalf of strong men, who could help themselves, but for those on whom the conditions of modern life pressed heaviest—the weak and helpless. I could subscribe wholeheartedly to a fine sentence of Burke's: "I do not call a healthy young man, cheerful in his mind and vigorous in his arms—I cannot call such a man poor; I cannot pity my kind as a kind, merely because they are men." There is no room to pity such; as far as a human being can be, they are masters of their own destinies, as I, even in the worst days of my weakness, felt that I was largely master of mine. But helplessness is the condition of the two ends of life, and for those who have lived past the days of youth and health into the days of age and feebleness, and are, whether by misfortune or fault, in danger of want or starvation, a new principle comes into play. The State has its claim on the individual in his years of health and vigour, and the individual has his claim on the State in his years of age and feebleness should either need the other's help; or, to put the idea in another way, as Mr. Calliaux, the French philosopher did: "If a human being entering the world finds himself a debtor to society, and in enjoyment of things it has done nothing to create, on nearing the time when it must leave the world, it has created enough social wealth to make society its debtor."

In the last result the accumulated wealth of a nation is the joint product of all the people in that nation, and not the product of any particular class. Some produce more than others, some have a greater knowledge of the conditions and the machinery of production than others, but no skill or genius which they possess will create wealth for them without the assistance of their fellows, and mutual obligations create mutual claims. Surplus wealth * is always being created by every successful nation, and it is an entirely equitable proposition that those who cannot produce, whether from childhood and weakness or age and feebleness, should receive support from the surplus wealth if the need arise. It is not a question of desert. The starving sinner is just as hungry as the starving saint, and wealth can only help starvation, and not virtue. If old eyes come before old age, and they often do, or our ears do not perform their functions, and

* I mean by that, wealth for which we have no immediate use.

we are struck down by the motor we could not avoid, they do not ask at the hospital about desert; they only see the human sorrow and the human needs, and—out of the surplus wealth—do what they can to help and to heal.

With these arguments I did my work. The only sound principles of taxation that I could recognize was that of spreading the tax as thinly and as widely as possible, so that all should contribute and all might claim. The political expedient of earmarking I refused to consider. It was unsound. I was not in politics, and therefore not bound to compromise, and I would not advocate it.

I met all classes of society alike with these arguments, and got amusement, as well as knowledge, from watching their attitudes towards my work. Officers of friendly societies, or of co-operative stores, and deacons of dissenting chapels, were often far more conservative in their ultimate thinkings about the aged, than were the members of the Primrose League, and the few "habitations" that I visited were usually more interesting than were the meetings of the aforementioned bodies. Charming women, who could not argue and were not accustomed to much thinking, made often very picturesque audiences, and if they took an opposite view to my own usually took it in charming fashion. One night I was addressing a meeting of Socialists in a poverty-stricken slum, and a night or two after I was talking to a crowd of ladies in evening dress in a West End drawing-room. I made exactly the same speech at each meeting, and advocated the cause of the aged poor in exactly the same terms at the Socialist lecture hall and the aristocratic drawing-room, and each audience agreed with what I said.

People who, like the men of Athens, always wanted to hear some new thing always gave me welcome, and among these the ethical societies amused me most. The first Ethical society was founded at Toynbee Hall, and I was present at its foundation. It never came to anything, and after a little while it was easy to see why. No dynamic can be got out of abstract morality, and the formula of a workman who belonged to it—" Be as good as you can and don't bother "—expressed this in a sentence, and showed its failure to touch either the heart or the imagination. Old ghosts from eighteenth-century sermon-books and echoes of Sandford and Merton and Mrs. Trimmer's stories seemed to be all about me as I listened to the ethical preachers, but they offered me their platforms to talk on Old Age Pensions, and I went. It was a new movement, and I hoped to find sympathetic souls for my new reform. I did not, but the fact was more due to lack of knowledge than hardness of hearts. Ladies were usually in the majority at their meetings, and once I found myself the only man in a room full of pretty but quite incapable girls. They were grateful when I took the meeting into my own hands and became chairman, lecturer, and everything else; but well-to-do young ladies, the majority perhaps in their teens, could hardly be expected to have very much enthusiasm for Old Age Pensions.

XXIV

SIDE ISSUES AND MANŒUVRES

AGITATION for Old Age Pensions taught me many things; and among these was the use and value of the varied elements in my previous career. Co-operators, Trade Unionists, and Friendly Societies men alike knew me in some way as connected with their work, while what I had done in the world of education gave my name an influence in circles outside those of the industrial classes. I had to convert the nation to the truth of a great idea and—without in the least knowing or intending it—had followed a career which exactly fitted me for the work, and had followed it for the purely selfish reason that I liked it. There were pleasures in the ten years' agitation of which my audiences knew nothing. Travelling about the country meant—for me—seeing England, much of Wales and Scotland, and something of Ireland as well. I am English to the core of me, the life of my nation is in my blood, and her ancient cities and buildings, historic corners, and places made famous by poetry and old romance had a charm and a controlling power for me that transcended all class ideas, and it sometimes surprised those who the day before had listened to me on the platform to find me the next day in the cloisters of an ancient cathedral or reading old literature among the stones of a ruined castle, but their surprise mattered nothing to me. It was my nature to do these things, and I let my nature have its play.

Usually my literary and historic tastes were counted among my vices, or at any rate among my weaknesses, by many of my friends in the Labour movement, but there were times, not a few, when I found sympathetic souls who were workmen as I was, but who saw other things as well as the workman's ideal. "I can't stick him: you never see him without a book," was the remark made about myself at a Congress, and which I overheard. But at that Congress, as delegate, was a pale, sickly youth who made friends with me because of the book, and he was scarcely more happy that I was as we walked together in the churchyard of a Norman church, listened to the music of the worshippers therein, and talked poetry and social problems.

Many a happy hour have I spent with men like this one—who were sympathetic enough with the ideals of their militant and often noisy companions, but who had a vision beyond them which the others never saw. Such work was worth more than all my agitation, for often the tragedy in these lives was awful, and I could but give them a few moments of intellectual pleasure to lighten it, but to them the pleasure was great. Sensitive, noble natured, often weakly in health, and not understood by their fellows, they found life a weary thing, and sought pleasure in literature and in the lore of the past. So had I in other years, but I never suffered as they did, for I could usually laugh—cynically or good-humouredly as it might happen—and go on my way.

During very nearly the whole of the agitation for

Old Age Pensions I was vice-Chairman of the Conciliation Board of the London Chamber of Commerce, and am still, Sir Samuel Boulton being the Chairman. The idea of conciliation and arbitration in labour quarrels forced itself on me during the Bookbinders' Strike of '92; the Conciliation and Arbitration Board of the London Chamber of Commerce grew out of the great Dock Strike of 1888-89. That strike was a cleansing storm which has long since spent its force, but it uprooted many old notions that needed clearing away, and cast into the ground the seeds of many new, and some true, ideas, and among them was the idea of arbitration and conciliation in the disputes between capital and labour. The Conciliation Board consists of an equal number of employers and employed connected with London trades, the employers being elected by the Chamber of Commerce, the employed by their respective trade unions. If a dispute arises in the London area, the employers and employed in dispute are invited to avail themselves of the services of the Board. If they agree—and action on both sides is purely voluntary, the Board having no compulsory powers—a panel of arbitrators is formed from both parties on the Board, care being taken that in neither party of the arbitrators are there any persons interested in the trades in dispute. Sittings take place, which may last a few hours or many days, and a decision is given. The work of the Board has been justified by results: none of its decisions have proved failures, none have been set aside.

Many ardent spirits on the labour side of the Board have always favoured compulsory arbitration, which presents itself to them as a new idea. It is as old as human quarrelling. This fact becomes curiously apparent in considering the various schemes of conciliation among the cities of ancient Greece. The difference in numbers between the smaller Greek states and the larger trade unions could hardly have been considerable. Strife among these ancient states called forth many schemes of conciliation, and, reading them, we realize that whatever changes in a changeable world the essential elements of human character remain the same. The tough and lasting quarrel over Salamis contributed something to literature and showed the same virtues, vices, and human difficulties and quarrels four hundred years before Christ as we meet at the conciliation boards to day. Ancient Greeks and modern Englishmen show exactly the same facility in failing to keep to the terms of an agreement. Exclusion from the Pythian games, as punishment for such failure, seems to have its parallel in exclusion from trade union circles, which includes trade union festivities as well. In the Amphictyonic Council the parallel between trade strifes and trade conciliations grows closer, and its methods are surely the first attempts at compulsory arbitration known to the world. It was a confederation of nations, and labour has its federation of trades. It aimed to embrace all the Greek states as the federation of trade seeks to embrace all trade unions; and the Amphictyonic Council, as the States-General of Greece at that time, had power to arbitrate and enforce its decisions; but when it tried to do so its power broke down, and thereby hangs a moral for compulsory arbitration always and everywhere.

A Spartan king is credited with the utterance that it is not lawful to treat as a wrong-doer one who is willing to arbitrate. Sound or unsound, the principle is far nobler than that of the modern cynic who says men will only arbitrate when they are beaten. The only sound way of settling a dispute is to hear both sides, get all the facts, weigh their value, and decide on the balance of evidence. Passion and hasty thinking are against this, and these qualities are pretty equally divided among all classes alike. But the world gets nearer to sanity with every revolution of the sun—even in the settling of labour disputes.

Twice during the Pensions agitation I was asked to contest a seat in Parliament. I refused. I meant to get Old Age Pensions through, and came to the conclusion that I could do this better outside Parliament than in, and the results of the agitation did not prove my calculations wrong. The non-party attitude of our movement made a strong appeal to me, but it disgusted orthodox politicians on both sides of the House. We were kicked by both parties, but having decided on a policy we were ready to pay the price. To those who made politics their religion we seemed unprincipled and unscrupulous, and those who only treated politics as a game were certain we should fail. There was something to be said for the latter view. Other committees had been formed to agitate for Old Age Pensions, had been ushered into the world with a much greater flourish of trumpets than had greeted the National Committee of Organized Labour, and had found in oblivion their graves. They had failed because their methods were unscientific. The Rt. Hon. Joseph Chamberlain, M.P., had talked continuously about Pensions, and in this way helped to keep them in the front; but all his speeches show conclusively that he had never thought the matter out. The committees, however, whether their lives were long or short, were evidence of zeal for the success of a principle even if—as usually happened—the zeal was tempered by the spirit of the party politician, and their economic knowledge was limited.

An excellent evidence of this lack of economic knowledge was afforded by the short-lived National Old Age Pensions League. This was inaugurated at Birmingham on October 24, 1894. Its object was "to advocate the restoration to the people of tithes, dole charities, and other national property, and the conversion of the revenues therefrom into a national fund for providing old age pensions." Sir James Kitson, M.P., was its President, and its Secretary was a Nonconformist minister, whose great idea was to provide pensions for the aged out of the funds of a disestablished Church. It got little support outside Nonconformist circles, and never got beyond holding a few meetings. To exploit the misery of the aged poor for the sake of running an agitation for the disestablishment of the Church was a fraud too transparent to escape being seen through. When it was seen that our Committee meant business I was approached by members of this League, but I refused to be led away by any such wild-goose chase.

Crowds of pamphlets on our subject were published. In the majority of cases their authors were clergymen whose experiences in poor relief were at first hand, and others were written by politicians or by trade union leaders. All of them proved useful in one way or another, and perhaps the most useful were those written by our foes. They convinced me more completely than anything written by our friends that I was riding a winning horse. The politicians, of all parties, regarded old age pensions entirely from the point of view of the success or failure of their own political party. The aged were a spent force in the affairs of life. They could bring no political capital to any party, and therefore they did not count. And we who were fighting their battle showed an utter disregard of the value of party influence, and made no use of the stage properties of political agitation, so that it was really not to be wondered at if politicians showed little regard to us or to our work.

And at the back of the Pensions agitation was a force as yet unmeasured by the pundits of the political world: the new and growing force of Labour organized to realize political ideals. In alliance with this force, and born of it, our committee wielded a power far greater than either Liberals or Conservatives knew. Side by side with this power was another, more ancient, and more potent than anything in politics—the power of organized religion. Religion in Great Britain is a mosaic of many patterns. The two greatest religious forces are the Church of England and the Church of Rome. Except for the larger among them, the sects, so far as we were concerned, were a negligible quantity. Two resolutions of the Congregational union helped us, but to each of the great ecclesiastical bodies we had an appeal. To the clergy of the Church of England had fallen a large proportion of the administration of the Poor Law. It was an accidental development, but it gave them a great advantage in a reform like that we were fighting for. They knew the Poor Law in its merits and its defects. They were sometimes heartless enough in its administration, but sometimes, too, they were the only sympathetic voices raised on behalf of the poor on a board composed of farmers, small tradesmen, and such like persons, and they could not alter the arrangements which gave the aged in one parish one and ninepence a week to live on and another five shillings a week. Many of the clergy were among our warmest supporters, many had pension schemes of their own, some were among our opponents; but pensions for the aged was a subject the Church in England knew something about, and a deputation to Frederick Temple, then Archbishop of Canterbury, was resolved on.

The Roman Catholic Church had—in the Middle Ages—through its monastic system made considerable provision for the aged poor, and had always inculcated such provision as part of a Christian's duty. His Eminence the Cardinal Vaughan, at a meeting of the Catholic Truth Society in 1899, had spoken of the poverty of the aged as a scandal, and had said that the time was coming when the wealthy classes must either tax themselves or be taxed to bring this state of things to an end. Rambling about the ruins of St. Mary's Abbey, York, and looking at the glorious old minster as it towered above them, and thinking of the condition of our aged poor, I wrote the two following sonnets, which, I like to believe, had something to do with influencing the public mind in the direction I wished it to go. They were printed and reprinted, and certainly had a larger circulation than anything else I ever wrote:—

A CONTRAST

I

Grey minster, hoary with the rime of years,
Whose heavenward-lifted towers bid souls aspire,
Thine aisles have echoed to our prayers and tears—
Have passed the agonies of purging fire!

Still standest thou mute symbol of a time
When men in faith and hope looked up to God—
Their hope—to fit them for a holier clime;
Their faith—that they might come to that abode.
And in that faith they reared thy stately walls,
And by them set God's hostel for the poor,
Whose servants tended to the sufferers' calls,
Nor drove the weary hopeless from the door.
  "Faith without works is dead!" Let their faith live
  Who for their Master's sake themselves did give.

II

The workhouse is the poor man's home to-day;
Men scorn the minster and the minster's faith;
The worn and aged fallen by the way,
In the drear day-room wait for kindly death.
The car of Juggernaut which Mammon drives
Crushes the souls of men, nor heeds their tears.
In greed of gold we waste our sordid lives,
And to the plaint of sorrow dull our ears.
O Galilean, Who with us wast God,
Our nation hath not touched Thy garments' hem,
Else had we cleansed us from our sins of blood,
Else had we learned to help our fellow-men.
  Is our faith dead alike in Thee and love?
  Purge as with fire, our dross or gold to prove.

Deputations to the two chief ecclesiastics in England were an entirely new departure in political agitation, and puzzled politicians and journalists alike. Cardinal Vaughan received a deputation of trade unionists at his house at Westminster on September 30, 1899, introduced by Mr. Herbert Stead; and Archbishop Temple received the same deputation at Lambeth Palace on January 27, 1900, introduced by myself. Three days previous to the deputation to Lambeth I had got a manifesto in favour of Old Age Pensions, signed by a number of the chief Labour leaders, into the columns of the *Times*. Such a thing had never happened before. The *Times* was frankly hostile to Labour, and the Liberal papers regarded manifestoes of that kind as their own special preserve. One worthy editor actually wrote and asked me why I had not sent it to him, and others were hurt at being left out of my calculations. A friend in the Labour movement, when the second deputation took place, assured me I was leading the working classes into wrong paths, and my reply was that on the contrary I was leading cardinals and archbishops into right ones.

The difference in the two types of ecclesiastical mind was very striking. Gracious, courtly, refined, and with something of a regal air, the Cardinal was, nevertheless, out of touch with the life of the world about him. He wanted to be sympathetic with us, but did not quite know how, and moved uneasily in dealing with our subject, as one who travels on unfamiliar ground. But he gave us his blessing in general terms, and the clergy of his Church were never among our opponents. Our deputation to him was worth, in influence, half a score of public meetings, but it excited to fury the Liberal Press, and a brief correspondence—to me amusing—took place between myself and the *Daily Chronicle*, in which I justified our position and our policy.

I had not seen much of Archbishop Temple since the days when I went, in company with Edward Baker, to hear him as the persecuted Bishop of Exeter. He was never very much of a martyr, as a smaller man would have been under the circumstances, but simply ignored his enemies and went on with his work. I had no idea when I wrote asking him to receive a deputation whether

I should have to count him as supporter or opponent, and Canon Scott Holland, whom I approached on the subject, bade me beware. "He is a tough customer to deal with, and will give you plenty of nuts to crack, so be ready." The old man had lost none of his ruggedness, nor his sledge-hammer methods of utterance, with the flight of the years. I did not want the deputation to miscarry; I thought I knew my case; but I was courteous and conciliatory by turns when I opened negotiations with him. "This is a magnificently historical building, Archbishop," said I, referring to Lambeth Palace. "Yes, if you don't have to live in it," came the reply. When the deputation was introduced it was soon apparent that the Archbishop was not on ground unknown. "He's a sharp old chap, but does he know anything about us?" said Mr. Will Crooks, afterwards the popular M.P. He did. The man was alive at every point, and the contrast between the rugged but withal genial Archbishop and the polished aloofness of the Cardinal was as complete as possible.

But both ecclesiastics had declared for our policy as regarded the aged poor. The archbishop knew where he was in every detail, told us he was certain the nation could afford the cost of pensions, bade us not to be too optimistic, but to remember that we had to convince the Chancellor of the Exchequer; and assured us that if a measure for Old Age Pensions came before the House of Lords while he was there it should have his support and vote. It was a second triumph for the committee, and those who desired to disestablish the Church in order to get Old Age Pensions said many bad things about us in consequence.

We were carrying out by our Pensions policy, entirely

unconsciously and unintentionally, a principle which had been often enunciated by Professor Samuel Rawson Gardiner in his history lectures to the University Extension Society years before. I had forgotten it in the days of the Pensions agitation, but the truth of it came back to me with overwhelming force when that agitation was done. He had always affirmed that for any solid and lasting reform there must be as foundation a combination of two principles, and they were reverence for ancient custom and respect for the expression of the popular will. We were manipulating both forces. Reverence for ancient custom made a strong appeal to me, and certainly our committee knew all about the expression of the popular will. It was spontaneously and overwhelmingly with us; it wanted what we were working for, and we were securing the support of " ancient custom " when we secured the support of organized religion, and meetings all over the country proved the unanimity of the public mind on our side.

There were other leaders of organized religion than the Archbishop and the Cardinal, and they were usually much more conservative in their tendencies, and more difficult to move in our direction than either Anglicanism or Rome, just as I have often found that for sheer hidebound conservatism an established Church is not in it with an old-fashioned Radical club or trade union. The other forms of organized religion ranged themselves on our side by degrees, and as success came in sight, but in the beginning they stood aside and watched. One of the most interesting of the Nonconformist leaders whom I saw on the subject of Pensions was the famous Wesleyan preacher, the Rev. Hugh Price Hughes. Mr. Hughes had the reputation of being a man of enlightened mind, and so in a sense he was, but his mind had never moved in our direction, and the interview I had with him in the Wesleyan offices in Bishopsgate was like an interview with a foreigner, so far were we apart.

And right at the beginning of our work the Boer War broke out, and soon after came the death of the great Queen Victoria. Against such distracting events public agitation was tremendously uphill. I had presented a memorandum to Mr. A. J. Balfour in March, 1900, embodying our scheme, which had been received by him; but war is the eternal enemy of every kind of social or domestic reform, and by every rule of political logic our committee ought to have gone the way of previous Pension Committees, and ceased. But, in spite of everything, there was a strange vitality in it which made its cessation before its work was done impossible, and other events were helping us. In the year 1900 was formed the Labour Representation Committee. It was the outcome of a resolution passed at the Plymouth Trade Union Congress of 1899, which recommended the fusion of all parties in the Labour movement in one organization, and under the direction of one committee. Trade Unions, the Independent Labour Party, the Fabian Society, and—as it was then called—the Social Democratic Federation, met together for the first time for a common purpose. Of this committee I was the first chairman, and in the second year was its treasurer. The secession of the Social Democratic Federation from the committee soon became inevitable, and, while I regretted their action, I respected their motives. They were workmen, living the workman's life, understanding the workman's mind, and so was I. They would have nothing to do with what seemed to them political compromises, were thoroughly loyal to what they regarded as the only sane policy for labour, and when they left the committee it was the poorer—from the workmen's standpoint—for their loss.

But for me the one thing of immediate and pressing importance was Old Age Pensions. The new committee supported me loyally in that, but I found it difficult to ride two horses at once, and after two years dropped away from the political organization, not from lack of sympathy, as so many believed, but because I was determined to win the Pensions battle, and feared that the political organization and its work would made this issue uncertain.

Meanwhile I was busy writing two books: one on Old Age Pensions, the other a study of literature dealing with the Seven Deadly Sins. My friends of the Social Democratic Federation,* to whom I was so strongly attracted on other grounds, were materialists, and the tendency of a great deal of socialistic thought was to place the material needs of life first. But I had found the secret of life's happiness in minimizing material needs, and had again and again reduced my dinners to the barest quantity in order to purchase a volume of poetry, or to hear an opera, and the enjoyment so got was far sweeter than that obtained without trouble. And in the pursuit of literature I found, not an increase of the business of life, but an increase of its joys, and a rest for the soul. My book on the Seven Deadly Sins grew naturally out of my studies of Elizabethan and mediæval literature, and my book on Old Age Pensions, which was published

* By fusion with a number of other Socialist societies, it is now the British Socialist Party.

in 1903, was the outcome of my work. It was attacked for its style and its facts were questioned—though they were never controverted—but its arguments were left untouched, and I realized once more that the victory of our cause would eventually be won.

But would it be won by me? Some of my friends thought not, and said often, "You are a pioneer, and your cause will win, but not till the grass is growing over you." I wanted victory before that, but with a war which cost 250 millions in progress, and likely to last no one knew how long, what possible chance was there for my committee and its ideals? And gradually the belief that we were fighting a losing battle grew among my audiences, and it became harder and harder to keep the Pensions flag flying; and the general election of 1900 was short and swift, with the war as a dominant factor in its issue. The Pensions agitation made itself felt in that election, and perhaps it was the only other political force that did. And through all those dark and weary years we kept steadily on, and never allowed our ideas to fall into the background. Many a workman, after his labours of the day were done, gave time and speech and service for a cause which men were gradually beginning to regard as hopeless; and as I watched the service of these loyal souls I knew that Old Age Pensions was a soldier's battle, and that if any history was made by our movement it would not be made by the leaders in politics, but by the rank-and-file.

And comedy, tragedy, and strange, sad pathos mixed and blended themselves in ours, as in all human work. Old men and women, "poor human ruins tottering o'er the grave," came to me, "willing to starve a little longer rather than go into the workhouse" if I could tell them that Pensions would come next year. Friendly society men, their natures narrowed by a lifelong worship at the altar of thrift, said that what I was aiming at could never, never be: the nation could never bear the cost. Supporters left us lured by the will o' the wisp of tariff reform, hoping to reach pensions that way. A freetrader through and through, I wanted any pension scheme I advocated built on a sounder basis than that, and I spoke in favour of Free Trade at the first meeting called by the Cobden Club, after the Rt. Hon. Joseph Chamberlain had declared himself. Everybody thought the new political cry would affect either the prospects or the policy of the Pensions agitation, and many were the prophecies that I should be captured by the Tariff Reform League. Neither happened. At all hazards we determined to keep our flag flying, and we availed ourselves of any platform open to us. There are a hundred platforms in England open to any gospel if people will speak on them without pay, and the only stipulation we made was that we should say what we liked, and if people did not like what we said they need not ask us again.

My book on the Seven Deadly Sins was published at a press that will one day be famous in the annals of literature—the Shakespeare Head Press, Stratford-on-Avon. At this press Mr. A. H. Bullen, first among Elizabethan scholars, has printed and published the most perfect edition of Shakespeare's works ever yet issued from the English Press. It is a worthy monument by a great scholar to the greatest of all poets. The press was started in the house of Julius Shaw, the friend of Shakespeare, and, with the exception of a rather commonplace eighteenth-century front, which replaces the old Tudor frontage, the house has changed little since the days when Shakespeare and Julius Shaw smoked their evening pipes together within its walls. On crossing its threshold you are in an Elizabethan environment at once. A fine marble mantelpiece forms a fitting adjunct to a capacious fireplace, in the centre of the room is a great oak gate-legged table, and against the wall near the mantelpiece stands an ancient oak settee, brought from the inn at " Piping Pebworth," where, if local tradition may be believed, Shakespeare often sat and " tossed his glass."

Here Mr. Bullen has produced an entirely handsome and accurate edition of Shakespeare's works. A beautiful handmade paper was specially manufactured, with Shakespeare's arms as a watermark. Old-face type is selected for printing the book, and uniformity of colour is a marked characteristic of every line of the printed page. The book was published at ten guineas the set of ten volumes, but a certain number of copies are printed on vellum. These are exceptionally beautiful, and it is Mr. Bullen's opinion that they will be as beautiful five hundred years hence as they are now. A complete edition of Shakespeare printed on vellum had never existed till Mr. Bullen's edition came into being.

He is responsible for the text, and also contributes a learned and most exhaustive appendix dealing with difficult and corrupt passages. Scholars from every part of the world supply contributions to make the edition of Shakespeare complete. M. Jusserand, Shakespearean scholar and French Ambassador at Washington, writes on Ben Jonson's views of the art of Shakespeare, the Rev. H. C. Beeching, Dean of Norwich, writes on the Religion of Shakespeare, and on the sonnets, Mr. Henry Davey contributes a memoir, Mr. Spielman writes on Shakespeare's portraits, Mr. Robert Bridges, poet laureate, writes on the Influence of the Audience, and Mr. Ernest K. Chambers on the stagecraft of the Elizabethan theatre.

The " Stratford Town Shakespeare " and the " Shakespeare Head Press " are incidents of great moment in the history of twentieth-century literature, and the man who made them actual deserves well of his countrymen. I have stood in the peaceful old Elizabethan " pleasaunce " fragrant with the scent of honeysuckle, and beautiful in the afternoon sunlight, which lies in the rear of the old house, and have sighed to think how little true scholarship is recognized, with all our noisy talk of education and our squabbles about its control. My association with Arthur Bullen and with the work which he has done for literature is an episode in my life to which I look back with unalloyed and exalted pleasure, and must ever be counted among the happiest of my literary memories.

SONNET ON A NEW YEAR

(1905)

Shadow of many shapes, what hidest thou
Beneath thy dusky and unlifted veil ?
Youth, with its golden heart of hope,
Sees roses in thy path, hears joy-bells clang,
And on thy brow beholds a halo gleam.
And grave maturity, who knows the years,
Catches the echoes of youth's song of hope
And bids thee welcome.   But age,
For whom the years are shadows that will pass,
Sighs wearily and awaits thy gifts.
And all must wait, for silent is thy tongue
And veiled the days that thou wilt usher forth :
Thou art their midwife ; not thine are they—
Part man's, part God's—base earth, but touched with Heaven.

XXV

PENSIONS ACHIEVED

In March, 1904, it seemed hardly possible for the Pensions movement to live. One of its best supporters ceased to subscribe, the trade union subscriptions grew more and more uncertain, and it seemed as though, after all we should end as other committees had done, and that our labour would be all in vain. There had appeared just about this time a very remarkable book entitled " The Temperance Problem and Social Reform," written by Joseph Rowntree and Arthur Sherwell, which had captured the imagination of a large number of social reformers, and it appealed to me because it was a new departure in temperance policy. The teetotal lecturer of my boyhood's days preached the doctrine that all publicans were rascals or else they would refuse to get their living by the sale of intoxicating drink. This was fanaticism, and not logic, and it was an argument that was bound to be seen through sooner or later. Messrs. Rowntree and Sherwell did not take this line. They said that the sale of alcohol was a dangerous trade, and ought to be classified as such, but did not fulminate against the sellers of it.

They advocated the system of the control of the liquor traffic which is practised in Norway. The trade is placed in the hands of private companies, and its sale is regulated by statute law. In 1904 they asked me to come and work with them and help them in developing their idea. I consented on the understanding that my Pensions work was not given up, and from April, 1904, to April 1905, joined forces with them, carrying on my Pensions work without salary. It was a strenuous but enjoyable year, and I came close to new forces in our social life, which I had not touched before.

The total abstainer I met was a different character to the man I knew in my earlier years. He had more imagination, more intellectual conviction, and if he had less of the popular touch and of the power to sway the multitude, he was nevertheless a power on the side of social righteousness that I was glad to meet. He had created new standards which were entirely wholesome, and when I met, as I often did, healthy specimens of young manhood, and young womanhood, who could say they did not know the taste of alcohol, I was ready to say at once, " Then don't trouble to know it."

There were always the defects of the quality, in this as in other things, and they were manifest occasionally. The total abstinence movement was a form of Puritanism for which its advocates could find thoroughly sound reasons if they desired to practise it themselves, and probably no man was ever any better for the use of alcohol, or any worse for its avoidance. But their logic was not so sound when they desired to force abstinence on other people. There is no doubt that it grew out of real moral enthusiasm, and on those grounds deserved every respect, and the prohibition of the sale of liquor wherever it succeeded, was not in any way a bad thing. But the lesson of most prohibitive legislation was, that though you may prohibit the sale of liquor you do not stop it.

The grime and gloom of so much of our industrial life are among the forces which make for intemperance, even though every principle of logic proves that a temperate life is an infinitely better thing than its opposite under any conditions. "Why do you get drunk Saturday after Saturday, ruining your life and destroying your character?" asked a temperance advocate of a Lancashire labourer. "Why, guv'nor, because it's the quickest way out of Manchester," came the reply. Let those who would condemn this man get some knowledge of the slums of Manchester or any other great city before passing sentence.

But taking up with the new idea caused people to say that I knew Old Age Pensions was a lost cause, and therefore I was getting rid of it as decently as I could; and so when my year was up I bade farewell—reluctantly, for they were people it was good to know—to the Rowntrees, and in July, 1905, took up the Pensions agitation. Things were no better for the aged poor then than in the previous year, but I always believed we should win. The Conservatives were in power with the expenses of the Boer War to meet, though it did not seem that they would keep in power long, and I could only keep up a kind of guerilla warfare at bye-elections. From my point of view they had done many bad things, but the immediate cause of their downfall was an entirely good thing.

They made an honest attempt to put National Education on a sane and solid foundation when they passed the Education Act of 1902, but their popularity began to wane from that date. To say that the Act had its defects is only to say that it was a piece of Parliamentary legislation. But it embodied the ideas of some of the most profound thinkers in the educational world, and a distinguished economist, who was also a Socialist, had the credit of framing it. I was not on the side of the general policy of the Government, but I was on the side of that Bill. My lifelong work for education had made clear to me the general muddle of our educational system, and the chief educational policy of Liberalism had been less a desire for education, than a desire to crush out Church schools. But it was quite evident by 1902 that Church schools would neither die nor be crushed by political malice. In 1884 I had written an article in the *Weekly Dispatch*, prophesying that the schools of the Church of England and of the Roman Catholics would die in a few years, and their places be taken by Board schools, but time and experience had converted me to the truth of George Eliot's saying that a good deal of prophecy is simply gratuitous impertinence.

On July 18, 1905, I wrote to His Majesty, King Edward VII., asking him for an expression of opinion on Old Age Pensions. I did not get it; but the letter was published in the *Morning Post* a day or two after, and served my purpose in another way. "You upset all my principles," said Charles Freak of the National Union of Boot and Shoemakers, and a leading East London Radical. "I thought by this time we should have got rid of kings and archbishops, and here are you trying to get their support for a democratic measure. But, of course, we know the democracy is stupid enough for anything, and I expect you'll do the job." Archbishop Davidson, who had succeeded Temple at Canterbury, had written a sympathetic letter to me which had been published in the Press, and Freak had seen it, but did not know if he ought to praise or condemn me for what I had done. He was a member of my committee, and they always gave me a free hand, as our cause prospered.

The General Election of 1906 was a complete revolution in politics, even the Prime Minister, the Rt. Hon. A. J. Balfour, losing his seat. We had no reason to believe that the Liberals would give us pensions for the aged, any more than the Tories had; we had not in any way laid ourselves out to please them, but had simply kept our cause to the front. I had said on a myriad platforms that I was ready to vote for a Conservative who *would* support Old Age Pensions, and against a Liberal who would not. The Liberals told me this was not politics. They were right, but then I was not fighting for politics, but for Old Age Pensions. When the election was over there were twenty-nine direct representatives of Labour in Parliament, and eleven of them were members of our Pensions committee. One of them, the Rt. Hon. John Burns, was a Cabinet Minister, and another, the Rt. Hon. Thomas Burt, was a member of His Majesty's Privy Council. We knew now the strength of our movement, and waited. The political wire-pullers of the party laughed as cynically at our ideals as did their predecessors on the opposite side a few months before, and the new Government talked an infinite deal of nothing to deputations of workmen who waited upon them on the subject, but these things, we knew, were just the shuffle of the political cards.

On March 14, 1906, a resolution was moved by Mr. O'Grady, Labour member for East Leeds, which asked Parliament to say that " a measure is urgently needed in order that out of funds provided by taxation provision can be made for the payment of a pension to all aged subjects of His Majesty in the United Kingdom." Vague and awkward as the terms of the resolution were, it was accepted by the House in a way that startled people. The new Parliament declared for the principle of Old Age Pensions with only one dissentient vote.

In 1906 the Liberal Government brought in their first Education Bill. Their majority was overwhelming, and victory for anything they brought forward seemed certain. Had the Bill been carried, Mr. Gladstone's "moral monster" of undenominationalism would have been the established religion of the schools, and this would have destroyed religion in education as effectively as the promulgation of atheism would. It assumes the existence of a certain residuum of religious principle about which all the sects are agreed, and that if this is taught in the schools there is an end of religious strife. There is no such residuum, and those who have given any thought to the subject of religion know this well enough. The idea was born in the Cowper-Temple clause of the Education Bill of 1870, and it has been the fruitful parent of the religious indifference which people deplore now. Its logic is more deadly than its preachers know. It assumes that all religions may be equally true, and it follows inexorably from this that all may therefore be equally doubtful.

As I had given some thoughts all through my life to problems of education, and had no political axe to grind, it did not take me long to see which side I had to take in the fight. Either I must stand outside and express no opinion whatever, or I must take my part with those who were fighting the Bill. I chose the latter alternative. I had been a member of the English Church Union for some years; and I went on to the platforms of that organization and helped it to fight the measure. This, to my political friends was worse than tactless, it was the destruction of Old Age Pensions. But I knew better than that. I had been too close to the public mind on this matter, during my eight years of agitation to believe that Old Age Pensions depended on me. They were so real in the public mind that sooner or later they would *have* to become a fact even if I were swept aside and forgotten. I was a paid servant of a committee, the majority of whom were Trade Unionists, and it was pointed out to me that they could stop my activities by stopping my salary if they chose. I had counted that cost, and was ready to pay it if it was demanded. It was not. What I was doing was known all over the country, but the National Committee of Organized Labour never interfered with me in the least. So long as I did their work as they wanted it done they were satisfied, and did not concern themselves with anything else.

It was a splendid fight, and the great battle was at the meeting of the English Church Union at the Albert Hall on June 19, 1906. That meeting was a fight for freedom, and for the rights of parents to have their children brought up in any faith which they believed. Socialist leaders denied this freedom to parents, and advocated the banishment of religion from schools. But to forbid religious teaching in schools was as much an outrage on individual liberty as to compel it. There had been, since 1870, a conscience clause, which my friend Ralph Young had availed himself of for his own daughter, and if there had been hardship under it he would have been the first to fight.

In the fight against Augustine Birrell's Education Bill I realized for the first time the danger to individual liberty that modern Liberalism was bringing into life. It was the Catholic party in the Church that laid bare the monstrous injustice of that measure, but they were nobly seconded by the Evangelicals. Standing on their platforms I realized that the fight was between principle and political trickery. The Church refused all compromise with materialism and rationalism, and stood for the Christian Faith as part National Education. It had a definite Christian conception of the State.

Nonconformists, on the other hand, gave up—in this battle—every principle they had stood for since the Reformation, for the sake of a political victory, and did not get the victory after all. It was a Socialist leader on Whitechapel waste who told me the Nonconformists were the Jesuits of the modern world, but it was the Parliamentary Socialists who were not also genuine workmen who were the real foes to liberty, and denied in the House of Commons the rights of parents to have any creed taught that was not sanctioned by the vote of the majority. The old proverb about eternal vigilance being the price of liberty needs an eternal affirmation, and the " enemy " may come as easily in the form of a Socialist leader as he came to Faust in the form of a travelling scholar.

A result of the fight is that there has gradually grown up in the popular mind a clearer understanding of educational problems, and fairer temper towards those who are permanently in opposition to popular shallowness, and this spirit of fairness began characteristically enough in the Labour movement. In February, 1906, I was asked by Mr. Isaac Mitchell, then secretary of the General Federation of Trades, to put my views on the education question before the Trade Unions, in the pages of their quarterly journal. No paper in the Liberal press would have given me the same opportunity. The article, which I called "A Just Policy in Elementary Education," appeared in the quarterly journal of the General Federation of Trade Unions of March, 1907, but by that time the Bill was dead. I was heartily glad to have been one of its executioners.

My Pensions work never slackened, and by the side of the Pensions movement there was growing up another which was needed, and therefore came into being—the Church of England Men's Society. I was drawn to it by sympathy, and because I thought I saw in it just the sort of influence that was wanted among certain sections of the working classes. There were men whom I was constantly meeting in the Labour movement who were churchmen, but who were largely exiled from Church activities, partly by reason of the prejudices against a workman active in the affairs of his trade among middle class churchmen, and partly because of the old-fashioned and cumbrous Church machinery. The men's society gave opportunities to men of this kind, and for their sakes I went on to its platforms.

Actually the society was started in 1900, but I was too busy in those early years to do anything with it, and it was not till 1906 that I went on to its platforms. I soon found that it was fine work to take a hand in, and I did it with a zest that I was never able to get into political work—except Old Age Pensions, and I never really thought of that as political, though other people did.

To me it was work for the cause of Labour, and in that spirit I carried it on, and for three years went up and down the country, with the Bishop of Stepney, who is now Archbishop of York. It was a men's society, and not a workmen's society, but there were large numbers of workmen who were members of it, many of whom I knew. Like other workmen they were bringing their intellectual powers to bear upon the industrial conditions in which they found themselves. But with a clearer view usually of the value of experience in national affairs, they responded more readily to the appeal of history and tradition, and the political filibuster found no welcome among them. They were often very good Liberals, though they were considerably sneered at by official Liberals and the Liberal press, because they were churchmen. Their thinking was often slower than that of workmen outside Church circles, but it probably gained rather than lost on that account, and the Church of England Men's Society as a whole was a valuable asset to the social movements of our time.

In the midst of activities like these I had the supreme satisfaction of seeing Old Age Pensions become the law of the land. Its chronological developments were as follows. Mr. Asquith's Pensions Budget was introduced on May 7, 1908, its second reading took place on June 16, the third on July 9, and on the 10th it was read in the House of Lords for the first time. On the 20th it came up for the second reading in the gilded chamber, and was returned to the Commons with certain amendments which they refused to accept. The peers made no fight, they knew well the measure had practically the whole strength of the nation at its

PENSIONS ACHIEVED

back, and they climbed down rapidly. For the second reading there was a unanimous vote without a division, and a wrecking amendment during the debate was defeated by a vote of 417 against 29. For the third reading 315 votes were cast for and 10 against, and on the first of August the Bill received Royal Assent, and the battle on behalf of the aged poor was won.

During the progress of the measure I was watching with keen personal interest the working of the legislative machine. Our committee had been collecting facts and building up arguments during their ten years' work, and showering them down upon the legislators, and now our own missiles were being hurled by them at one another across the floor of the House of Commons. Mr. Herbert Stead, in his book "How Old Age Pensions Began to be," writes thus of the scene.

It was a curious experience. We watched with a feeling that the battle had long been won, and that we were but witnessing the full-dress parade of victory. There was scarcely a new idea advanced during the whole course of the two eventful months. The only novelty was in the speakers and the Parliamentary environment. The arguments on which we had ridden to battle were brought out again for the use of unfamiliar riders. Old ghosts and bogeys which we had laid years ago were flaunted across the floor of the house as brand-new apparitions. Our thunderbolts were being hurled by alien hands. The amusing thing in many of the speeches was the air of discovery with which were announced the platitudes of our agitation worn with continual use.

The humour of the conflict was—to us—delightful, but there were other aspects. Behind all the comedy it was very apparent that the great body of feeling, even among our opponents, was on our side. The party game had to be played, but humanity, not party politics, was going to get the victory. Austen Chamberlain spoke against the Bill, and marshalled in excellent order all the party arguments, but his heart was with the aged poor. Harold Cox spoke against us with a glittering brilliancy which charmed everybody, and convinced nobody. Mr. Balfour—under the necessity also of worshipping the party idol—lost himself in a cloud of misty arguments, and did not succeed in convincing the House that he believed in them himself.

Among the supporters of the Bill, Mr. Asquith lifted the whole debate to a high moral and intellectual level, and after him in importance came the Labour members. Mr. George Barnes stung the Conservative benches to fury when he spoke of "speeches of no importance, and frivolous amendments," and among the stalwarts who did yeoman service for the cause, were Mr. Thomas Burt, member for Morpeth, and Mr. Frederick Maddison.

A curious meanness of spirit marked the debates on pensions in the House of Lords. The speeches were often abler and more polished than those in the Commons, but they were less living, and many of the peers were entirely ignorant of the subject they discussed. Not all of them, however. The speech of the Primate was a noble utterance, the logic of Lord Wolverhampton was unassailable, and Lord Rosebery described the Bill as a revolution. It was, and it was one of the quietest and most beneficent of revolutions ever carried out. Without shrieking or shouting or posing in the limelight, and by nothing but steady and determined work, Old Age Pensions was achieved.

And for me the moment of victory was clouded by the shadow of death. On the night of the third reading in the House of Commons, I left with the shouts of victory ringing in my ears to stand by the deathbed of my father. The Bill was carried at midnight, and at seven the following morning he passed out of life. An old dock labourer, at war with the world as he knew it, he was nevertheless a staunch Conservative, and a protectionist who had never been converted by Cobden. Self-taught in everything, emotional and imaginative, he had been in his early years a sailor before the mast. He knew something of literature, loved Byron's sea descriptions, regarded Falconer's "Shipwreck" as a great poem, and had a passionate admiration for Dibdin's sea-songs. In his closing years when he was past work, he found much happiness in wandering about the docks where he worked as a labourer in East London, and, like Dauber in Mr. Masefield's poem he loved to paint, chiefly ships, but flowers appealed to his imagination sometimes. Ships and flowers were his chief subjects, for landscape he had no eye. Kind-hearted and lovable and able to the end of his life to win the friendship of the young, there was yet an element of sternness and hardness in his character which could become manifest on occasions. He had in him those character qualities which make our army and navy strong, and had he possessed wealth would have probably made an excellent mid-Victorian county magnate of the narrow dogmatic order, the autocrat of the country-side. As it was he was an honest workman, who did his duty in his own sphere of life, and lived his fourscore and six years honourably and without blame.

THE BLACKBIRD

Silent they watched him on the bed of death:
  The grey old man whose life was ebbing slow.
Beheld the mystery of the parting breath,
  And the soul's struggle newer life to know.

"God in Thy mercy," sighed the dying voice,
  And the chill Presence, with its shuddering gloom
Mixed with the darkness, and a breath of ice
  Passed o'er the watchers in that silent room.

The grey of morning mellowed into gold,
  And light and sunshine flooded all the earth,
Darkness no longer nor the presence cold:
  Silent the prayer now: was it death or birth?

Then on the tree-tops in the morning air
  A blackbird carolled forth its matin song,
And in a moment all the world was fair,
  Nature's sweet music 'welmed death's touch of wrong.

Sing on, dark chorister, thine hymn of joy!
  It tells of hope and strong triumphant life,
And of a world passion that shall tears destroy:
  A Love with death eternally at strife.

XXVI

OF BOOKS AND OTHER MATTERS

ONE of the chief joys of victory when at last the Pensions Bill became law was that all alike were now prepared to work together to make its administration a success. Conservatives and Liberals, Socialists and individualists, were at last in agreement as to the value and importance of what had been done, and the first few months of 1909 were full of delightful experiences both to my friend Herbert Stead and myself. " You promised us a pension and they said we should never get it; but we have, God bless you," said an old Walworth woman to him in the first week of the year. " I'm seventy-six, mister, and my wife is seventy-four, and we *could* do with that pension: think it'll come in our time?" said an old country labourer to me in the last year of our fight. He was a character in his way: this old peasant, fresh-coloured, healthy, and with a merry note in his voice, but without a single hair on his head. He had lived his long and uneventful life as a tiller of the soil, asking nothing of any man but his simple wage, and as age and feebleness drew near, poverty and the grim shadow of the workhouse seemed likely to close the scene. But the pension did come in his time, and the last few years of the old people's life were lived in peace.

It was for such as these, it was "for the comfortless trouble's sake of the needy; and the deep sighing of the poor," that we had worked, and I had learnt many things in doing that work. And foremost among them came home to me the fact that without sympathy, without looking on the human as well as on the economic side of things, the poor are not to be understood. It is a fatal defect of Socialism that it ignores utterly the human side of things, and emphasizes only the economic, and therefore it is rejected as an interpretation of life by the thoughtful poor. They have their own ideals of life, and they find no help in either the fireworks of the street orator, or the patronage of the district visitor. There is a pride among them that often refuses sympathy, and when that quality is found among the rich and the middle classes it is usually recognized as a dignified and honourable thing. But it is just as dignified and as honourable in a charwoman as it is in a countess. The poor and the rich share the same virtues and vices and commit the same sins, whatever variations may exist as to method and degree, just as they contract the same diseases and share the same flesh and blood. Saints and mystics are found alike in the slums and the squares, even as rogues and rascals are; and if ever humanity rises above its civilization to a realization of the common and universal qualities which make "of one blood all the nations of the earth," then, and then only, will it begin to understand itself. But its tendency in these modern days is to sink below it.

One such case of pride among the many I have known was that of a poor old London washerwoman. A little shrivelled forlorn-looking creature, she got her living by going out to daily washing or charing among people nearly as poor as herself, and her wages were probably never more than two shillings a day and a little food. A solitary soul, who had lived alone for years in a tiny attic where there was just room for a bed, table, and chair, but conservative in her ideas, and proud as Lucifer himself. Like Dogberry, the poor soul had "had losses," and made much of the fact. Her husband had been well off, she said, and had left her with money when he died; but a rascally nephew had got it from her, and she never saw him any more. Her story was truth; but she quietly endured uncomplaining, and worked on, honest as the air and the sunshine, content so that she could live and ask no man for charity. "They ain't intelligent," was her scornful comment on the Labour members, whose portraits appeared in the *Daily News* at the election of 1904, and "They ain't honest," her comment on the Liberals. Life could have had but few joys for her, and that which alone made it tolerable was that which the world would have laughed at—her pride. She never took the old age pension—death reached her before her seventieth year—but the poor little, quiet, unnoticed soul, with her pride in her better days, had a kinship of blood with the grand dame of society and her pride in her ancient lineage.

The Act in its working proved a splendid testimony to the uprightness of the English poor, as I found, and as hundreds of others found, when they took part in its administrative work. There was malingering, of course, but its proportion to honesty was that of Falstaff's ha'porth of bread to the intolerable quantity of sack. There was a graded scale of pensions, according to income, beginning with one shilling and finishing at five shillings. We had fought for 65 as the pension age, and had got 70;

probably in imitation of the German pension scheme. Once there came before the committee of which I was a member an old blind beggar, well known as standing at a street corner for many years. He spoke no word, but stood there in eternal darkness and held out a little tinpot for alms. At seventy he claimed his pension, but was still able to beg. He was asked his average income from begging and told the truth about it—it was eleven shillings a week, and he could only claim a two-shilling pension. He was a dull-witted commonplace soul, and could not understand that his own honesty gave the law its opportunity and its reason for reducing his pension by three shillings, where another beggar with less honesty and more knowledge could claim five.

"Now that the battle has ended you will find new worlds to conquer," said Mr. Keir Hardie to me, but for a time the desire was strong upon me to rest. Not that this was entirely practical, for the victory of pensions meant the cessation of my salary as Pensions Secretary. I was not in the position of a member of my own trade who was made secretary of a Scottish Liberation Society. "I've got a job for life," was his remark; "the Scotch Church will last my time." It did. The pull of literature was strong upon me once more. In the room at Browning Hall which had been my office were a large number of the volumes of the Early English Text Society. No one looked into their pages but me, but to me they were a source of inspiration from the moment I discovered their existence. Andrew Lang says: "Readers, like anglers and poets, are born to be so, and when born under a fortunate star do not need to be allured or compelled to come into the muses' Paradise." Nor did I.

I had often been interested and amused to notice that when a workman had risen to eminence, journalists in search of copy often pounced upon him to know what book influenced him most, with various other matters concerning his literary tastes. The poor man has never thought about such things before, but "bearing his blushing honours thick upon him," and willing to oblige, does his best. I have never been asked the question, and could hardly have answered it honestly if I had.

A book, if it is to impress a man profoundly, must come at the right time. I have been under the spell of many books, and because in the surgery of Dr. Watkins I came under the spell of the English Prayer-book, I understood every word of Macaulay's eulogy of it when I read it twenty years later. Byron, on his romantic side, and Shelley after him, had their periods of influence on me, and then Browning and Tennyson, and when at last W. R. Morfill and his University Extension lectures came into my experience I knew what literature meant, and order made its way into the intellectual chaos of my mind.

A centre of active intellectual life in the City of London was South Place Chapel, Finsbury, and it was all but inevitable that I should come into touch with it sooner or later; but my first visit to it was made in quite my youthful days in company with Edward Baker. Under the ministry of William Johnson Fox, leader writer for the *Dispatch* and some time Member of Parliament for Oldham, whose lectures to the working classes I had read in the Guildhall library, but whose sermons were "without form and void," the congregation had for its religion a nebulous deism; but when Edward Baker took me there in 1870 Moncure D. Conway was minister, and it was impossible to define his belief at all. He had literary charm but no inspiration, he was critic and rhetorician by turns, he was a rationalist pure and simple, and reason was for him the final court of appeal in all things.

Many of the young fellows of my own age whom I met at South Place were as little convinced by Conway's arguments as I was, but they fell under the charm of his style and his oratory. Many went to listen for a little while and then left, and they were men from all churches. If they stayed long faith disappeared entirely, though I knew several who lost belief while listening to Conway and found it again in the Church of Rome, and one who is a hard-working priest there now. Young journalists came to hear one who, like his predecessor, William Johnson Fox, was a fairly successful journalist himself; and weird women, overflowing with words, sometimes took the preacher's place on the rostrum, and Hindoos, Theistic or anti-Theistic by turns.

But I wounded the hearts of friends when I compared Conway to the Rev. Mr. Windrush in Charles Kingsley's "Alton Locke." The description of Mr. Windrush is in the chapter called "An Emersonian Sermon," and reads as follows:

I for my part was charmed with Mr. Windrush's eloquence. His style, which was altogether Emersonian, quite astonished me by its alternate bursts of what I considered brilliant declamation and of forcible epigrammatic antithesis. I do not deny that I was a little startled by some of his doctrines, and suspected that he had not seen much, either of St. Giles' cellars or tailors' workshops either, when he talked of sin as "only a lower form of good." "Nothing," he informed us, " was produced in nature without pain and disturbance, and what we had been taught to call sin was, in fact, nothing but the birth throes attendant on the progress of the species. As for the devil, Novalis, indeed, had gone so far as to suspect him to be a necessary illusion. Novalis was a mystic and tainted by the old creeds. The illusion was not necessary—it was disappearing before the fast approaching light of philosophic religion. Like the myths of Christianity, it had grown up in an age of superstition, when men, blind to the wondrous order of the universe, actually believed that supernatural beings like the Homeric gods interfered in the affairs of mortals. Science had revealed the irrevocability of the laws of nature—was man alone to be exempt from them ? No. The time would come when it would be as obsolete an absurdity to talk of the temptation of a fiend as it was now to talk of the weir-wolf or the angel of the thunder-cloud. The metaphor might remain, doubtless, as a metaphor, in the domains of poetry, whose office it was to realize, in objective symbols, the subjective ideas of the human intellect ; but philosophy and the pure sentiments of religion which found all things, even God Himself, in the recesses of its own enthusiastic heart must abjure such a notion.

Kingsley saw men with clear eyes, and in Mr. Windrush he described a hundred rationalistic preachers. They created in shoals the type of character known as the " superior person," but the " growing good of the world " owed nothing to them; and they were never in touch with the facts of life. The slum priest battling with poverty, the friendly society man preaching thrift, and the trade unionist fighting evil conditions in the world of labour, were on the lines of progress and religion, while the preacher's rhetoric in the " unfettered pulpit " was full of sound and fury, signifying nothing.

There was always a good deal of religion in the workshop, usually of the narrow and ultra-dogmatic order, though the people who professed it were much better specimens of manhood and womanhood than those who posed as enlightened and broad-minded. The dogmatic folk were a little too prone to court what they called persecution, and to make themselves martyrs for conscience' sake, if they got half a chance; but, even so, they were usually a force on the side of wholesome living and of righteousness. One such I knew in my early years, with whom I broke many controversial lances, who was full of angularities, but whose character I learned to respect. He was a strong Calvinist of the old-fashioned school, and was quite certain that he was one of those whose election was sure. This belief certainly increased his personal egotism, but it did not make him a bad man, although workshop logic declared it ought to have done so. But it did make him an intolerable nuisance, as he was always vaunting his election before other people, and expecting them to recognize him as a saint on the way to glory, and if they laughed at him and poked fun at his self-conceit, he straightway declared he was being persecuted for his religion.

It was all very absurd, but he probably regarded himself as being as genuine a martyr as St. Lawrence on the gridiron, and whenever I have had a chance of running these victims of religious persecution to earth I have found the basis of their so-called martyrdoms self-conceit and conviction mixed in pretty equal proportions, as was the case with the old stationer's warehouseman here referred to.

But he did one good piece of work that needed a strong man to do it in that warehouse. Young fellows in those days, and for that matter girls too, were foul-mouthed, and the old warehouseman made a dead set at swearing, and, being an old man and head-warehouseman to boot, his view finally prevailed. But it was not before there had been some terrific battles between him and a woman who was known among us as "mother dirty-mouth." She beat him easily in the matter of filthy Billingsgate, but he won at last. He did not convert her; he simply crushed her. By strong, manly logic he gradually got the men on his side, and the woman became gradually but surely more wholesome in speech in consequence.

A great deal of the so-called religious persecution in our social life which has made such excellent copy for religious journals has been due not to the opinions expressed, but to the aggressive and sometimes brutal way in which they were put forth; or, as an American preacher in South Place said with cruel precision, they were "not persecuted for their religious opinions, but for their bad manners." The Protestant lecturer who insulted Romanists and lied about their faith had no cause of complaint when he was hooted and mobbed, any more than the atheist had when he made himself equally disagreeable. I worked at my trade, however, with one kindly old soul who was an ardent disciple of Mr. Bradlaugh. He was a man without knowledge of any kind, beyond his trade, and might just as easily have been a Calvinist or a Catholic for all he knew about his creed; but his nature was good, clean-minded, wholesome, and honest, and I occasionally met atheists of his type in the congregation of Mr. Conway.

XXVII

AMERICAN LITERATURE

WHAT I got from my visits to South Place was a knowledge of American literature. They were a fine group of men and women who, in the second quarter of the nineteenth century, began to lay the foundations of the intellectual life of America. Hawthorne, the giant of American literary life, I loved, but could not wake enthusiasm among my friends for him. Longfellow I loved, and in early years thought him a great poet; and my children love him now as I did then, but Conway's literary heroine was Margaret Fuller.

It is unlikely that future generations of Americans will ratify the judgments of Emerson, W. H. Channing, and James Freeman Clarke upon the merits of this lady, and Henry James has said that she left behind her simply the same kind of reputation as that of a popular actress. That there was a great deal of pose about her is certain enough, but there was a solid foundation of sincerity behind the pose. She was a constant visitor to that charming Socialist failure the Brook Farm Community, but was not a member of the community, and might best be described as a critical sympathiser. Speaking generally, women are bad critics—except of one another—but Margaret Fuller had a mind of the true critical order, and she was probably a useful friend to the little group of amateur Socialists who set out to reform the world, but only succeeded in adding a few charming pages to American literature.

She was a leading spirit of what was known as the Transcendental Movement in New England, and as Conway preached her she might have been regarded as the typical American woman. She was not that, and perhaps Lowell's description of her under the *nom-de-plume* of Miranda, severe as it was, was more in accord with the facts of her personality than Conway's impassioned idealism.

> " Miranda meanwhile has succeeded in driving
> Up into a corner in spite of their striving,
> A small flock of terrified victims, and there,
> With an I-turn-the-crank-of-the-universe air,
> In a tone which at last to *my* fancy appears
> Not so much to be entering as boxing your ears,
> Is unfolding a tale (of herself, I surmise),
> For it's dotted as thick as a peacock's with I's."

James Russell Lowell when he wrote these lines was expressing the ideas of the young Americans of his day. I met him twenty-five years later at Toynbee Hall, and he was then a dignified American politician who wanted to talk about religion to me when I wanted to talk poetry.

The Transcendental movement was short-lived and bore a close resemblance to what has been called in England the New Theology. It was an outgrowth of a Unitarianism which was travelling past Christianity, and many of its followers gave up the Christian faith, or else joined the Church of Rome. But Emerson, the Channing family, though not William Ellery Channing,

Theodore Parker, George Ripley, and that strange genius Bronson Alcott, who bears a curious far-off resemblance to Walter Savage Landor, came under its influence. *The Dial* and *The Quarterly Review* were its two organs in the American Press. The first of these was edited by Margaret Fuller, and served as warning rather than example to later writers; and the second was edited by Brownson, who began his early life as a " sceptical democrat " and ended it as a priest in the Church of Rome.

To listen to Conway was to get into touch with these currents of intellectual life, among a people I had never known, and I found a pleasure in it. His congregation had a way of regarding itself as possessing all the truth in the world, and as representing the religion of the future, and as men and women of intellectual activity pass through the phase at some time in their lives of regarding themselves as superior persons it was natural to meet that type of character there. George Howell, a well-known Labour leader, and for many years a representative of Labour in Parliament, had his period of South Place influence; and George Jacob Holyoake, one of the pioneers of the Co-operative movement and the practical founder of the Freethought movement in England, was a lifelong member of the Society.

Another man of interesting personality whom I knew and first met at South Place was Arthur W. Hutton. Beginning life as a devout English Churchman, he, under the influence of Cardinal Newman, became a priest of the Church of Rome, and for some years laboured strenuously in that communion. After Newman's death he, to the surprise of his friends, gave up religion altogether and appeared as a preacher of Agnosticism at South Place.

I heard him lecture there on the "Attractions of Catholicism," and later he came to hear me discourse on Chaucer's "Canterbury Tales," and then I got to know the man. The mystic and the rationalist were curiously blended in his character, and he struck me always as easily impressionable, and—to use a workshop phrase—as being always under the influence of the next man. He was highly intellectual, and his secession from the Roman Church was undoubtedly sincere, though ill-natured critics suggested otherwise at the time. After many religious changes—among which was included a spell of profound admiration for the Society of Friends and visits to their meeting-house at Winchmore Hill—he returned to the Church of his baptism, was for a short period vicar of Kingsley's old church at Eversley, and died rector of St. Mary-le-Bow, Cheapside, in 1912. In the closing years of his life he was a much-honoured and respected city clergyman, his goodness remembered, his eccentricities forgotten, but beyond that he made no particular mark on his Church.

Conway's enthusiasm for Margaret Fuller led me to study the Transcendental movement in New England, and I saw it had many things in common with the Freethought movement at home. Neither movement led to anything of consequence, and both suggested a chase after a will-o'-the-wisp. Both represented an intellectual revolt, mixed incidentally with much intellectual blundering, against ideas that had become stiff and hardened, but were not on that account necessarily false, and however ossified they had become were infinitely better in their essential qualities than the ideas of those who revolted against them. The Freethought movement was lacking alike in poetry and imagination; the Transcendental movement retained both; a little too much of the latter, its enemies said. And, beyond all question, Margaret Fuller was its embodiment and interpreter. In her writings we see its aims as we do in the writings of no other person. From her we learn the ideas that created it, from her we learn, though she does not set out to teach them, the causes of its failure.

Its promoters believed they were founding a new religion, as indeed did Mr. Bradlaugh in his early career, when he had the beginnings of a ritual, with nothing at the back of it to give it meaning and purpose. "Robert Elsmere" had not been written then, but there was an Elsmerian touch in Bradlaugh's dedication of children to the Freethought cause, in the staff of office, and the credentials which, for a little while, were given to the lecturers of the National Secular Society.

But both Transcendentalist and Freethinker made the individual the centre of the universe. Outside themselves they saw nothing, and Margaret Fuller's "Infinite Me," of which James Russell Lowell made such rollicking fun in his "Fable for Critics," must have seemed grotesque indeed to a virile nature like his. Brook Farm was an attempt to put the new faith into practice. Like the congregation at South Place, and a good many other highly respectable religious and non-religious gatherings, its members did nothing of any practical value. They indulged in much theorising, some of it of a charming kind, but most of the theorizing was of the Rev. Mr. Windrush order, and their tradition is faithfully carried on, and Mr. Windrush is an eternal presence, in the Free Church Councils to-day. They did not form quite a complete parallel to my friend Jerry Hall, the printer's warehouseman, who was honestly happy in the salvation of his own soul, whereas at South Place, and in the Transcendental Societies of New England, they gradually came to the conclusion that they had no souls; but old Jerry and they had a good many points of similarity.

The theory of the Transcendentalist was that it was possible to return to a primitive state of society where all alike should hew wood and draw water, and all alike share in the pleasures of the intellect and the soul. The fact that all alike are not fitted to do these things, and that the square peg in the round hole is an eternal problem in practical life, and an eternal worry to practical men, never occurred to them. Margaret Fuller lived in the midst of this intellectual revolt in her beloved New England, and wrote thus of its meaning, and her words may carry truths and warnings to us fifty years later.

Political freedom does not necessarily produce liberality of mind, nor freedom in Church institutions vital religion; and seeing that these changes cannot be wrought from without inwards, they are trying to quicken the soul, that they may work from within outwards. Disgusted with the vulgarity of a commercial aristocracy, they become Radicals; disgusted with the materialistic working a "rational" religion they become mystics. They quarrel with all that is, that it is not spiritual enough. They would perhaps be patient, if they thought this the mere sensuality of childhood in our nation, which it might outgrow; but they think they see the evil widening and deepening, not only debasing the life, but corrupting the thought of our people; and they feel that if they know not well what should be done, yet, that the duty of every good man is to utter a protest against what is done amiss.

Transcendentalism failed to influence the life of America because the idea at the root of it was fundamentally unsound. It was this " Faith in the universal man as he comes out of the hands of the Creator, with no law over his liberty but the eternal ideas that lie at the foundation of his being." But the universal man, like the economic man, so dear to early generations of the Fabian Society, does not exist, and the individual man finds at the foundation of his being the stern fact of sin. Strenuous energy, moral enthusiasm, and fine religious passion, all devoted to the preaching of a creed that was contrary to the facts of experience, and belied by the teaching of every-day life, was the tragedy of Transcendentalism, as it is the tragedy of half the reform movements of the world. But in the midst of such traditions American literature passed from childhood to maturity, and took its place in the world.

It was during the Toynbee Hall activities that " Robert Elsmere " first appeared, and it was an event in literature. Not because it was a great novel, or because it was the first novel with a social trend, but it certainly was one of the first novels dealing with social problems that was vigorously discussed in the higher walks of literature. This was not because of its social ideas but because of its religious heresies. They were of a mild order, but Mr. Gladstone thought them dangerous, and made an attack on the novel in one of the reviews. Its success was assured from that moment. All his political enemies read the book to prove him wrong, and all his political friends read it to prove him right, and publishers and author rubbed their hands. I was never a great novel reader, but a friend sent me " Robert Elsmere," and asked my opinion of it. The book dealt with phases of life that I had been familiar with for many years, and my friends knew this. Robert Elsmere's copy of public worship, without any definite faith to give reason for worship, I had seen first at the Church of Progress in my boyhood's days, and in South Place Chapel, and had no illusions about it. No inspiration of a religious kind ever comes from a gentleman on a platform with only a glass of water and abstract ideas, even when there is a good supply of music as well. The lectures at workmen's clubs, and James Allanson Picton's Sunday afternoon lectures on history, and my own experiences as a lecturer all helped to make the Elsmerian ideas and experiments interesting to me.

I read the book carefully and sent my friend a criticism of it. I said little of its religious problems, but a good deal of its other aspects. My friend—all unknowing to me—was also a friend of Mrs. Humphry Ward, and my criticism, which was frank, found its way into her hands. The result was a letter from her asking me to call and see her. While reading her novel I associated her in my own mind with Margaret Fuller, but I found out when I met her that this was a wrong judgment, and that the two women had very few things in common. I had met several lady novelists of the minor orders and they had interested and amused me by turns. They were famous, and they knew it, and proclaimed it with the sound of a trumpet. It was far otherwise with the great novelist whom I met one evening after I left my work at the Co-operative Printing Society, at her house at Russell Square. We had a long and interesting talk on matters relating to Labour and to social life, and in the midst of our talk a long-haired and charming child in night attire ran in, all oblivious of the stranger, to bid her mother good night. "David Grieve" was not then written, but I knew its plan in that conversation. It was a fine novel, and a young Unitarian preacher, to whom I lent a copy, said he could not lay it aside till he finished it. But I could not get any workmen to read it in those days.

It was not a new world to conquer, but an old one that was being conquered, that met me when I again looked out on social life. An institution, that was full of fine industrial safeguards because it was based on religion, and not on science or philosophy, was gradually being destroyed by modern industrialism and pleasure-seeking combined. I refer to the world-old institution of Sunday. It was listening to the debates at the Trade Union Congress that first brought home to me the evils that had grown up around the modern Sunday. They had grown up in my own lifetime, and in my early years I had helped to create the evils which it was now my duty as a good trade unionist to fight to the death. A free Sunday had rivetted upon many callings in the industrial world the slavery of a seven-days' week.

I had always been in favour of a free Sunday, and early realized that those who complained of the dulness of Sunday had a case, though I never spent a dull Sunday in my life. But the revolt against the dull Sunday brought with it worse evils than the dulness it overthrew, and the price we were paying for the amusement of the dull few was the enslavement of the many, and a good deal of the dulness came, not from the institution of Sunday, but from the fact that the dull people had not learnt the art of utilizing their time to the best advantage. The Puritan safeguards, whatever their defects, did keep inviolate a seventh part of his time for the worker, but Puritan ideals were moribund or dead, and the humanitarian arguments with which Puritan preachers sought to replace them were things of straw which could not stand a moment against the forces of commercialism when the religious safeguards were gone.

But these arguments had their plausibility as such arguments always have, and appealed strongly to the working-classes. The argument that Sunday was their only day was true in my early years, and I advocated the opening of museums on Sunday, because I saw that. But it is not true now, and museums are usually more crowded on Saturday afternoons than they are on Sundays. And while I accepted the argument that Sunday was the only day the working-classes had, I went always farther than my teachers, and wanted to know whether they were for ever destined to labour with only Sunday for their rest-day, and whether it was not possible to conceive of a state of society when they would get more leisure than that. To this query Edward Baker, and Picton, and M. D. Conway had no reply, nor had the working-classes of those days. They thought they should like museums open, and they were open, but they never went to them much after the novelty wore off, and I had the experience on one occasion of finding myself in the Bethnal Green Museum on a Sunday afternoon the only other persons being the attendants in charge and a little child.

Another argument used in answer to the protest against Sunday labour which I have come to see the fallacy of, was this: "Yes, a free Sunday does mean Sunday labour, but what does that matter, if a man has to work on Sunday he can have a week-day in the place of it." But the man who is put off with a week-day in the place of Sunday is robbed in the process. A Sunday and a week-day are not of equal value. Sunday is, and always must be, worth more. Ancient custom, worship, social friendship, have given to Sunday a spiritual value which if destroyed can never be compensated for by material pleasure. Workmen realize this quickly enough when they are deprived of their Sundays by the industrial conditions under which they live, but it is not realized by those who can have pleasure on Sundays while their fellows have to work.

"The toad beneath the harrow knows exactly where each tooth point goes;
The butterfly upon the road preaches contentment to that toad."

The Labour movement of Great Britain must look to it that what it may win in a shortening of hours, it does not lose again in an increase of days. A universal eight-hours' day will be a very pitiful compensation for a universal seven-days' week—which inevitably works out at six days' pay as all experience shows.

In the closing months of 1909 I gave a series of lectures on economic subjects at Ruskin Hall, Oxford, and during 1910 I was Labour Secretary to the Imperial Sunday Alliance. In the same year I was made an Alderman of the London County Council. The new Council tried to make an experiment in London government, which appealed to every fibre of my being. The Moderates were in power and the balance of power was nearly equal, and before electing the Aldermen they made a suggestion to the Progressives to govern London on non-party lines.

It was a great idea, and would have been a great experiment, which might have marked a new departure in civic politics and presently have extended to national politics. But the Progressives could not rise to it, and I realized once again that they who shout loudest for liberty are the last to grant it when it goes against their own interests. I had won old age pensions because I had refused to make it a party question, and if I had fought my battle in any other way pensions would be still to seek. The idea was cast out by those who ought to have been its natural supporters and London politics ground on once more in the old discredited party mill.

My work on the Council did not last a year, for my health was failing when it began. Forty years of strenuous work took its toll of me at last. Mind and body alike rose in revolt against sitting on the Council till two in the morning and then going to business again at ten, and with a sense of weariness and general breakdown I gave up my aldermanship, and when I came to myself again was in hospital with the knowledge that the only way out was by the aid of the surgeon's knife. I was a coward with that before me. Would the body that had served me so well for sixty-six years endure what was to come? Perhaps, but I did not know, I knew I had worked " Brother Ass " relentlessly and without pity, but apart from that I had not used him ill. The crisis passed and life was before me once more. To the surgeon in whose care I was I owe a debt which can never be repaid. And the episode of pain was worth enduring for the revelation it brought of human sympathy, and kindness, and love, which surrounded me till health returned.

It is a compensation of the sick-room that if action

ceases thought remains, and the dreams and the realities of the days that had passed for ever filled my mind as I lay in the hospital ward and old ideals came up for correction by experience, and by the stern schoolmaster Time. The secular ideals about which Edward Baker and George Jacob Holyoake used to discourse so eloquently in my early years passed to and fro in my mind, but I saw them in a different light now. They were always a negligible quantity in the social movements in which I had worked, but the shadow of truth was with them and this made them attractive to those who could be content with shadows. "There is no difference between things sacred and things secular," said Holyoake to me as we travelled to the old City of Canterbury to open a co-operative store. I did not reply, but I knew when the words were spoken that we stood upon the dangerous edge of things. At bottom the words were true, but is our bias towards the mud or the stars? All life is sacred, says George Herbert, but we must see it from the right point of view; all life is secular, says the secularist, be content with that. But there comes a time when men cannot be content with that. They wrestle with the mystery and learn that the mud and the stars can never be the same. We see the foulness of the mud in the light of the stars, but if we turn our face from the stars and gaze only on the mud we are soon blind to the glory of the firmament.

That "all things are secular" makes a far stronger appeal to unregenerate man than the opposite proposition, is no doubt true, and it is also eternally true that if we look down we go down. Looked at in the proper light every natural function of life is clean, but the unclean is one of the ugliest facts in both the physical and the spiritual worlds. It is born of the mud and not of the stars, and whether choice or ignorance brings it to birth the results are the same. It is belief, not negation, that keeps life in balance and makes its meaning clear; the face set as though it would go to Jerusalem that beholds at last the vision of God. But outside Jerusalem was the valley of Hinnom; a sign and symbol of other things, things akin to those that Bunyan beheld in his vision when he saw " that there was a way to Hell, even from the Gates of Heaven as well as from the City of Destruction."

XXVIII

FOR BETTER OR FOR WORSE?

WHEN in 1906 I interviewed W. T. Stead for a Christmas number, we discussed, among many other things, the always fascinating subject, "Was the world getting better or worse?" I had seen sixty years of life, he just a little more. Each of us had his own point of view, and each of us had passed through different experiences, and if we did not reach identical conclusions the talk was thought-stimulating, and my memory has often gone back to the restless, excitable man who walked rapidly to and fro in his office and poured out a flood of strange, disjointed but wonderful talk, and did literally survey mankind from China to Peru.

He was a great soul with the instincts of a prophet, if he did not possess the prophetic voice. In many ways he was a creature of moods, catching at an emotion of the moment, and making it into a living and abiding principle by the very intensity of his grasp, and his mood at that moment was pessimistic. It was the changing elements in life, combined with the quickened speed of it, that obsessed him and filled him with gloomy forebodings. Our educational results were unsatisfactory; we had lost the habit of reading, had discontinued the habit of family prayer; the political outlook was uncertain, the Labour party had no mind of its own; and the outlook for the middle classes was chaos. Joined to this there would be a revolt of the women sooner or later, and the sanctity of the home would be invaded, but, after all, there was spiritualism and eternal life.

I had thought myself out to a definite position in regard to spiritualism years before, and have not shifted from it. The evidence had convinced me that in the séance room it is possible to open a door between this world and the next, but that when it is done you do not know whether things good or evil are passing through. I did not feel any call to discuss spiritualism with him, but I thought I knew the mind of the Labour party better than he did. I knew it had a very definite mind of its own indeed on my subject—old age pensions—and a good many other things as well. And I knew also that it was not half so revolutionary as it believed itself to be, and that its great danger was that of being befogged by the ritual and ceremonial of Parliament, and of eventually being swallowed up in the crowd of ordinary politicians. About the middle classes I was not concerned. The young man of the middle classes as I knew him at the various educational centres was always pretty well able to take care of himself, and the young woman of the middle classes had a much better chance of gathering in the flowers of life than had the girls of working-class parents.

But George Meredith's words, " Who can really think and not think hopefully," have always embodied for me a sound philosophy. The true test of optimism is, I have no doubt, the sight of evil, and I have known as much of the evil of life as anybody. I could agree with my friend's criticisms of our educational system and of other social tendencies, could share some of his doubts about the Labour party and yet be hopeful. The workshop is infinitely better than when I first went into it, and this I say knowing many kinds of workshops now in many parts of Great Britain. In spite of the increase of speed and competition, there is more sobriety, idealism, and individuality therein, and workmen have found many ways now of breaking up the monotony of their lives, and are doing it without the aid of the philanthropist, though the latter, usually under the inspiration of religion, has taught them how. Brilliant young journalists who browse about on Sunday and say they do not see working men in this, that, and the other place, do not see them because often on Sunday the workman is as much a gentleman as his employer—and by nature he is sometimes more.

There is more idealism in every form of industrial life, and therefore more tragedy. New thoughts bring not peace but a sword, and because of this those of conservative temperament say, " Why, then, all this pother about education ; let the industrial classes alone and they will be happy." It is futile reasoning. New ideas will come and will capture new minds, whether they bring peace or strife. They are among the forces which man can chronicle, and perhaps on which he can pronounce judgment and say whether they are good or evil, but which he cannot control. Time may balance them and give them their proper place ; it usually does, but meanwhile the thorns and thistles that flourish so plentifully in the human garden will surround their growth. I vividly remember a young fellow coming to a class conducted by me in the beginning of my educational work who had the same passion for knowledge that I had in my teens.

There was about him a shy reserve that made him difficult to know, but he was well built, handsome, and of gentlemanly manners, and was generally liked. That he was a young workman of some sort I was sure, but he kept his business to himself and stuck to the class. And then one day I met him with a butcher's blue smock on, carrying a tray of meat. He blushed scarlet when he saw me, and I held out my hand and chatted a few moments with him and went on my way. But he never came to the class any more, and although I tried to get into touch with him I never could. There may be those who will only see matter for mirth in this episode, but the sensitive soul of a young workman is a point of pain in the welter of the world as acute and as real as the soul of a poet.

Two brothers I knew of a different order to this lad. One of them was a clerk in a business house with, I always thought, very limited wages, and the other was a waiter. They were very intellectual young men, both of them, and keen on history and literature, but much older than the lad above mentioned, and the waiter had a knowledge of the world not always to be found among men who attend classes for working men. One day the waiter, who was physically rather a weak creature, fell out of work. He came to me, as people in difficulty have always had a way of doing, for help or advice. I knew nothing of waiters as a trade, and could be of little use to him. Then, to my startled surprise, he assured me he should try journalism. I gave him no advice there. I knew the man and the world he strove to enter too well. He was honest, plodding, steady, but with very little imagination and no idea of writing at all. At last, however, he returned, I believe successfully, to his old calling.

The raising of our educational standards has created an enormous crowd of people who will not, if they can help it, labour with their hands. This does not come from any contempt of labour, but from a dread of the conditions under which it is carried on. The professional classes complain that their standards are being lowered, and the working classes complain that their labour is so uncertain that they cannot live. And yet it is true to say that the workman who has a good trade and is in constant work is better off than many curates. He is not called upon every second day to give in charity, and is not obliged to keep up an appearance. He is as well off as a number of newspaper men and many among the lower ranks of professional men, and if he makes the best use of his opportunities may get his full measure of human happiness, a measure that is often more wholesomely filled than that of those whom he may envy because they have a larger share of this world's goods.

But there has been a steady deterioration in the quality of handicrafts going on for many years past, and this is not the fault of the working but of the employing classes. Speed, machinery, and a hundred other things contribute, but it is by the labour of ill-trained but not always ill-paid youth that much of the handicraft work of our nation is done : youth that when it reaches manhood is cast out, its place to be supplied from the inexhaustible crowd of young lives which are turned out year by year from our elementary schools. It is thus that the quality of our handicrafts is lowered, and our nation made to take a back seat in the industrial workshops of the world.

And yet the workman is an idealist now, and because of the uncertainty of the social forces by which he is surrounded tragic shadows dog his footsteps and kill his ideals through life, as the evil shadows dogged the footsteps of Bunyan's idealist when he turned his back on the city of Destruction. Let us take the modern workman, having left school behind him, and with his manhood just opening out, and see what life means and how it shapes before him.

He is, we will say, an ordinary average man with ordinary qualities, with nothing to mark him off from hundreds or perhaps thousands of his fellows. Honest, straightforward, manly, but otherwise entirely commonplace. He reads a little perhaps, but like games and amusement best. He is easily impressionable and caught by the popular newspaper article or the popular speech, and not given to original thinking very much; in fact, the chief characteristic in his nature is the desire to enjoy, and this he does if he gets regular work and has decent wages, thinking as little about saving for the future as any other young fellow of his own age—actor, barrister, medico, or what not. Youth is the time to enjoy so long as it be done in manful fashion, and he fulfils the law of his being. But presently a new force enters into his life, and he knows what is meant by the glamour of sex, becomes either the pursued or the pursuer in the game of love; other ideas broaden out before him, his manhood becomes a wholesomer, stronger thing, and marriage is now the wish of his heart.

It is perhaps then, for the first time, that he comes up against certain economic facts, and the whole future of his life and happiness will depend on whether he is able to grapple with them or not. It is the time in his life when his ideals are at their highest, and he desires the best he can reach for the girl he loves, but he realizes all of a sudden that, while his income may be satisfactory for himself as a single man, even if he lives up to it, it will become straitened if two persons are to depend on it, and still more so if at any time there are more than two. But he is in love, he risks everything, is married, and life takes on another outlook henceforth.

It is pretty certain that, although the workmen's wages are larger than when I was young, their spending power is less. Thrifty Edward Baker, with his wages varying from eighteen to twenty-five shillings a week, had some guinea shares in the Crystal Palace—five, I think—and had saved up some twenty odd pounds, he told me, which his wife stole when her chance came. I should be surprised to find a man earning that money now who got as much out of life as he did and saved that amount. And it by no means follows that this is due to deterioration in the character of workmen. The price of living has risen or is rising all over the civilized world. No one can pronounce with any certainty as to the cause of this change, but it presses hardest as usual on the man at the bottom of the ladder. It is variously charged to the depreciation in the price of gold, the rise in the standard of living, the passing of money into fewer and fewer hands, the increase of the wages of labour and what not, but nobody really knows the cause and nobody can ignore the fact. I do not say that workmen as a class are worse off now than when I was young, but it is quite easy to show that large sections of the working classes are no better off.

Things are easier in many ways for the modern workman, but whether he gets any more value out of life in consequence of this is again a highly debatable matter.

His children are educated free, and if they care for educational things as they grow up these things can be had for the asking. And there are more pleasures at the public cost now than ever there were, which all classes alike can enjoy. But things are harder for him, too, especially as the years pass and time makes his mark upon the workman's brow. Taxation is immensely higher, and will not decrease. There are more calls on his weekly income the more thrifty he may be. If he is a trade unionist and insures against being out of work that is one tax on his weekly wage. If he belongs to a friendly society and insures against sickness that is another. If he goes to church or chapel that is still another, so that, combining these with occasional illnesses, from which no family is immune, the chances of workmen saving against the proverbial rainy day seem to decrease with time. And yet they do save, and the savings bank returns prove this up to the hilt. Saving, however, is often determined by the accidents or the misfortunes of life. A steady run of work, not too large a family, a wife who is a good chancellor of the exchequer: all these things count and add to the chances of family thrift, but slow limbs and grey hairs inevitably ring the workmen's knell of independence at last.

It is believed by many workmen that wages can be influenced by votes, but such a belief is a fallacy and a fraud, and those who attack the wage system root and branch have the soundest logic in their contendings. The silly women of the political world, who seem bent on proving the truth of Schopenhauer's dictum that the woman is the inferior animal, believe—or, think they do—that wages can be influenced by votes, but when votes and wages are brought together the result is corruption and monstrous births. But it is still true that women's wages in most industries in which they are employed are a scandal and a sin, though the cause of this has perhaps a deeper reason than economics can show: like the workmen's demand for a living wage, it belongs to the human side of things.

Many things have passed from the world of everyday work, if its sad background remains, and some mirth has been gained and lost in their passing. There is often a tendency to primness, not to say priggishness, among gatherings of workmen now which stimulates the risible faculties, and they occasionally suggest a Bohemian assembly suddenly inspired with a passion for evening dress. The man whose wife makes his clothes has gone from among us, and with him we have lost many interesting studies in the grotesque. Edward Baker's wife made the clothes he came to work in, and the honest-hearted man grew eloquent at times about her sartorial abilities. But young men said wickedly behind his back that he suggested the fifth of November, and there was but little exaggeration in their words. The Calvinistic workman of a good type was interesting and he of a bad type amusing, but both are gone. One of the latter class, whom I knew in my 'teens, seemed to me then to have a tremendous knowledge of Calvinistic theology. He was a vellum binder, and rather proud of the fact that he had a brother who was a Baptist minister. The poor parson worked at his trade as skipping-rope handle maker and got five shillings every time he preached. It was what I got later on for my lectures at the clubs on history and literature. My shopmate, who in his early years had been a soldier, had a soldier's pension in addition to his salary in the trade, but the pension did him little good. He disappeared regularly on his pension day, and returned the day after with a splitting headache and the temper of a fiend. Apart from these escapades he was not a bad man.

The poor creatures who can never help themselves, but are eternally leaning on others for support, are always with us, and probably always will be. If they are wealthy they add to the vice of the world, if they are poor they add to the burdens of those who are only just one degree removed from their poverty. The man who can never take advantage of his opportunities is as plentiful after our forty years of popular education as he was when education was among the luxuries of life, and did not reach the poor unless they fought for it. And yet it is a proven fact that any man can earn enough for his own needs if he gets the chance, and has the will.

Wife-beating was never a monopoly of the working-classes, and it has all but disappeared from every form of social life that I know. It is quite an ancient custom, dating probably from primitive times, and all classes have indulged in it. There is an entry in the church books of John Bunyan's chapel at Bedford which tells how a member of the congregation was reprimanded at a church meeting for beating his wife *when she did not deserve it.* In the street where I lived as boy and young man we were in an atmosphere of wife-beating, and yet it was a street that prided itself on its respectability. At a house next door to me a man flung his wife out of a ground-floor window, and one man I knew, in a good position in life, intellectual and educated, who was kind to me as a boy, was in the habit of giving his wife periodical thrashings.

Her female neighbours used to say she richly deserved them, and she certainly was a confirmed dipsomaniac. People seldom interfered between a man and his wife; it was a dangerous thing to do, as the contending parties usually joined forces and turned on the person who interfered with, " And, pray, what business is it of yours ? "

Drinking is as old a vice as wife-beating; is there not a splendid temperance sermon in Piers Plowman ? Are they going out together ? About the reduction in the consumption of strong drink there is no manner of doubt, and if it continues the outlook is excellent. But there is other evidence which points in a contrary direction. The advent of the woman into the labour market is changing many social customs, and in many ways the change is for the worse. I have always been an advocate of letting a woman do any work for which she showed capacity, and I advocated women factory inspectors when my fellow trade unionists in London held the idea to be anathema. There is nothing in the fear, not uncommon in trade union circles, that she will displace man. She has been able to compete with man not because she is better than he is, but because she is cheaper and more easily driven. It is her weakness—moral, mental, and physical—that makes her the prey of the sweater, and, although in many ways she has gained by expanding her industrial sphere, in others she has greatly fallen. She is showing a tendency to copy masculine vices, and they become lower things and worse as vices when she imitates them. Years ago a woman lost caste among her sisters of the working classes if she was seen drinking in a public-house with other women, but to-day the " Friday night pint " is an institution in many factories where women are employed, and it by no means stops at a pint. I have worked in shops where it was a rigid rule to allow no young fellow to drink with the men until he was twenty-one. But young girls suffer petty persecution who refuse to drink with older women, though to their honour, be it said, many do suffer it rather than give way in a matter which they regard as right.

The illegitimate child is no longer regarded as a child of shame in many social circles, and it is women, not men, who have broken the wholesome moral standards down. The powerful Lancashire play of " Hindle Wakes " leaves a worse savour behind it than does the horrible magnificence of John Ford in his great Elizabethan play, but is as true to life as Ford's story of Giovanni and Annabella was true to the decadent Italian life of the Renaissance. But Ford made the consequences of his story tragedy to the last item. It will be a tragedy going farther down into the roots of life than any blood and lust story of the Renaissance ever went if we breed a race of men and women in our generation who can have neither honour nor respect for the mothers that bore them.

I had seen for many years past without knowing it that it was better for intellect and heart alike to be in the great currents of national and social life rather than to be separate from them even from the best of motives, though I do not say that mine were always such motives. Something of personal egotism and self-assertion, and of the desire to have truth on my side rather than to be on the side of truth was always with me. But the beauty of life humbled me, and it was always flashing across my path. As a child I was impressed by my mother's attitude to a clump of trees that grew some distance from our

x

little front room window in the East London street. She used to stand at that window ironing; she was a good ironer, and in her younger days got plenty of work. She called them her trees and talked to them and of them, and pointed out their natural beauty to me summer after summer, and built up in my character a sense of beauty in life which remains still. It was nature, not art, that appealed to her, and nature as a vision of God, and she would have understood, had she ever met with them, the words of the mediæval monk who defined happiness as "doing little things for God and not minding because they are little."

It was listening to Lord Halifax at a Nonconformist P.S.A. in Stepney in, I think, 1896, that brought home to me the need of being in touch with the great currents of life, if one would get life's full measure. I had been reading Matthew Arnold a good deal and sifting the truth from the fancy in his books, and going through East London I saw Lord Halifax down to speak at a P.S.A. which was being run by Mr. Howard Kennedy, a gentleman who in those days was on the staff of the *Times*. The chapel was full, the speaker being a lord, and I listened to a noble address which finished for me the sifting I was making in the thoughts of the great critic and poet whose mark is deep on the literature of his time, and I went home full of new energies and new ideas.

In the Labour movement I was watching the influence of the work of the Christian Social Union. I had heard members of that Union express doubts as to the value of its work, but I never felt any. It is largely to them that the Labour movement owes the religious leaven which works in it more and more. Religion among its individual members there is and always has been, but it is due to the members of the Christian Social Union, men like Bishop Stubbs, Canon Scott Holland, Charles Gore, now Bishop of Oxford, and Percy Dearmer going to trades congresses and preaching in the local churches, that the congress sermon became a fact and that the Labour movement in England has never become what it often is on the Continent, an atheistic thing. True it has its atheistic leaven, but the yeast is bad and the leaven doesn't work.

There never has been a time in history when men have not said that religion was dying, and they are saying it now. And truly our civilization in some of its aspects is such a horrible welter of wickedness that the statement seems justified up to the hilt. But out of the sin of the world comes the prayer of the world, and of prayer faith is born. New theologies make a mock at sin, but it is they who are mocked in the long run, and old philosophies define sin in terms of logic as something other than we think, or explain it in such a fashion as to explain it away, but definition and explanation alike are evidence of the reality of the fact which called them forth. And St. Paul's words about sin and grace abounding side by side have only had their truth emphasized, not minimized, in the course of two thousand years.

But if the evil angels of life are never absent from our world the good are there too. The heroic is with us to-day in large and increasing measure, even though the shadows of warfare and the lust of blood follow hauntingly in its path. The spirit of the Elizabethans lives in those young souls who crowd into the new science of aviation, fearlessly navigate the air, and take a horrible death as part of the day's work. It is the same spirit as that which in the days of the great Queen circumnavigated the globe, discovered new worlds, and filled our England with a new and abounding life. Eternally true are the words of the greatest of all the Elizabethans, " The web of our life is of a mingled yarn, good and ill together; our virtues would be proud if our faults whipped them not, and our crimes would bid us despair if they were not cherished by our virtues."

XXIX

"IN THE MIDST O' THE BIGNESS O' THINGS"

The business of life is largely concerned with little things, and our happiness or our insight alike can be choked by the dust of small detail. "What shadows we are, what shadows we pursue!" said Edmund Burke midway in a great career, when the sudden death of an opponent gave him an effortless victory. But a shadow can be the reflection of a glory as well as of a shame, and dust can cease to be dust when it is touched by a breath from heaven. Nature and civilization are eternally at war; again and again Nature is defeated, and yet she is infinitely the greater of the two. Much of the sordidness and the squalor of modern life comes from the too rapid victory of the artificial over the natural, and the noise of life which deafens, and the dust which chokes us are born of the conflict between the town and the forests and fields, between natural and human instincts, and civilized conventions which hold them in check. And yet Nature is essentially barbaric: it is always true that the state of Nature is less perfect than the state of grace; and this is so because life began, not with Nature, but with that which was before Nature: "And the Lord God formed man out of the dust of the earth, and breathed into his nostrils the breath of life, and man became a living soul."

When a sickly boy, scarcely knowing if life were to be mine or not, I found a summer joy in lying on the grass and gazing dreamily into the sky; there came to me often a sense of the limitless greatness of the world in which I lived. I knew Shelley's "Skylark" somehow or other in my teens, though I knew nothing of the poet till long after, and have watched the bird till I lost him in the clouds, and chanted half unconsciously to myself as I watched,

> "Higher still and higher
>   From the earth thou springest,
> Like a cloud of fire
>   The blue deep thou wingest,
> And singing still dost soar, and soaring
>   Ever singest."

Lines I loved stayed in my memory with scarce an effort, and I had found all unwittingly a law of compensation which never ceases to work in the world. The merriment of my young companions I was not strong enough, or perhaps I was too morbid, with the morbidity that comes with a lack of health, to share, but I found a compensation my joyous comrades never knew, I was "in the midst o' the bigness o' things."

I have never thought of life at any time as being founded on anything but a supernatural basis. But I always loved the intellectual wrestling with that idea which I got in my early 'twenties in Edward Baker's cottage in Rodney Road, Walworth, and sometimes with my father at home. I was often thrown in the struggle, for Edward Baker's friends were matured and sometimes educated men, and I had a greater love for education than I had a knowledge of it, but I came up smiling and went at it again. Of religious experience or of conversion I had none that the religious people I knew in those years would have recognized. The truths of religion grew into my nature, so to speak, and the free-thought pamphlets, of which I saw so many, only served to convince me of their own shallowness. But they were kindly hearted men who gave them to me, and might just as easily have been religious men giving me religious tracts, and the tracts they distributed were not at a very much lower intellectual level than those which devout ladies carried round from house to house each week in the belief that they were doing good. Whatever good they did, however, came when the spirit of kindliness was at the back of their action rather than from the tract.

Two strains of heredity were in my nature—my father's scepticism, and my mother's faith. Many and happy were the Sunday evenings I spent with my father in my boyhood's days, laughing over the "Ingoldsby Legends," talking politics, and listening to his sea stories while my mother was gone to chapel. He hated every kind of religious teacher, revelled in such character-studies as Stiggins and Chadband, and the only cleric he ever had a good word for was Robert Aspland, the minister of the chapel to which he was taken when a child. It was a Unitarian chapel in the gravel pits at Hackney, where, according to tradition, Rogers the banker-poet took Benjamin Disraeli when the famous politician was in his childhood. Of Aspland's benevolence and general goodness of nature he was never tired of talking, but he never had a good word for any other teacher of religion. Captain Marryat was his favourite author, he described the sea life my father knew; and of later sea writers than the author of "Jacob Faithful" he refused to know anything.

I have often laughed at a remark of his, made years ago when he was turning over a medley of free-thought pamphlets and religious papers in my rooms, "If the Devil ever gets among your books he'll go raving mad about them. He will feel certain he ought to have you, but won't know whether he has got you or not."

Two strains of religious thought have been dominant in the development of the Christian faith—Catholic and Puritan—and they are found among nearly all Christian peoples. They vary according to national characteristics or individual idiosyncrasies, but they exist because they stand for two ways of regarding the problem of life, and they present two entirely different aspects of that problem. All that is true in Puritanism is found in the Catholic idea, but the Puritan remembered what the Catholic had forgotten—hence his success—but he remembered nothing else. The Catholic idea bears witness to the fact that the ultimate truth of things is infinitely greater than our conception of it; but Puritanism has whittled away every expression of ancient truth, and following its teaching men have reached agnosticism instead of faith. The Puritan strain of thought in England culminated quite naturally, and with an entirely logical completeness, in the Hall of Science, and Charles Bradlaugh was the last of the English Puritans.

The gradation was easy as I saw it in my early days; but it is going on, on a much larger scale now. From Dale or Spurgeon to Picton, from Picton to Conway, from Conway to the Hall of Science; and then came the end of all but individual ideas and individual work. It was

"IN MIDST O' THE BIGNESS O' THINGS" 313

the Puritan temper—the temper that destroyed beautiful windows; broke up carvings, and burnt pictures—that manifested itself in Charles Bradlaugh when he set forth as Iconoclast to destroy other symbols than these. But it was only Puritanism that yielded to his backwoodsman's blows; in the principles of the Catholic idea he made no breach, and none knew it better than himself.

The man was great with all his dogmatic assumptions and crude reasonings. He had a small band of devoted followers, but they all dispersed at his death. Representing as he did both their principles and their prejudices, as life deepened with him and experience grew, it was principle and not prejudice that determined his actions, and this his followers did not always understand. He saw with clearness and precision the power of the Catholic idea, and never concerned himself greatly with the opposition of the Puritan side of religion; in fact, at last, he found many of his political supporters in its ranks. But he said in 1883, " It may be far off; it may be near; it may be to-morrow—the fight between the Church of Rome and rationalism, between the fullest assertion of the right of private judgment and the most complete submission to authority."

But he did not see that when men have followed this principle to its final goal, they do not concern themselves any longer with the abstract right, which is conceded, but with the value of the private judgment in the intellectual sum of things when it is expressed. The rubbish heap of thought which has been created by the refuse of private judgments is the biggest rubbish heap in the world, even though it has attained some picturesqueness by the moss and lichen with which it has been clothed by time and the imagination of man.

The religious instinct is as eternal as humanity itself, and will cease only with the human race. And its most complete expression is found in the Catholic idea. The Papacy stands condemned at the bar of history, and it is difficult to see how that sentence can ever be reversed. But the religious principles on which it was erected respond alike to the needs of intellect and heart as no other principles yet discovered can; will it be that some day they will emerge cleansed from the blood and lust that has stained the Papal throne, and answer again to the spiritual needs of a world? The Catholic revival in the Church in England gives an unhesitating and affirmative reply.

But the Catholic idea does not touch the life of the common people. Reared in the atmosphere of the Protestant sects the English democracy does not possess a Catholic mind.

If, however, the Catholic idea does not appeal to the multitude, the appeal of the mystic who is not a Catholic does, and the career of General Booth is evidence of the fact. He had no new theology to bring them, and if he had it would have left them cold. His appeal was that of the old faith. All he said and all he did was based on his absolute faith in God, and in the atoning power of the blood of Jesus Christ, and he reached more men and women by the Gospel of Christ than any leader of men in his day did by any other Gospel; in the truest sense of the word he reached the masses. He had seen the Divine Vision, and seen it as truly as Augustine, or Athanasius, or Behmen, or Fox. He did not seek to destroy other forms of religious life; he only sought to save souls from sin. His methods must be judged by results, both now and in future years, but he was a genuine mystic, and the light he saw was the true light.

Two religious movements and a scientific principle have moulded the most active and virile thought of my lifetime: the Oxford Movement, the Salvation Army, and the doctrine of Evolution. Against the first I was warned from the beginning as an evil thing, and as a boy ignorantly sympathized with the drunken ruffians and bullies hired in the name of Protestantism to make riots at the church of St. George's in the East and elsewhere. I had—like a good many more people—nothing but prejudice to back up my sympathy, but when knowledge came with later years I found I was—as I had often been—on the wrong side, and that what I ignorantly vilified was a noble movement inspired by a true faith. The Salvation Army had to suffer much the same persecution as the ritualists, though it was never persecuted with quite the same bitterness as they were, but it kept true to its ideals, never exchanged its faith for politics, and finally lived down opposition and found at last its place among the genuine religious forces of the world.

The doctrine of Evolution was expected to destroy religion a generation or two ago. Some of this fear may be found in Tennyson's noble poem of "In Memoriam," and in my younger days the poem furnished many weapons for free-thinkers, who used its lines in a way undreamed of by the poet. But Evolution is an empty mockery to the soul that seeks redemption; its theories received some shrewd blows when the Abbot Gregor Mendel's discoveries became known to the world, and it is hardly likely that the doctrine that the centre was created by the circumference will always command intellectual respect. That it is among the best working hypotheses of science there can be no manner of doubt, but to regard it as having any relation to religion has always been absurd. On the deeper things of life it is dumb.

It is always true that those who believe are saved: it is only the sincere idealist that can move the world. Ideals are born of belief, and we are always nearer to ultimate truth when we affirm than when we deny.

An ideal is a conception of life different from that which exists, and which is, or seems to be, better than that which exists. It must be or seem to be better, else it would have no power to draw men to its pursuit. Ideals are partly the result of imagination, partly of experience. Imagination in its completeness is a higher form of seeing. It is an old metaphor that the imagination of a sculptor sees in the unknown block of marble the perfect statue which, working according to ascertained principle and scientific method, he will presently chisel forth. Imagination shows the ideal, but experience is needed before the ideal can be perfectly realized. And imagination does not show the hidden flaw in the marble; that only experience can discover, and when it is discovered it may render all the sculptor's work null and void. The imagination of the reformer brings before his eyes the new social order which, working according to principles he believes to be sound, he hopes to call into being. But no imagination can reveal to him the faults and weaknesses, the folly and the evil, that may be hidden in the natures of the men and women out of whom his vision must be realized, his Utopia be built up. Experience is eternally correcting our ideals, but it is a law of our nature that we must be for ever seeking that which transcends experience, and herein lies the secret of the unrest of the human race.

> "Ah, but a man's reach should exceed his grasp,
> Or what's a heaven for?"

wrote Robert Browning, and when he did so he gave utterance to one of those immortal phrases that enrich the imagination of the world.

But always amid the unrest—which was surely a part of the Eternal design and purpose—men are seeking for a solid foundation, a rock of ages, on which to rest their souls. "Our heart is restless until it find rest in Thee," wrote St. Augustine more than a thousand years ago: his yearning is born of an eternal passion, and from it has come the spiritual riches of the world. Those who would find the secret Augustine found can do so if they fulfil the conditions of the search, and often it may happen that the strong and simple soul fulfils these conditions without knowing it, and reaches the rest towards which the intellectuals, their minds wearied by the speculations of our tangled modern world, labour painfully and in vain.

Always and from the beginning a Divine light has been in the world, and some have seen it in glimpses, some in full vision, and some have known without seeing that the Divine light was there. The religious consciousness of the Jew has been a priceless heritage; the mysticism of the Eastern faiths has not yet found its proper estimate in the thought of the Western world, but Christ has brought the answer to every problem human life has known. Always and from the beginning there has been a deposit of faith, something that has not been discovered by the intellect, but which stands in no hostility to intellect and is apprehended by the instincts of the soul, something that has been revealed in moments of intuition when the veil which covers the spiritual from the material world has been lifted up. Always and from the beginning men have sought fellowship with God in the act of corporate worship, which other men have called the worship of the unknown. But to the true worshipper God is never unknown.

Unexplained by every form of human philosophy still stands the mystery of the power and personality of Jesus Christ, the central figure of the religious life of the world. Pericles and Socrates were finely touched spirits and to fine issues, but not to them has come the inspiring power, and the radiance of Divine glory which enshrouds the person of the Nazarene. They were great among the greatest, He obscure among the poorest; their memories gild with a fine glory the records of a nation. He is the light of the world. Only one reply can be made in answer to the question, "What think ye of Christ?" and that is the ancient one:

For the right faith is, that we believe and confess: that our Lord Jesus Christ, the Son of God, is God and Man;

God, of the substance of the Father, begotten before the world: and Man, of the substance of his Mother, born in the world;

Perfect God, and perfect Man: of a reasonable soul and human flesh subsisting;

Equal to the Father, as touching his Godhead: and inferior to the Father, as touching His Manhood.

Who, although He be God and Man: yet He is not two, but one Christ;

One, not by conversion of the Godhead into flesh: but by taking of the Manhood into God.

It is by belief in the Incarnation and the Deity of Christ, and by this belief alone, that religion will be saved in the intellectual turmoil of our day, and those who turn away from it into by-path meadows of new theologies, or amiable moralities, have their faces set in the direction of the final negation.

Much of that part of the religion of England which is embodied in the Protestant sects is turning its face in that direction, though it is largely unconscious of the fact. Its adherents and followers may never reach the final goal which was typified so completely in the Hall of Science, or in a much more cultured form at South Place, but their descendants will if they are not saved by some power which is not with them now. It is the Church in England that is preserving the principles of the Christian faith, and the Catholic revival, which was born of the Oxford Movement, is the dynamic force which has created anew the religious life of the Church. It was not until I got into close touch with the Church in England, and saw its life in relation to other activities in the religious world, that I came to this conclusion, but then it was driven home to me with a force I could not resist, and, listening to Arthur Henry Stanton at St. Alban's, Holborn, and Charles Edward Brooke at Kennington, I found the solution of life's difficulties and the answer to all its problems.

XXX

EVENING

And now, as life's evening approaches, if perhaps I am a little tired with its work, and am glad of such rest as the destinies will allow, I am in no way tired of life itself, and have never understood the temper of the pessimist which sees in it something to be shuffled off and got rid of as soon as possible. It is well to have lived, to have helped one's fellows, to have enjoyed the sunshine of the good old earth, and that larger sunshine of the intellect and the soul. And life as I see it beyond death is an endless vision for ever and for ever opening out into greater and still greater glory; but there must needs be a passing through of penal fires for the purging of the sins of the soul, and I would not if I could escape any future penalty which I may have earned by the wrong-doings of the life that now is. Looking back on that life, I half wish that I could do something more yet for the country which gave me birth.

When Canon Barnett died on June 17, 1913, I realized that death sometimes teaches us more than life. I had known him intimately since 1877, and my love and reverence for him deepened with time, even when our intellectual paths diverged. Something of the paradox which manifests itself in all great souls manifested itself in him. No one saw more unerringly than he the deadly influence of evil environment on life and character, and no one fought it more strenuously. But in the evil environment that surrounded him in the slum parish he found a stimulus to vigorous action. It was something which called forth the finer qualities of his nature, and not a hindrance to the work he meant to do. Not many young men could have faced as he did " the worst parish in my diocese "—which was how Bishop Jackson described the parish of St. Jude's, Whitechapel, in 1872.

But he was not among those workers who quarrel with their tools, he used what was there to his hand, and in the worst parish he did his best work. From there radiated influences that touched the universities, the press, and politics for more than a generation and created ideas and enthusiasms which still live and work among us. I found the secret of his success in a remark he made to me when we were discussing a small appointment that had just been given to a great man : " Any position is strong when the man is strong." And he was strong, though not indeed in the way the multitude counts strength. His strength was in the humbleness of his mind and the sincerity of his soul. He broadened the scope of religious activities, not by talking about being broad-minded, but by affirming principles which men had forgotten. " Greatness," he said once at an annual address at Toynbee Hall, " consists not only in doing great things, but in doing little things in a great spirit."

His work was great and far-reaching in its character, but it was not for what he did that men sought his counsel, but for what he was. Politicians came to him because he was able to touch with new and living inspirations their barren world, and give them ideals they could not reach otherwhere. Young men fresh from the universities came to him for direction and advice, and went away with a new light on life and its duties. Something of genius there was in his clear vision of what was sincere in a man. You could differ with him, but you could never doubt him. He was full of sympathy for all that was sound in the Labour movement and its ideals, but he was no court chaplain to King Demos. He could be a deadly critic of any idea which he regarded as false, and yet his criticisms never seemed unkind. In the last book he wrote he described himself as "one who has no claim to be a 'thinker,' but has learnt most by 'doing.'" Characteristic humility is in the words, and perhaps he never quite realized himself how his thoughts helped other minds; but when I read the sentence I thought of more ancient words: "If any man will do His will he shall know of the doctrine whether it be of God."

Quiet-natured, but full of a soul-supporting faith, he refused to let himself be daunted by failure even when at times men seemed to be against him. He did not believe that many men consciously and intentionally did wrong, and he had faith in the appeal of goodness to the worst soul.

In the year 1875 he wrote to the parishioners of St. Jude's:—

The Christian Gospel is not popular and cannot advance rapidly. Those who cover it up in attractive language, who offer to converts worldly comforts and happiness, who stir up a tide of emotion which carries a listener in one night from degradation to perfection, produce results which seem great: but such results bring the world but little nearer to God's

Kingdom. Those tempted to leave one form of self gratification by the promise of another, have not learned to value goodness before all things; those who are borne along by the tides of their emotions when the tide falls are left with all their old doubts and temptations as strong as ever, they cannot have that memory of daily fights with, and conquests over sin, which will make them sure that God is always near them, and victory always in their power.

I would urge you, therefore, as followers of one whose work ended in seeming failure on the Cross, to work without haste, to look for no success, but just to do every day what you know to be right, and

> "To throw on God
> (He loves the burden),
> God's task to make the heavenly period
> Perfect the earthen."

Work done in this spirit assuredly finds its place in the values of the world, though it may be never seen amid its fogs, or heard of amid its turmoil. Here is no worship of success or failure, here is an insight that looks beyond them both, and appeals to the heroic in man. Not the things of the moment, but "the vision that is very far off," inspired the work of Samuel Augustus Barnett.

Ordained priest in 1872, the same year as Samuel A. Barnett was appointed Vicar of St. Jude's, Whitechapel, the work of Charles Edward Brooke, Vicar of St. John the Divine, Kennington, and Canon of Rochester, covers the same period of time as that of Canon Barnett. It was different, as the two men were different, but both men were strong. Each man was profoundly conscious of the value and the need of work for education, and Toynbee Hall, Whitechapel, is a monument to the genius of the one, and St. Gabriel's College, Kennington, to the genius of the other. They were not intimate, but each knew the other, and each—as I know from personal knowledge,—held in admiration the work of the other.

Brooke's work was to build up a new parish in a growing London suburb, and the slum grew in the suburb as well as the school. He was in no sense a slum priest, but it was well for the slums of that district that he was a power in it. He was ready to do anything for the welfare of the locality except lower his principles. Chance drew me to his church when I went to live in South London, and I was at once impressed by the magnetic personality of the man, and what he was preaching was what I wanted to hear. I did not get to know him till the education fight of 1906. We met on the platform of the English Church Union at the Albert Hall, and the man who had helped me as a preacher I admired as a fighter. We were on opposite sides in politics except in the matter of education. He was a staunch Conservative, I a member of the Labour party. But he was a man who hit hard and fought fair, and when the battle was over he had usually won the respect of his adversaries. He fought for his Church and its faith, and he had proved his devotion to both by generous donations and sacrifice for the cause in which he believed.

Sane, shrewd, level headed, and full of an abiding religious energy, he added to his work at home a no less energetic zeal for work abroad. He was a mission priest with something of apostolic fervour in his desire to spread the Faith abroad. "The missionary church is the only good church," said Canon Barnett to me, and to this doctrine Brooke subscribed with his whole heart, though his ideals and those of Barnett were not the same. The religious needs of our Colonial Empire called forth all his vigour, and the influence and the name of St. John the Divine, Kennington, lives in our new and growing empire in its Canadian territory.

In his church at Kennington he created, as such men do, a religious atmosphere, and it was born of the faith of his own ardent soul. His death in 1911 left the world poorer; his was the kind of life that creates faith, purpose, and activity in other lives, and helps to make that music which is " the gladness of the world."

I have loved to see the struggles of my own class to get rights which are assuredly theirs; they are the noblest struggles of our generation, and now and always I shall wish them Godspeed. It is in struggle that character stands revealed, and it is a poor idealism, after all, that dreams of a world without struggle.

The struggle that will purify our social life will be a struggle for justice to the bottom dog. Included in that struggle will also be the effort to prevent him from casting himself back into the mire out of which he has been raised. Because he is the bottom dog we never quite see him in his true perspective. To some he is a scapegoat on whom the sins of society are cast. Others picture him as the creature of an evil scheme of social life, and others still, as a degraded being whom society, for its own safety, must watch and guard against, casting him from time to time such crumbs as it can spare from its usually well-furnished table. All these theories are true, and none of them contain the whole truth. But this is true, that the bottom dog has no vices which the dogs of the palace or the drawing-room do not share. He is as they are; he loves, hates, resents oppression, sins, suffers, and sometimes dreams and hopes. And for whatever else that may appertain to him, is it not true that Cain and Abel were children of the same mother, and that Judas dipped his bread in the dish of the Lord Christ?

The story of England in the history of the world is a glorious episode, and nothing can dim that glory if England is true to her national traditions. Her colonies love her with a love which no other nation in the world commands from its dependencies, and the love is born of the freedom which is part of their national heritage. A wound given to the old Mother Country would vibrate across the globe, and find nerve centres in all parts of the earth. Not second to ancient Greece in literary glory, the thought and imagination born of her brain have fed the souls of untold millions of the human race, and will feed those of millions yet unborn. She has her own particular manifestations of original sin; she would be lacking on the human side of things if she had them not. By other nations she has been called hypocritical, but she need not concern herself with the opinion of other nations; her career in the life of the world can justify itself. Its chief characteristic has been a passionate desire to do justly by all men—even her enemies, and if sometimes she has missed her mark it has not been because there has been failure in the integrity of her aim. The nation is only the individual writ large, and shares in the human blunders and mistakes which manifest themselves in a greater or less degree in the units that make its multitude.

Life is a symbol of that which is eternally greater than

itself, and it is only when humanity realizes this and becomes humble that it reaches its true *stature*. "Do you see yonder wicket gate?" said Evangelist in Bunyan's parable, and the man said, "No"; but when the question is asked, "Do you see yonder shining light?" the answer came very humbly, "I think I do." Loyalty to the Divine Vision, even when all he could say was that he thought he saw it, carried the man safely to the end of his journey; he believed and was saved, and those who were his companions and did not believe were left by the way.

It is a hopeful outlook for the future that a conviction of social sin has arisen among us, and most of us are practically agreed that humanity stands in need of salvation. A sense of sin and a desire for salvation are the vital dynamics of progress. We are not, however, agreed as to how it is to be saved, or what it is to be saved from, though many use old words and talk vaguely of "a change of heart." Some there are who picture humanity as turning away from its age-long visions as delusions of the senses, and finding happiness in the only life left to it: a life on this earth. This is the modern gospel, and it is preached often with sincerity and charm. But it is empty and false. It narrows the human outlook, and destroys spiritual standards and possibilities. We can only find redemption from the baser elements in our souls, in ideals that are not for time, but for Eternity.

INDEX

Advanced Unitarians, 28
All Saints, Margaret Street, 114
"All Sorts and Conditions of Men," 95, 102
American literature, 280
Amphictyonic Council, 241
Anderson, James, 7
Annie, 48
Asquith, Rt. Hon. H. H., 119, 179, 266, 268
Athanasian Creed, the, 224, 318
Atkinson, Miss, 7
Aveling, Edward, B., 175, 176, 177
Aviation, 307

Bad literature and boys, 10, 11
Bailey, the Old, 12, 13
Baines, Charles, 70, 71
Baker, Edward, 22–31, 63, 77, 112, 122, 125, 289, 292, 300
——, James E., 160, 189
Balfour, Rt. Hon. A. J., 250, 261
Baptism, 5
Barnett, Rev. Canon S. A., 79, 88, 91, 104, 109, 142, 156, 221, 227; death of, 320
——, Mrs. S. A., 109, 221
Barrett, the Fenian murderer, 13
Beaumont Institution, 107, 108, 109
Becket, Tennyson's play, 171
Bedford, Bishop of, 71
Bell Inn, the Old, 89, 90
Besant, Mrs. Annie, 72, 161
——, Sir Walter, 95, 96, 170, 171
Bethnal Green Museum, 289
Birmingham, Trade Union Congress, 215
Blackbird, the (poem), 270

Blacklegs, 191, 192
Blackley, Rev. Canon, 233
Blatchford, Robert, 32
Bookbinders, the Co-operative, 118, 119, 145
—— Strike, the, 173 to 195
Books in the workshop, 137, 138
Book Society, the, 61
Booth, Rt. Hon. Charles, 221, 222, 223, 233, 234
——, General, 13, 314
Borough of Hackney Club, 66–71
Boulton, Sir Samuel, 240
Boyle, Hugh, 232
Boys and brutality, 13, 14
Bradlaugh, Charles, 23, 161, 284, 313
Brooke, Rev. Canon C. E., 51, 319, 323, 325
Brook Farm, 280
Browning's poetry, 44, 157, 204, 205, 206, 310, 317
Browning Hall, 203, 205, 222, 274
—— Robert, 40, 44, 74, 161, 163, 165, 204
Bullen, A. H., 253, 254, 255
Bulwer Lytton's plays, 131, 132
Burgin, George B., 171
Burns, Rt. Hon. John, 214, 215, 261
Byron, Lord, the poetry of, 44, 275

Catholic Church, 245
Catholic ideas, 205, 314, 315
—— Truth Society, 245
Calvinistic workmen, 278, 302
Canterbury, city of, 160, 164, 292
Celeste, Madame, 135
Chamberlain, Austin, M.P., 268
——, Rt. Hon. Joseph, M.P., 242, 253

Cheap swimming baths, 114
Chevalier, Albert, 175
Child of the Toys, the, 174
Christ and Modern Commercialism, 196
——, Deity of, 319
Christian Social Union, 306
Church Congress, 220, 233
—— of England, 18, 23, 319
—— of England Men's Society, 265, 266
—— of Progress, 24
City churches, 6, 33
—— of London Theatre, 7
Clarence, Duke of, 184, 194
Coffee taverns, London, 111, 112
Coleridge, the Lord Chief Justice, 161, 163
Colston Hall, Bristol, destruction of, 218
Commercial travelling, 110, 118, 145
Commonwealth Club, 51, 95
Conciliation Boards, 240
Congregational Union, resolutions of, 244
Contrast, a (poem), 245
Conway, M. D., 276, 282, 283, 289
Cook, Sir E. T., 145, 180
Co-operative Bookbinders Society, 118, 119, 145
—— News, 118, 226
—— Printing Society, 146, 178, 179, 182, 287
—— Wholesale, 178, 203, 220
Cowham, W. H., 189
Cowper Temple Clause, the, 262
Cox, Mr. Harold, 140, 268
Craigen, Miss Jessie, 72
Creighton, Bishop, 85, 233
Creswick, William, 7, 129, 130, 131, 132.
Crooks, William, M.P., 248
Cynicus, the studio of, 175

DAGONET Ballads, the, 137
Daily Chronicle, the, 214, 247
Daniel Day, 3
Davidson, Archbishop, 260, 268
Death of Canon Barnett, 320
—— of my father, 269
—— of Queen Victoria, 250

Denison, Edward, 76–78
Dennard, T. W., 70, 71
Derelicts, human, 46, 47, 48
Deterioration of handicrafts, 298
Dickens, Charles, 27, 103, 227
Dleny, Frank, 183, 184, 194
Don Quixote, 11
Drinking, increase of among women, 304
—— decrease of among men, 304
Druid tradition, 3
Dumas, Alexander, novels of, 15
Dunbar, William, 211

EARLY English Text Society, 274
—— memories, 1
Education Act, the First, 49, 53
—— Act, 1902..259
—— Act, 1906..262
—— Meeting at Albert Hall, 1906..263
——, no enthusiasm for, 52
Educational Standards, the raising of, 298
Effingham Saloon, the, 7, 9
Eliot, George, 78, 260
Elizabethan Society, the, 156, 159, 160, 167
Elizabethan Stage Society, the, 169
Elsmere, Robert, 286, 287
Emerson, R. W., 281
English Church Union, the, 262, 263, 324
Errand boys, London, 10
Essays and Reviews, 26
Ethical societies, 237
Evening, 320
Evolution, 38, 315, 316
"Everyman," 170

FABIAN Society, the, 140, 141, 221, 250, 286
Fairlop Fair, 3
—— Friday, 2
—— Oak, 3
Fair wages clause, the, 209
Falcon Square, City, 16
"Faust," Goethe's, 11, 264
"Faustus," 166; Marlowe's, 169
First Education Act, the, 49
First London School Board, the, 51

INDEX

Ford, Onslow, R.A., 165, 166
—— John, plays of, 305
Forster, Rt. Hon. W. E., 49, 89
Fox-Bourne, H. R., 99, 111, 114, 118
Free Sunday, fraud, the, 288, 289
Freethinker, a, 23
Freethought lecture halls, 27
Fuller, Margaret, 281–286

GALLOWS, the, 12, 13
Gardiner, Samuel Rawson, 81, 249
Gaston, Richard, club actor, 135, 136
General Election of 1906..261
—— Federation of Trades, 265
Gladstone, W. E., 25, 26, 49, 121
Goodmans Fields, 2, 103
Goschen, Rt. Hon. G. J., 83
Gower's walk, 2
Green, John Richard, historian, 76
Grieve, David, 288
Guildhall Library, the, 43, 44, 45
Gutter boys, 6, 11

HALIFAX, the Lord, 306
"Hang Theology" Rogers, 64
Hardie, J. Keir, M.P., 195, 211
Harriet Lane, the murder of, 108
Hawthorne, Nathaniel, 280
Heath, Miss, 7
Herne, the Hunter, 55
"Hindle Wakes," 305
History, the teaching of, 81, 85
Holyoake, G. J., 118, 292
Home Rule, 121, 147, 153
—— —— Bill, the, 121
House of Commons, 266, 269
House of Lords, 268
Howell, George, M.P., 282
Hughes, Rev. Hugh Price, 250
—— Thomas, Q.C., 79, 155
Hutchinson, William George, 189
Hutton, Rev. Arthur W., 282
Huxley, Prof., 24, 50, 51
Hyde Park, 45, 125
Hyndman, H. M., 140, 184, 210

IGNATIUS, Rev. Father, 32, 34
Imitation martyrs, 77, 147, 278, 279
Imperial Sunday Alliance, 290

Independent Labour Party, 210, 211
Industrial idealism, 64, 126, 226, 239, 296
Infant mortality, 216, 217
Ingomar, 7
Irish peasantry, 148, 149
—— priest, an, 150, 151
Irving, Sir Henry, 128, 130, 131, 133, 164, 165, 171, 172
—— controversies, 133
Irving's influence on the drama, 133

"JOE RAY'S beast," 47, 48
Johnson, Dr., on taxation, 213
Jones, Rev. William, 104
Journalism, 95–115, 179
Journalist, an old, 122
Justice to the bottom dog, 325

KEAN, Mr. and Mrs. Charles, 7
Kennedy, Rev. Dr., 38
Kingsley, Charles, 276
King Edward VII., letter to, 260
King's College Chapel, 104
Kirkus, Rev. W., 35

LABOUR leader, a, 52
—— movements, 63
—— Representation, 115, 116
—— —— Committee, 250
Lambeth Palace, 248
Lang, Andrew, 274
Lansbury, George, 147
Le Galliene, Richard, 173
Liberalism, 127, 187, 261
Liberal Party, the, 116, 117, 120
Life a symbol, 326
"Little Bethel," 103, 104, 128
London County Council, 290, 291
—— Chamber of Commerce, 180, 240
—— the charm of, 44–47
London Journal, the, 10, 118
Lowe, James, 66–70
Lowell, James Russell, 161, 281, 284

MANFRED, 44
Mansion House, meeting at, 89

INDEX

Marlowe, Christopher, 159–167
—— Memorial, the, 161–167
Marriott, Miss, 7, 133
Marryatt, captain, the novels of, 15, 311
Marston, Henry, 7
—— Philip Bourke, 173, 174
Martineau, James, 38
Marx, Eleanor, 176, 177
Massinger, Philip, 170
—— window, the, 170, 171
Mazeppa, 44
Medical College, London Hospital, the, 80
Melodrama, 9, 10
Melville, Henry, 23
Meredith, George, 295
Middle Ages, the, 158, 172
Mile End Road, 3, 4
Miller, Mrs. Fenwick, 51
Milner, the Viscount, 139
Miners' hecklings, 229, 233
—— imagination, 231
Mining villages, 232
Mitchell, Mr. Isaac, 265
Montefiore, Leonard A., 79, 82
—— Claude E., 142
Morfill, W. R., 84, 275
Morning Post, the, 260
Mother in the factory, 215, 216, 217
Mullins, James, execution of, 12, 13
Myers, Ernest, 79
Myers, F. W., 79

Nash, Vaughan, 178
National Committee of Organized Labour, 222
—— Reformer, the, 189
—— Old Age Pensions League, 243
Nature and civilization, 309
Neale, Edward Vansittart, 155
New Theology, the, 281
"New Theories and the Old Faith," 37, 38
Noel, the Hon. Roden, 172
Nonconformists and Education, 49, 60, 264
Northumberland miners, 100, 101, 230, 232

Obscene journalism, 112, 113, 114
Odger, George, 127

Old Age Pensions, 138, 140, 225–237
—— Age Pensions Act, 267, 273
—— Age Pensions Committee, the, 222, 223
—— Age Pensions resolution, 261
Oxford, the charm of, 56, 57, 142
—— Movement, the, 315, 319
——, a walk to, 54, 55, 56

Paracelsus, 44
Parker, Rev. Dr. Joseph, 39
Pall Mall Gazette, 95, 99, 118, 144, 153, 180
Paterson, Emma, 92, 93, 94, 218
Patmore, Coventry, 174
——, Milnes, 174
Parnell, C. S., 152, 153
Pavilion Theatre, the, 7
Pennywinkle Joe, 46, 47
Pensions Budget, the, 266
Penwiper woman, 47
Phelps Samuel, 7, 129, 131
Pickersgill, E. H., 72, 73
Picton, James Allanson, 35–38, 49, 53, 85, 116, 117, 287
Pilgrim's Progress, The, 6, 10, 293, 327
Poel, William, 168, 169, 170
Policy of Cardiff, the, 213, 214
Poor Law, the, 244
Prayer Book, the, 18, 23, 39
Primrose League, the, 236
Private Schools, condition of, 58, 59
Progressive Club, 70, 71
—— Review, 78, 82
Prostitute's funeral, a, 3
Puritan and Catholic, 205, 206, 312
Pythian games, the, 241

Radical Club, a Sunday morning at, 95–99
—— Club, The Tower Hamlets, 72, 95
Raleigh, Sir Walter, at Youghal, 152
Religion in the workshop, 278
Renaissance, the, 205, 206
Reynolds, G. W. M., 15, 138
Reynold's Miscellany, 10
Ridley, Bishop, 221, 222
Rock, the, 18, 21, 35
Rosebery, Lord, 268

INDEX

Rowntree and Sherwell, 257
Rowsell, the Rev. Canon T. J., 5, 108
Ruskin Hall, 290
Russell, the Rt. Hon. George W. E., 123
Rutherford, Mark, 27, 120

SADLER's Wells theatre, 129
Salvation Army, the, 13, 315
Sawford, Sam, 9
School management, 54
—— Board elections, 50, 51
Science, Hall of, 23, 161
Scott Holland, Rev. Canon, 71, 248, 234
Sedgwick, Amy, 131
Seven Deadly Sins, the, 251, 253
—— days' working week, a, 290
Seventh Day Baptists, 104, 105, 106,
Shakespeare, 15, 72, 96, 157, 159, 308
——, Head Press, 253
Shelley's monument at Oxford, 166
—— Skylark, 310
Shilling Browning, the, 167, 168
Shoreditch Town Hall, classes at, 79
Sick folk at Falcon Square, 19, 20
Simcox, Edith, and Trade Union Congress, 208, 212
Sims, George R., 25, 102, 137, 138
——, Thomas, 184
Sloper, James, 86–90, 110
Socialism, 115, 119, 138
Social ideals, 137, 301
—— kaleidoscope, the, 138
—— life in the workshop, 41, 42, 138
Sonnett on a New Year, 256
Southwark Cathedral, 170
South Place Chapel, 275–286
Spinosa, Benedict, 117
Spiritualism, 295
Stage supper, a, 171
Stanley, Dean, 73, 74, 75
Stead, F. H., 203, 204, 224, 267, 271
——, W. T., 204, 294
Steadman, W. C., 219
Strike leaders, 183, 184

St. Jude's Whitechapel, 79, 88, 321, 323
Stratford Town Shakespeare, the, 255
Sunday morning at a Radical Club, 95–99
—— labour, 288, 289
Surrey Theatre, 129, 131
Swimming baths, cheap, 114

TAIT, Archbishop, 53
Taxation, increase of, 301
Temperance problem, the, 65, 257, 258, 259
Temple, Archbishop, 245, 246, 247
——, Bishop, 26, 27
Tennyson, Lord, 40, 171
Terry, Miss Ellen, 164, 172
"Tom Brown's Schooldays," 79
Total Abstinence Movement, the, 258
Toynbee, Arnold, 85, 109
—— Hall, 109, 140, 141, 142, 144, 156, 321
—— Journal, 145
Trade Union Congress, 186, 187, 188, 207, 208, 209
—— Unionist, the, 178, 182
—— Union ideals, 187
Transcendentalism, 281, 286

UNIONISM, 121
Unionist Club, 121
University extension, 76–85, 89, 100
Unveiling of the Marlowe Memorial, 164, 165

VAGABOND Club, the, 174, 176
Vaughan, Cardinal, 245, 246, 247
——, the Rev. C. J., 23
Valley of Hinnom, 292
Vellum Binder's Society, 63, 115, 185, 209
Vezin, Mrs. Herman, 7
Victoria Park, 45
Village priest, a, 149, 150, 151

WAINWRIGHT, Henry, execution of, 108
Walsham How, Bishop, 71

Wapping, 3, 4
Ward, Mrs. Humphry, 287
Washerwoman, an old London, 272
Watercress girl, the, 8
Waterlow, Sir Sidney, 127
Watkins, Dr. John, 16–21, 35, 76, 275
Weekly Dispatch, the, 99, 102, 110, 111, 112, 113, 115, 118
Westcott, Bishop, 232
Whiskey, a tax on, 225
Whitechapel, 7, 79, 80, 264
—— Committee, the, 79
Wife beating, decrease of, 303

Wilkinson, Jeanette G., 93, 95
Wills, Rev. Freeman, 191–194
——, W. G., 193
Windrush, the Rev. Mr., 276
Wolverhampton, Lord, 268
Women's Trade Unions, 93, 94, 95
Working Men's Clubs, 26, 66–74
Workmen's ideals, 40, 41, 42, 43, 64, 124
Workmen's wages, 300
Workshop life, 41, 42

YOUNG, Ralph, 231, 263

THE END

Biography and Reminiscence

With a Portrait. 2nd Impression. Demy 8vo. 10s. 6d. net.

Jane Austen: Her Life and Letters. A Family Record.

By William Austen-Leigh (Fellow of King's College, Cambridge) and Richard Arthur Austen-Leigh.

Sunday Times.—'A model biography in its way, and as the work of relatives may claim to be authoritative and exhaustive.'

Liverpool Daily Post.—'Apart from the interest of its subject, it has much to commend it. A thoroughly interesting and most informative biography.'

With 2 Portraits and 2 Plans. Large post 8vo. 10s. 6d. net.

'J.' A Memoir of John Willis Clark,

Registrary of Cambridge University, and sometime Fellow of Trinity College.

By Dr. A. E. Shipley, F.R.S.

Master of Christ's College, Cambridge.

In the Cambridge Review, The Provost of King's says:—'A book of permanent value to Cambridge men and of vivid immediate interest to the generations who knew "J." Dr. Shipley has told his story with a combination of true appreciation and perceptive humour.'

Country Life.—'Everybody with a direct or indirect connection with Cambridge University will read this modest biography with absorbing interest. Mr. Shipley is to be congratulated on having produced so worthy a memorial of his friend.'

With Portrait. 2nd Impression. Large crown 8vo. 3s. 6d. net.

Recollections and Impressions of the Rev. John Smith, M.A.

For twenty-five years Assistant-Master at Harrow School.

By Edward D. Rendall & The Rev. Gerald H. Rendall, Litt. D.

Late Headmaster of Charterhouse.

Manchester Courier.—'One need not be an old Harrovian to catch something of the magic spell of such a man as John Smith. Both authors bear witness to his humanity, his generosity, his unaffected humility.'

Large post 8vo. 6s. net.

The Adventures of a Newspaper Man.

By Frank Dilnot.

Author of 'The Old Order Changeth.'

Daily Citizen.—'Mr. Dilnot has the seeing eye and the understanding heart, and withal a happy knack of description that renders all his "adventures" intensely interesting.'

Daily Mirror.—'An excellent piece of journalism, he plunges at once into the middle of things. There are no dates and no dulness in him.'

London: Smith, Elder & Co., 15 Waterloo Place, S.W.

Recent 6s. Fiction

Mrs. Humphry Ward's Successful Love Story.
With 4 Illustrations by Charles E. Brock.

The Mating of Lydia.

By Mrs. Humphry Ward.

Author of 'Lady Rose's Daughter,' &c.

The British Weekly.—'I shall be surprised if "The Mating of Lydia" is not one of the most popular books of the Spring.'

Daily Telegraph.—'Written with the old charm and ease of style, and exhibits, as many of her novels have done, an exquisite perception of the beauties of Cumberland scenery.'

Standard.—'As chronicler of country-house life Mrs. Humphry Ward has only Mr. Galsworthy for rival.'

Daily Citizen.—'A fine story. Mrs. Humphry Ward has not, in my judgment, done a better.'

Agnes and Egerton Castle's New Volume of Stories.

Chance the Piper.

By Agnes and Egerton Castle.

Authors of 'If Youth but Knew,' 'The Grip of Life,' &c.

Liverpool Daily Post.—'All the stories contained in this book are of exceptional merit, and display Mr. and Mrs. Castle at their very best. The reader is impelled to read on and on, and will find it difficult to set the book aside until the last page has been turned.'

His Dear Desire.

By Margaret Watson.

Author of 'Under the Chilterns,' 'Driven,' &c.

Scotsman.—'Miss Watson's charming idyll. There are traits and touches in the story that for insight and faithfulness of delineation of "South Midland" scenery and character are not unworthy of George Eliot.'

Northern Whig.—'Miss Watson's next venture will be warmly welcomed merely on the merits of this.'

The Dominant Race.

By W. H. Adams,

Late District Commissioner Gold Coast Colony.

Times.—'Mr. Adams has a masterly way of telling a story. A straightforward and exciting piece of fiction without undue sensationalism. The whole novel is really admirable.'

Barry and a Sinner.

By John Barnett.

Author of 'The Prince's Valet,' 'Eve in Earnest,' &c.

Pall Mall Gazette.—'Mr. Barnett, with his usual lightness and fineness of touch, has here given us a comedy touched with farce. The satire is keen but always good natured.'

London: Smith, Elder & Co., 15 Waterloo Place, S.W.

Recent 6s. Fiction

A New Novel by the Author of 'Peter's Mother.'

Michael Ferrys.

By Mrs. Henry de la Pasture (Lady Clifford).

Author of 'Master Christopher,' 'Erica,' &c.

Times.—'Mrs. Henry de la Pasture's novels always have an engaging charm about them which is partly due to the environment, and partly to her sense of delicate humour.'
Daily Telegraph.—'It is a beautiful romance, touched with comedy as well as tragedy, and told with the author's usual skill and pathos.'

Mrs. Pratt of Paradise Farm.

By Katharine Tynan.

Author of 'Love of Sisters,' 'Honey, My Honey,' &c.

Times.—'Another of Mrs. Hinkson's endearing idylls of the country.'
World.—'A combination of charm and delicacy. Told with a tender grace which makes of the simple story an artistic achievement.'

The Confession of Richard Plantaganet.

By the late Dora Greenwell McChesney.

Author of 'Cornet Strong of Ireton's Horse,' &c.

Edited by L. Maye.   With a Prefatory Memoir by Lady Macdonell.

Times.—'More than a romance. Every one in the book seems real, and there are moments when the story is deeply affecting.'

Napoleon Boswell: Tales of the Tents.

By Herbert Malleson.

With a Preface by Lady Arthur Grosvenor.

Observer.—'The book has a singular charm.'
Aberdeen Daily Journal.—'A faithful and interesting presentment of gipsy life and character. Not only a book to read, but to buy.'

The Secret of Sarm.

By the Hon. H. B. Money-Coutts and W. R. Macdonald.

Nottingham Guardian.—'A clever romance based upon the familiar dread of German schemes for the invasion of England. This supplies the motive power to a very pretty love story.'

London : Smith, Elder & Co., 15 Waterloo Place, S.W.

History and Politics

With a Portrait of Captain Cook. Crown 8vo. 6s.

The New World of the South: Australia in the Making.

By W. H. Fitchett, B.A., LL.D. Author of 'Fights for the Flag,' &c.

Public Opinion.—'Few men could "gather up the fragments into history's golden urn" in a more attractive style.'

Oxford Chronicle.—'A retrospect well worth the telling, and which could not have found a more faithful or picturesque narrator.'

Dedicated by gracious permission to His Majesty King George V.

The Annals of the King's Royal Rifle Corps.

Vol. I. 'The Royal Americans.' By Lewis Butler. Formerly a Captain in the Regiment.

With Portraits, Illustrations and Maps. Royal 8vo. 25s. net.

Appendix dealing with Uniform, Armament and Equipment, by Major-General Astley Terry and S. M. Milne.
With numerous coloured and other illustrations. Royal 8vo. 15s. net.

The Volumes may be purchased separately.

With 8 Maps. Crown 8vo. 2s. 6d. net.

Common Sense in Foreign Policy:

A Survey of its Present Outlines and its Possible Developments.

By Sir H. H. Johnston, G.C.M.G., K.C.B.
Author of 'The Uganda Protectorate,' 'The Nile Quest,' &c.

Scotsman.—'The plain unvarnished opinions of a practical mind, of a well-travelled man of affairs, on questions which sooner or later must call for solution by the Powers. The book is distinctly stimulating.'

Letters from the Near East. Crown 8vo. 3s. 6d. net.

By the Honble. Maurice Baring.
Author of 'With the Russians in Manchuria,' &c.

Times.—'Mr. Baring records vividly and modestly the conditions of the Balkan countries as he saw them. By far the most moving chapter in the book is the description of the cholera hospital and camp at San Stefano—a tragic theme which impresses the more deeply because it is handled with restraint.'

2nd Edition. With 20 pages of Illustrations. Crown 8vo. 3s. 6d. net.

With the Bulgarian Staff. By Noel Buxton, M.P.

(Chairman of the Balkan Committee), Author of 'Europe and the Turks.'

The Globe.—'A very terrible book. It is war with the gilt off. But it is of the most absorbing interest, and no one who wishes to know what war really means should fail to read it.'

Large post 8vo. 6s. net.

Studies in British History and Politics.

By D. P. Heatley (Lecturer in History, University of Edinburgh).

Times.—'In his general reflection Mr. Heatley shows the philosophic temper, but in handling historical events and characters he shows a knowledge and a grasp of their significance which will commend the studies to the intelligent student.'

London: Smith, Elder & Co., 15 Waterloo Place, S.W.

Recent Publications

Crown 8vo. 5s. net.

Russian Sketches: Chiefly of Peasant Life.

Translated from the Russian by Beatrix L. Tollemache.
(The Hon. Mrs. Lionel Tollemache.)

Scotsman.—'There will always be room for a book so fine in its literary quality and so faithful to its Russian originals as this volume. Graceful and polished renderings into prose of some poems and short stories that are conspicuous in Russian literature.'

Songs from Leinster.   Crown 8vo. 2s. 6d. net.

By W. M. Letts.
Author of 'A Rough Way,' and 'The Mighty Army.'

Times.—'Singing with true insight and often with much beauty the thoughts of the simple Irishman or Irishwoman.'

Scotsman.—'Good English verse, with a natural and affecting brogue that harmonises fresh and sweet cadences of poetry with racy local idiom.'

Shakespeare's Hamlet: Large post 8vo. 6s. net.

A New Commentary with a Chapter on First Principles.
By Wilbraham Fitzjohn Trench, M.A. (Dublin).

Scotsman.—'It is both studious and enlightened; and cannot but prove helpful and instructive to anyone who reads it side by side with the play.'

The Ring of the Nibelung. Crown 8vo. 2s. 6d. net.

By Richard Wagner.
A new rendering in English Verse by Randle Fynes.

Globe.—'Many passages of real beauty are to be found scattered through the volume. His book should receive a warm welcome from the increasing number of English people who are interested in Wagner.'

Halfpenny Alley.   Crown 8vo. 5s. net.

By Marjorie Hardcastle.
With a Frontispiece by Lady Stanley, and an Introduction by
Alexander Paterson, Author of 'Across the Bridges.'

Scotsman.—'Plain tales about people on the border between the workhouse and the world outside. The stories interest by sheer force of actuality. Pictures so accurate and yet so cheerful.'

Socialism Rejected.   Large post 8vo. 7s. 6d. net.

By Bernard Samuelson.

Scotsman.—'Touches so nearly upon matters that concern everybody nowadays that it should not fail to attract and interest.'

Money Changing: Large post 8vo. 5s. net.

An Introduction to Foreign Exchange.
By Hartley Withers.
Author of 'The Meaning of Money,' 'Stocks and Shares,' &c.

The Financial News in a 3 column review says:—'Mr. Withers makes the topic interesting in spite of its obvious and irrepressible technicality. Occasionally he renders it really amusing.'

London: Smith, Elder & Co., 15 Waterloo Place, S.W.

WORKS BY SIDNEY LEE.

A LIFE OF WILLIAM SHAKESPEARE.

SIXTH EDITION. With a New Preface. Large crown 8vo. 7s. 6d. With Two Portraits of Shakespeare, a Portrait of the Earl of Southampton, and Facsimiles of Shakespeare's known Signatures.

BLACKWOOD'S MAGAZINE.—'This masterly work is an honour to English scholarship, an almost perfect model of its kind, and it is matter for great national rejoicing that the standard life of Shakespeare has at last been made in England. Rarely have we seen a book so wholly satisfying, so admirably planned, so skilfully executed. . . . It is an absolutely indispensable handbook for every intelligent reader of the plays.'

ATHENÆUM.—'There is no doubt that for some time to come, probably for a long time, it will be a general text-book.'

SPECTATOR.—'Unquestionably one of the most remarkable achievements of modern English scholarship. . . . The mass of obscure and tangled controversies which he has ravelled out is immense.'

TIMES.—'A marvel of research, and, on the whole, remarkably temperate, judicious, and convincing. . . . Never before has learning been brought to bear upon Shakespeare's biography with anything like the same force.'

PALL MALL GAZETTE.—'A definitive biography.'

Also the ILLUSTRATED LIBRARY EDITION, profusely Illustrated with Photogravures, Facsimiles, Topographical Views, &c. NEW AND CHEAPER EDITION. Medium 8vo. 10s. 6d. net.

And the STUDENT'S EDITION. With a Photogravure Plate and 4 Full-page Illustrations. NEW AND REVISED EDITION. Crown 8vo. 2s. 6d.

SHAKESPEARE'S HANDWRITING.

Facsimiles of the Five Authentic Autograph Signatures of the Poet. Extracted from SIDNEY LEE's 'Life of William Shakespeare.' With an Explanatory Note. Crown 8vo. 6d.

QUEEN VICTORIA: a Biography.

NEW, REVISED, AND CHEAPER EDITION.

With Portraits, Map, and a Facsimile Letter. Large crown 8vo. 6s.

QUARTERLY REVIEW.—'Mr. Sidney Lee has performed, with marked success, a work which required, in no common measure, a combination of assiduous labour, skilful arrangement, and unfailing tact. . . . Our interest is sustained from the first page to the last.'

*** Also the FOURTH IMPRESSION (SECOND EDITION) of the Original Edition. With Portraits, Maps, and a Facsimile Letter. Large crown 8vo. 10s. 6d.

London: SMITH, ELDER, & CO., 15 Waterloo Place, S.W.